Butterfly on a Pin

ALANNAH HILL

Our memories make up the ongoing experience of our lives and provide us with a sense of self. Your first kitten or pup, the sound of your baby's first cries, the taste of your grandmother's sponge cake. These are memories that make us who we are. Our memories tie our pasts with our present and provide us with a framework for our future. I understand our memories are personal and that we all remember people, events and feelings differently. The events, people and places I have written about here are real and true memories for me. There are some instances where I have changed people's names to protect their identity and privacy. Without memories, dear reader, we cease to exist.

Butterfly on a Pin

A MEMOIR OF LOVE,

LOSS AND REINVENTION

ALANNAH HILL

hardie grant books

Published in 2018 by Hardie Grant Books, an imprint of Hardie Grant Publishing

Hardie Grant Books (Melbourne)
Building 1, 658 Church Street
Richmond, Victoria 3121

Hardie Grant Books (London)
5th & 6th Floors
52–54 Southwark Street
London SE1 1UN

hardiegrantbooks.com

A catalogue record for this
book is available from the
National Library of Australia

Butterfly on a Pin
ISBN 978 1 74379 425 8

10 9 8 7 6 5 4 3 2 1

Cover and text design by Evi O. / OetomoNew
Typeset in 11/17 pt Baskerville by Post Pre-Press Group
Cover photograph by Georges Antoni
Printed by McPherson's Printing Group, Maryborough, Victoria

For Mum

Prologue

The day my mother attempted to kill herself was not like any other day I'd known. I was five years old. I remember the darkening clouds gathering in the foothills of the small ghost town, a ghost town where my family lived, a ghost town in Tasmania called Geeveston.

I was desperately frightened.

My mother was very, very sick. She looked sick, she couldn't move her head, and in my rush to get to her I slipped on my own footsteps. Breathless, I crept quietly into her bleak and sombre bedroom. Mum was lying on her marital bed, staring at the ceiling, tears falling from her brown eyes, crawling down her face and onto her neck. I watched the chaotic mess and when the priests told me to get out, I couldn't. Somebody picked me up and dropped me onto the floor in the room next door where my three siblings were eating stale honey sandwiches. We began rocking backwards and forwards, backwards and forwards, humming my mother's favourite Catholic hymn: 'Nearer, my God, to Thee, nearer to Thee, nearer, my God, to Thee, nearer to Thee.'

I couldn't hear my mum breathing. All I could hear was the sound of violent hiccups.

All we could do was rock back and forth, eating our honey sandwiches, waiting for the gigantic stranger, who was often seen glowering from corners or hurling raging aggression after drinking in the local pub. The stranger was my father.

A biblical hymn sounded from the marital bedroom and so my own hymn to God became even louder. I was shouting 'Nearer, my God, to Thee', shouting it with my stale honey sandwich trapped in my throat, rocking with my siblings in perfect timing, as my giant father arrived home with his imperfect timing. A flurry of noise, a farmer's hat thrown onto the floor, boots thrown against a wall and there he was, my father: the man I believed was the reason Mum was lying on the marital bed in a state of Catholic exorcism.

I wanted to die. I wanted the whole world to die. My eyes were blurred from tears and I heard him shouting at my mum.

'For God's sake, Aileen. This again! Jesus, Mary and Joseph, Aileen, what the fuck do you want?'

I knew even then what my mother wanted. I knew it and I never spoke up. I wondered why my father couldn't see it for himself.

The truth is that my mother, over a period of forty-five years, was almost sent mad by my father's dismissal of her, and his own unhappiness, which, like the plague, spread death of one kind or another at a rate of a mile or more a day.

When I left Tasmania in 1979, I had never been on an aeroplane. Three decades later, it was not uncommon to find me in seat 1A, flying first class on one of Qantas's fanciest new fleet of aeroplanes. I'd be bound for London, Paris, New York City, Singapore and Tokyo – trips that took in five cities in fourteen days. My bespoke sherbet-bomb diary was filled with high-flying career-girl fabric appointments, dinner invitations, posh fashion shows, art gallery openings and VIP tickets for Première Vision,[1] the famous Paris fabric and trim fair. I was chauffeured from the airport to a fancy boutique hotel.

I'd climbed to the top of the mountain, climbed and climbed and climbed. Looking down from the clouds at my life in the broken-down houses of my childhood, I'd wonder if it was all true. *Did I really make it?* I would immediately fret, thinking, *God, if I lose this – if my impossible dream gets taken from me – I know I'll surely die.* I'd be overwhelmed by a sense of nothingness, the unjoined girl of my childhood never too far away.

My mother was always two dark steps ahead. Her superb wit always ready, always in waiting, to put a little two-bob snob like me in my place. To Mum, I would always be a sixteen-year-old runaway shopgirl. On my visits to Tasmania, she would often tell me of her desperate attempt to die, changing the time it had happened, the number of pills she swallowed, and why she was covered in a strange plum sauce.

'I remember seeing priests hovering over your bed, Mum. Who looked after us? Why did Dad look so angry? Why, Mum, why? Tell me everything, Mum. Why, Mum?'

'Lan, what do you remember, dear?' she would ask. 'You came home from the orchard coughing, coughing, coughing, coughing, remember that, Lan, I was in and out of consciousness, Lan, in and OUT of consciousness. You know I nearly died, don't you, Lan? You know you nearly lost me, don't you, Lan? You do realise I was almost DEAD, don't you, Lan? What a dreadful man I married – a heathen, a philandering liar with insipid eyes. NO, I don't know why he didn't want you, Lan, I don't know why he wouldn't look at you! You were such a plain little thing. No personality, dear, you didn't have a speck of personality. Not a SPECK! You must have been frightened seeing your dear old mum lying

---

1 Pronounced *Premiaaiir Vizeeoon.*

on the marital bed DYING in front of your very own eyes, Lan. Dying! Right in front of your eyes, Lan!'

Yes, dear reader, I *was* frightened, and the terror from my childhood has never left.

TASMANIA

1962–1979

'Even now I can't trust life.
It did too many awful things to me as a kid.'

CLARA BOW, IT GIRL OF THE '30S

1

Shadow Doll

It was an early June morning in 1968. The trees were holding on to their dizzy green leaves – leaves that would soon fall under the cold grey skies of the bitter Tasmanian winter. The beginning of each day seemed dead, almost forgotten, before it had even begun. The day would come to life midafternoon, only to die another lingering death until the new dawn woke the world up to reflect upon its forlorn, bewildered state.

There were four rooms in the apple orchard house where we lived in Scotts Road, Geeveston. My father, an orchardist, was asleep in a small cupboard area separated from the lounge room, loud snores blaring from beneath the newspaper he placed over his head to shut out the constant disappointment of the world he inhabited.

Mum had been mopping the floor with a small bucket and an ancient mop. Whenever she began any housework, a quiet pleading sigh would escape from somewhere inside her as she prayed to any saint she believed could help her escape her life. On this particularly dark day, Mum had been praying to St Anthony and occasionally stooping to pick up some object – a piece of dust or the lid of the tomato sauce bottle. I dreaded the pick-ups as these would be the times when Mum yelped her histrionic squeals, assuming a statue-like position with one hand superglued to the small of her back.

'My BACK'S gone! My BACK HAS GONE! I can't go on like this, dear Lord. I CANNOT go on like this, dear LORD! The BACK area has GONE! MY BACK HAS GIVEN WAY! It's my SCIATICA!'

Now, dear reader, I am still unsure whether this outcry was to gain my father's attention or if it was simply so one of us children could relate the saga of Mum's aching sciatic nerve to Nan, her mother.

When the word went out, Nan and her four sisters[2] would start telephoning frantically to see how poor, worn-out, unhappy Aileen was managing with the terrible burdens and cruel tricks that God had played on her. The burden of motherhood. The burden of dreadful mongrel children. The burden of marrying a lapsed Catholic, womanising drinker. Poor Aileen, they all said.

Nan's sisters had all entered the Catholic nunnery at one stage or another in their lives. Auntie Sherry stayed on for seventy years as a real-life alcoholic nun. She had four complete nervous breakdowns and disliked anyone who was less than forty years of age. In fact, she disliked all of her sister nuns and all of the priests, but most of all she disliked Mum's children. We were lazy little unfit mongrels. I was often taken into a small room, my hands placed by my side while Auntie Sherry, wearing the full nun's regalia, reminded me again and again what a colossal burden we were.

'Are you being a good girl for your mother, Alannah? Your poor mother is a very, very sick woman, and I am not going to watch that beautiful woman fall into another nervous breakdown. Your father is a mortal sin – a wretched lapsed Catholic who does not own a set of rosary beads. I hope you know, young lady, that God is watching

2 Aunties Brenda, Sherry, Joan and Jean. There was also Uncle Bob, who became a priest, and another brother, Maurice, who died at four years old.

everything you do. Can you see him watching you? Because he is. Now, I hope you're helping your poor sick, ailing mother!'

My knees were given little nun-like slaps. Auntie Sherry's forehead had tiny beads of nun-like sweat beginning to drip onto her nose, and her lips were quivering. I could only see part of her face, most of it hidden inside the nun's headdress, giving her a godly gargoyle nun-like demeanour.

Slap

Slap

Slap

'Off you go then. You're a naughty little girl. Now go and help your poor mother.'

And on this June morning, Mum mopped and mopped, praying while glancing at my sister and me. Bernadette and I were grimly engaged in a tug of war in the kitchen. We were fighting like two Tasmanian devils over a discarded doll that I'd found a few days earlier, dying in a puddle of water.

I hadn't yet been able to find a name for my bunged-up rag doll. I had names in my heart such as Velvet, Chenille, Gypsy Girl Doll Dead, and even my own name, Alannah, but none of them seemed right. I knew my doll had no real place in the world, no light shining into or out of its discarded little soul. It lacked any real doll essence – it was a shadow doll.

The doll was my shadow.

My shadow was the doll.

My sister wanted Shadow Doll.

'Let me hold the doll! I want to hold the doll!'

We pulled each other's hair, kicked each other's shins, hissed and spat, slapped each other with our bare hands and tried to strangle each other's necks. I secretly hoped that I might see a bruise appear suddenly on my sister's knees. But my sister was a force. A year older than me, she was much stronger, and she wanted to hold my dying relic of a doll for five minutes.

But five minutes was an eternity.

Mum froze as our screams and cries became louder, her hands going to her hips. She held a cigarette in each hand, both of them alight, a black mood erupting across her face. Her prayers stopped, replaced with a high-pitched scream that seemed to rise like a biblical demon from hell itself.

'God give me strength to go on! God give me THE STRENGTH, dear St Anthony! Help me, for GOD'S sake, HELP me to struggle on through this day, dear GOD!'

Mum hollered toward us, her eyes sunken into her face, her mouth stretched into a perfect O. One of us was going to be slapped, and I sincerely hoped it wouldn't be me.

'GIRLS! Give me that stupid doll! If you wake your father God ONLY knows what will happen – STOP your shenanigans! I told you MY NERVES HAVE GONE! God give me strength, dear Lord. STOP or I will THRASH BOTH of you from one side of this room to the other. STOP! Are you going to STOP?'

I yanked Shadow Doll out of my sister's hands and held it close to my chest. My sister yanked it out of my hands and held it close to her chest. It was as if neither of us could live unless we held that doll. And as we pulled at Shadow Doll, its seams began to fray further until its stuffing lay strewn across the slippery floor.

And then he appeared.

My father emerged from the gloomy space behind the lounge room with his titanic presence, one thousand feet high, the conductor and composer of the immortal '1812 Overture', cannons and all. With his gnarled hands on the buckle of his belt, he had one look that had the power to paralyse all my thoughts.

I waited for the roar. It was always the same. 'Get those mongrel basdards out of my sight, Aileen. I told you to keep them quiet … Jesus, Mary and Joseph, I can't stand this!'

He left the room as quickly as he'd entered, muttering about how children should never be seen or heard, leaving his tornado of a shadow across my shrinking heart.

My mother flew through the air and threw both of us against the wall of the kitchen.

Mum slipped on Shadow Doll and severed its head.

My sister's arm cracked as she hit the wall.

It was almost as though a child's pop gun had been fired point-blank. Her little wrist flopped, her arm stopped moving. I saw her pain so clearly, her face tight with an indescribable look of fear.

I spied my broken Shadow Doll lying on the ground, the cottonwool stuffing spilling out of its cloth belly. A tear ran down my face and tumbled onto my stained hand-me-down tartan skirt.

I murmured, 'Oh *Mum* … what have you done to Bernadette's arm, Mum? It's like my doll, it's just hanging there all loose and …'

My mother and I were quick to blame each other.

'YOU did this, Alannah.'

You did this, Mum, I thought.

'You NAUGHTY, naughty girls! How DARE you fight like that, and Lannah – give your sister back the doll. She's the oldest so she gets to keep the doll.'

'No! Mum, no! It's my doll! I found it! It's my doll! It's not her doll!'

Wide-eyed, I sensed that Mum felt guilty for Bernadette's arm, so I gathered up the doll parts under my arm and stared at Mum, who glared back at me. I could feel Mum's confusion and chaos – the realisation that she had thrown Bernadette against the wall, snapping her arm in two.

She grabbed hold of us both, dragged us outside and thrust us into the green Holden. Mum had never driven a car before. We hurtled madly over speed bumps, reversed into a chicken-wire fence and ran over a small bird before careering into the doctor's surgery car park.

There was a flurry at the surgery when we arrived: a broken arm was a major injury in the Geeveston of 1968. There were X-rays and it was announced that my sister's small arm was broken.

The mummifying of my sister's arm was soon completed. The local doctor appeared 159 years old to my young-girl eyes, and he had Mum erratically explaining to him that it was the mopping and the slippery wooden floors that had conspired to make Bernadette trip and fall onto her arm.

'I'd just finished mopping and then Bernadette just slipped! She SLIPPED! Silly girls running across the floor when I TOLD them not to! They both DEFIED ME!'

Bernadette swanned out of the surgery holding a red lollipop, her arm cast in beautiful cream plaster suspended in a glorious fashion from a perfect white linen sling. I thought she looked like a walking broken doll and I made a little wish that, in the very near future, I too might break my arm.

Much fuss was made of my sister's arm when we arrived home hours later – even Dad came out to inspect the damage, and I watched as he picked Bernadette up and kissed her on top of the head.

I watched as he held her in his arms and sat her down on the green settee, patting her perfectly cast arm while whistling an Irish tune. I felt unsteady. My older brothers – the boys – moved like strangers between the shadows of the broken arm and the secret of how it came to be broken, and the sudden quietness in the house over Bernadette's wondrous new plaster development seemed symbolic, religious almost.

I sat on a wonky chair with my legs under my chin, staring at my arms, wondering what they'd both look like in a creamy plaster cast with a perfect white sling.

But mostly …

Mostly …

I sat on high alert.

Too afraid to live in the light, too afraid to live in the dark. To my father, I was invisible.

Many years later I would occasionally speak of this very early memory with Mum.

I'd sit on her green couch, asking her the same question over and over again, looking for a chink, a blink, a memory that was real.

'Tell me again, Mum! Tell me again how Bernadette broke her arm. How? How did she do that again?'

'I KNOW what you're getting at, Lannah! I KNOW what you're trying to make me say, and maybe I DID push her. Maybe I DID! NO, NO you did NOT have a dummy, Lannah! We couldn't afford a dummy, and why do you KEEP asking me about PHOTOGRAPHS, Lannah? There are NO photographs of you, dear – we didn't have a CAMERA, dear, and why SHOULD there be photographs of you all? WHY?'

Then I would ask, 'Mum, tell me about the box again?'

My mother's father had built Mum a wooden box when we were four children under four and always running away from her. The 2 by 2–metre box was apparently the most beautifully made wooden box anyone had ever seen. When we stood up we could just see over the top of the box, and Mum told me we'd all spend hours and hours inside the box being 'good little kids'.

'It was a beautifully made box, Lan. You kids played in the box for hours and hours. No, you did NOT have a doll, there were some old cow bones from Uncle Hayden's butcher shop that you played with. You LOVED it in that box, Lannah. You all LOVED it!'

'Mum! That is so bleak!'

Mum stared back at me through a cloud of cigarette smoke.

'You wait until you have four kids under four and a WRETCHED drunken husband. I hope to God you never have children, Lannaah. You would NOT manage! You'd go MAD with four kids and a lying, cheating husband. You'd put your kids into a box too, Lannaaaaah … kids LIKE being in a box! You did!'

Mum's face quietened, her tone gentler. 'I guess it was a bit bleak, Lan. I guess it was.'

But Mum hadn't finished.

'You always wore your sister's hand-me-downs, not a sign of any airs or graces. Not now with all your Chanel perfume and your expensive cars and all the FRIPS you buy yourself, Lan. I bet you've done your kitchen up again, Lan. You have NO idea how to SAVE, do you, Lan? You've SPOILED yourself ROTTEN, but you WAIT – YOU WAIT, it's ALL going to come tumbling down, you mark my words, Lannah – as TRUE as I'm a CATHOLIC – you will end up with nothing! NOTHING!'

2

The Lapsed Catholics

I believe that once, long before I was born, my father was a curious young man with clear blue eyes and a bright future. But somehow he fell afoul of life's twisted highways, and by the time I knew him he had become something else, an entirely different entity. The real-life father who lived with us was the man I feared the most. I was certain I was the cause of my father's anger and his silent, scalding moods. I would roam from room to room to avoid him.

My father didn't like children, marriage or ordinary life. My mother didn't have the patience for children either and yet within seven years of marriage, Mum had accidentally given birth to four of them. There were the two brothers, Mark in 1958 then Joseph in 1959. Bernadette came along in 1961, and me a year later, almost to the day. My younger brother, Martin, arrived much later in 1969. For seven years, I was the youngest.

My brothers moved stealthily through our smoke-filled house, never speaking, never interacting with anyone, silent as ghosts and yet larger than life. The boys were referred to as 'the boys' and Bernadette and I were spoken of as 'the girls'. We were dutifully trained to steer clear of each other.

There would be no unnecessary talking, no laughing, no family holidays, no counter lunches, no counter teas, no Sunday drives and no games. Of any sort. We had no pencils, no pens, no music, no radio, no books, no toys, no friends and no hobbies. In Geeveston, by 5.30 pm we were in our narrow beds, lined up against one wall in the small porch.

Dad's announcements about how we had ruined his chance of a grand and noble life were withering. Despite being an orchardist, my father held a series of regal visions. In his mind, he was the owner of a cattle farm and had come from a long lineage of Tasmanian royalty. In another time and another place, he would have been a Liberal Party prime minister. The shock of seeing himself holed up in a Geeveston shack, stuck with a wife and kids, was enough to turn a man to drink. An Irish Catholic, he appeared to the outside world a larrikin, a mysterious, well-read, insightful drinking man. Despite all the odds stacked against him, in high school he had earned a scholarship to St Virgil's Catholic school in Hobart. The whole town had cheered for him.

My father held many secrets. It was rumoured Dad had accidentally kicked a football into his mother's eight-month-pregnant stomach – the baby was stillborn. I remember hearing that Dad's mother drank whiskey by the bottle from that day on.[3] There was a formal wake and the beautiful stillborn baby girl lay angelically for an entire day on an aluminium bench alongside freshly slaughtered meat bound for my uncle's butcher shop. The little girl, named Ita, was eventually taken to the Franklin hospital morgue, but I believe the wails of my grandmother haunted Dad for years to come.

I remember waking to his own piercing howls for her.

---

3 Legend has it that my father, like his father, like his grandfather before him, was a man of the drink. There was much heavy drinking in the Hill family tree. Perhaps this is why I have never been drawn to the drink?

'Mum! Mum! Mum!'

He would howl for his mother over and over again until I heard my own mother slapping him, telling him to shut up.

3

The Hills Are Alive with the Fumes of Tioxide

I was about six years old when my three siblings and I were roused at the unholy hour of 3.30 am with cold water being poured onto our foreheads. My father was acting in a quite peculiar manner. There was a slight spring in his step, a gentle wink in his eye. For the very first time in my short girl-child memory, my father seemed happy, even whistling a merry kind of tune like a pretend-normal person as we piled into the emerald-green Holden and he sat down behind the wheel. With a turn of the key, he fired the engine into our new future.

The Hill family was on the move. We were to leave our falling-down house in Scotts Road, Geeveston, abandoning the apple orchard. I felt a keen apple-sadness not knowing who was going to pick the fruit. There would be no turning back – an adventure was about to take place in a faraway land I could scarcely imagine: Chasm Creek.

The four of us squeezed into the back seat of the Holden. We were told to sit quietly. I smacked my sister on her legs for something to do and then plaited her hair. I ignored my two brothers by listening intently to the Holden slicing through the Tasmanian silence. My father whistled occasionally and my mother silently passed him hot tea from a thermos, scalding his hands. I continued plaiting my sister's fine, straight hair, marvelling at her composure and how well her hair seemed to plait. She stared straight ahead so I smacked her on the legs. I wanted her to look at me. She wouldn't look at me. And so I gave her another little slap.

Dawn broke over the midlands of Tasmania, fitfully sunny and unseasonably cold, dark clouds tumbling across the sky in sudden heavy squalls of rain and sleet. I remember the pitiful sight of the farmers' battered crops, the skeletal trees shaking in erratic gusts of wind that screamed across the heartland deep into my own heart.

The drive seemed endless until we stopped at Uncle Bob and Auntie Sherry's presbytery in remote and beautiful Campbell Town for a ten-minute toilet break. I peered through a stickybeak window into the presbytery, spying Auntie Sherry pouring what I now know was sherry into tea, while speaking piously of faith and devotion. Bored, I pulled the rope of the great bell that hung by the steeple, causing my father to rush outside and bellow. Eventually the boys tired of searching for gravestones to stomp on and I tired of my bell-pulling and we dozed in the back of the car until the exploding roar of the engine awoke us and we continued our six-hour drive.

At last we arrived in Chasm Creek, a bustling community of three small houses next to a factory. My mother turned her head to check on us as we sat wide eyed and expectant in the back seat. My mother's prayers to the good Lord had finally been answered – my father had been accepted as an employee at the Tioxide factory!

Much later, I would discover that the infamous Tioxide plant was a Tasmanian ecological disaster. It was a pigment, clay and titanium dioxide manufacturer, and the discharges of effluents were allowed to flow directly into Bass Strait. It would become well known that if you dared hover your toe above the poisonous waters you'd turn into a painted statue – either that, or your toe would neatly detach itself and fall off.

I remember my father arriving home covered in a suffocating white ash, his overalls covered in the same white ash, strange toxins and paint fumes seeping from his skin. I believed my father was working as an industrial scientist but in real life he was a shiftworker at the factory.[4]

Eventually, my brother Joseph would work at Tioxide sweeping floors. My brother Mark would also work at Tioxide. My sister also worked part-time at Tioxide as a secretary. My mother and I never worked there.

Many years later, Mum would tell me how much she loved living in Chasm Creek. During the day, it was just the two of us, Mum and me: my siblings were attending and hating Stella Maris, a Catholic school in Burnie.

Mum told me that I did ordinary things like make mud pies, line up sticks from the back creek, or wash little pieces of paper and peg them onto a child's clothes line, a relic left by the previous tenants. That I helped chop the wood, combed her wavy black hair and once made thirty-two cups of watery tea in a morning. I remember that we'd both walk to the house three doors up to collect our weekly supply of mince, potatoes, milk and frozen peas.[5]

And then the Hill family were on the move once again.

There seemed to be no reason for this move, but move we did, from one creek to another. There were 8 kilometres between Chasm Creek and Sulphur Creek.

---

4 The talcum powder–covered Tioxide factory produced up to 3500 tonnes of titanium dioxide a year – the poisonous titanium that I grew up believing was real-life kryptonite. The fact that titanium had nothing to do with Superman came as a terrible blow when someone cruelly informed me it was merely a pigment, a byproduct if you like, of house paint. The Tioxide plant closed down in 1996 amid one of the biggest scandals of ecological damage in Tasmania's history. By 1998 it had been completely demolished. Nothing has been built on the toxic land since due to health and safety reasons.

5 One of the houses in Chasm Creek opened its back door from midday until 2 pm three days a week to double up as a temporary butcher, milk bar, hairdressing salon, op shop and second-hand uniform store.

And then, dear reader, just like that, I was seven years old and my mother had accidentally given birth to a baby boy, Martin. And my father was almost killed in a dramatic tractor accident. So dramatic in fact that the tractor he was driving flipped over, trapping him in its iron embrace for three hours. I remember Mum opening the door to a man's solemn voice, followed by the startled histrionic cries of my mother. I don't believe we visited Dad in hospital, and we were told he might never come home. But while he was banged up, with almost all of the bones in his body broken, sprained or torn, he was overcome with a brilliant money-making idea. We were going to be rich! A milk bar slash service station came up for sale for $10,000, 12 kilometres away in the beachside town of Penguin. After the eight weeks it took my father to recover, we were once again on the move.

Mum would often tell me how Dad promised he would help out in the milk bar whenever she needed, and it was on this condition that Mum agreed to run the 'family business'. Dad would continue to sell insurance all over Tasmania but the milk bar in Ironcliffe Road would be our salvation.

Looking back, it seems to me that the careless piece of string holding back Mum's wavy black hair was the only thing holding her together. Her brown eyes constantly searching, she was barely able to smile. I couldn't see it then, but I surely can now – my mother's face was the face of a woman who had been cheated.

Cheated, although she wasn't quite sure how.

My mother was about to have a Catholic milk bar meltdown, a meltdown from which none of us would ever really recover.

4

Free-Floating Anxiety

I am by nature a solitary girl. A solitary girl with a free-floating anxiety.

The dreary little free-floating anxiety is defiantly indifferent to your hopes and desires; it dares to waft through your heart like a spectral cobweb on a cool summer morning, antagonising your very soul and turning your skies dishwater grey. You never can anticipate where it will land. It comes in different forms: it can take your breath away, make you gasp in unexplained horror, set a fierce pain ripping through your stomach, turn your voice into a squeak, cause your skin to burn and itch and your eyes to swell with tears that refuse to fall, denying you even this small relief.

It's hard to pin this free-floating anxiety down. Just when you think you've grasped it, it shapeshifts, confusing and possessing you at the same time. If you suffer from this affliction, dear reader, please allow me to advise you that the only way to manage it is like a descending flu. Watch the storm cloud as it settles in, and free-float with your anxiety as you wait for it to pass. It simply dissolves into pale, cloudy wisps of unrequited love, lost opportunities and shattered dreams … until the next time the sky turns and the winds change and it comes to visit you once again.

Once you recognise how fickle your free-floating anxiety is with its alightings here and there, its transparent unreality, it begins to lose its power. Eventually, it loses interest and turns away to greener pastures. But it never, ever leaves for good. Like an earthbound spirit in a haunted house, it's here for the long haul – eternity.

My mother had this same free-floating anxiety, although in her case it presented more as an unpredictable spasm or reaction. Mum would often broadcast her current mood-state with a histrionic scream shrill enough to alarm the entire Penguin township. My mother's wails for help echoed through the graceless hellhole, the hellhole of …

THE MILK BAR.

Our milk bar was known as 'That Shocking Milk Bar', run by 'That Hill Family'. We gained an appalling reputation within two weeks of taking over the milk bar on Ironcliffe Road.

Our pasties were never hot enough, our drinks never cold enough and our meat pies a constant disappointment. Not only were they *not* hot enough, they also appeared to be very, *very* dry. Our two breakfast cereals, Weet-Bix and Creamoata porridge, were often out of date, the dairy-fresh milk curdled, the petrol bowser empty, and the motor oil for the hotted-up Toranas gluggy. Solidified.

Half a mile away, our opposition milk bar was doing a roaring trade. The proprietors of the roaring-trade milk bar were a gentle couple with perfect manners, *hot* pies and Chiko Rolls! Their window display was filled with fresh lamingtons and colourful advertisements. Classical music whispered gently from unseen speakers, a phenomenon I'd never encountered before. It was a far cry from our milk bar's sad bell of doom, held together by ten-year-old string.

It was during the early years of the milk bar that Martin, aged three, climbed into Dad's car, released the handbrake and roared down a hill, sideswiping two parked cars and delivering himself and my father's

Falcon into a ditch full of water. The lower part of his body was crushed. For five weeks he was in traction in the Launceston hospital, where it was discovered that he had Perthes disease, a childhood hip condition. He returned home covered from his neck to his knees in thick white plaster, a little mummy on a homemade trolley with wheels. It was decided after the traction and the plaster hadn't worked that Martin would need calipers, calipers with a built-up left shoe to ease the pain in his hips. Little Martin moved stiffly in his antiquated steel legs and would often collapse from the energy it took to run. I felt sorry for my young brother with his young boy hip condition.

I took it upon myself to look after Martin. I found a broken pram at the local tip so I could wheel him up and down the high streets of Penguin, ringing the rusty little bell on the pram's rusty handle.

Viewed from the street, our milk bar was an unremarkable brick tomb. Peeling white paint added to the effect. The front windows no longer beckoned light inside. It seemed no light could lift the gloom shrouding our family business. A spectacular giant sheep that lit up after dark (donated by Golden Fleece because we sold their petrol) had been winched onto the milk bar's tin roof. A handmade sign was nailed to a small space underneath reading: *JH and AY Hill. Milk Bar*. We had no fence, for there was nothing of any value to fence in: a derelict backyard with clumps of weedy lawn, a garage resting crookedly on a muddy slope, a falling-down Hills hoist holding two towels and three pairs of Mum's black polyester slacks.

Our milk bar shuddered from the inside out. A stained couch was the dismal showpiece in a space the size of a laundry. Mum liked to call this room 'the lounge room' although I cannot recall ever lounging or even sitting on the stained brown couch. The couch sat against a window that seemed eerie and out of place, almost as if the window understood the terrible joke it had turned itself into, because the window didn't look out to a garden or a garage or even onto a street. Instead, this misplaced window was the view into my three brothers' shack-like bedroom.

A single bed sat solemnly against one wall opposite bunk beds. A broken plastic back door swung against the bunk beds with a monotonous banging that changed pace according to the winds. A handmade sheet with orange and brown swirls was tacked across the bunk beds to create a private oasis for my brothers – the door to their room often being a late-night milk bar stop for unruly rural teens wanting three packets of Barbecue Shapes, Iced VoVos or a bottle of Fanta.

Each morning the boys' view of the new day dawning was the lounge room with both Mum and Dad slumped against the mantelpiece, itself a brown stain of horror with scorch marks from hundreds of cigarettes burnt into the wood.

Our parents' heads would be thrown forward into their hands, their red filter tips glowing dimly in the wintry Tasmanian dawn. Mum's black hair would be flattened into her head, her dressing gown threatening to catch fire from the gas heater, her feet swollen from one of her ailments; Dad would stand frozen in a white singlet, blue polyester slacks and bare white feet, a piece of bloodied toilet paper stuck glumly onto his chin. Their curved spines a heartbreak of sorrow, they would stand side by side, separated by an entire universe as their internal worlds collapsed like two slowly imploding stars.

Somewhere in the far distance an insistently dripping tap dripped, a lone sea wind suddenly gusted, a chained dog barked.

I believe my mum at this time was teetering on the edge of life and, little by little, scream by scream, she was moving further and further away from the happy girl she told me she had been 'BEFORE I met YOUR FATHER!'

'YOUR FATHER' was expressly spoken with extended vowels to imply it was our own fault that he was the man who had fathered us. 'YOUR FATHER! YOUR FATHER! Everything was alright until I met YOUR FATHER! My nerves have GONE, Lannah, get Martin into the bath – DID YOU HEAR ME, LANNAAAAAAH? Get him INTO the BATH!'

Mum's fury at being left alone in the milk bar, at Dad's *staggering* drinking and his week-long drives selling life insurance would often end with Mum standing in the middle of the milk bar and letting out a loud scream. 'JIMEEEEE! Where is YOUR FATHER?'

He'd often come home empty-handed before disappearing to a 'meeting' at the pub. The meetings were titled 'I'm trying to fucking sell life insurance, Aileen! Life insurance! That's where the money is, Aileen! Life insurance. Jesus, Mary and Joseph, get those fucking kids out of my sight before I go fucking mad!'

5

The Great Fleeing

Mum was a raw open wound from the twelve-hours-a-day, seven-days-a-week shiftworking in the milk bar. Her heart could be sliced open at any moment by a snag in the arrangements of the day triggering some half-forgotten pain or repressed horror, some ancient hurt.

Nan, her mother, lived five hours away in Hobart, a drive on an endless concrete freeway. I could tell by Mum's breathing when her anxious need for her own mother was rising. I'd sense her mind working frantically to rise above the Valium hangover haze and the three-packet-a-day smoking habit.

It was always the same. Mum's frantic telephone calls would begin at 6 pm in the hallway of the milk bar. Dad had hammered a telephone onto the wall of the dimly lit hallway, lined from floor to ceiling with large pods of Coke, Fanta, sarsaparilla and lemonade. The phone had a small lock on the side – my father didn't want any of his mongrel children using *his* telephone. He'd storm around the milk bar when the $35 telephone bill arrived. We were *not* to use the phone for *any* reason – the telephone *must* stay locked.

I'd stay perched on my stool in the milk bar wearing a scowl and my scorched-pink chenille dressing gown, serving the townspeople of Penguin their cigarettes and Tip Top bread. I was slightly hysterical with any customer who dared step onto the acid-yellow linoleum floor. Often the customer would take one look at my wretched little face and just walk straight back out again. I took it as a compliment that I had the power to turn people away.

I would hear Mum in the hallway, the voice of a woman on the edge of a colossal Nervy B.[6]

'Is Jimmy Hill at the bar?'

Silence.

'I SAID, is JIMMY HILL AT THE BAR?'

I'd hear the muffled sound of a hang-up on the other end of the telephone and the sound of Mum's neurotic finger redialling.

'IS Jimmy HILL at the bar, Fred?'

Mum would be hung up on or met with more silence. Waiting for the next part, I would eat two dozen cream butters, all the raspberry frogs, and four packets of Chickadees while her neurotically nimble fingers dialled demonically again, and she spoke with an ever sharper edge to her voice.

'GET ME Jimmy, Fred, I KNOW he's there. Get him home now, Fred, or I'll send Lannah down for him.'

'He's not here, Aileen. I'm sorry, he hasn't been in all day but I'll tell him you called.'

'How DARE you! I hope you rot in HELL, Fred Hindes. You're a lying, rude heathen and if I ever see you in this MILK BAR I'll take a Bible —'

Mum never finished her sentence – the phone was always slammed down just after the word 'Bible'.

My voice would tremble. 'Will I go down and get him, Mum? I'll go down and get him?'

---

6 Mum named her condition 'Nervy Bs' – shorthand for nervous breakdown.

'Get down there, Lan, dear! You know what you have to do! Get yourself down to that RSL club and BRING your BASDARD father back HERE!'

I'd watch Mum, her body heavy with sadness, fall into her cell of a bedroom along with a packet of Bex powders and a glass of water, snatching a handful of red raspberry lollies as she limped past. She'd slip her op-shop shoes off, heave her burning heart onto the unmade bed and light another cigarette. In darkness illuminated by the lone circle of red fire, I would see her teeth resting in the greasy glass of water along with the Bex powder, and I became even more determined to leave my family.

My brothers were angry strangers, never home, and if they were their presence was loaded. My sister was often found reading and twirling her hair beneath a faded orange chenille blanket in the bedroom we shared.

I didn't have anywhere to go and not a lot to do, so I tried to be invisible.

But I'd walk ever so proudly into that giant concrete tomb, the Penguin RSL Club, wearing a cotton dress, my mouth sticky with cheap glossy lipstick, clutching my new op-shop bag to my hips for protection. I seemed to go utterly unnoticed – not a single RSL drinker would acknowledge my presence.

I'd cast my eyes over the room, wary of the condition my father might be in or the damage he may have caused. I would spot him immediately, reciting repetitive jokes and spouting delusions of grandeur. The bartender would help me get him outside, where he'd fall into the back of a taxi. I would feel his anger building.

'Your fucking mother and you, ruining my night. Why can't you just let a man have a few effing ... *arghhhhhh* ... trying to make money for you mongrel basdards and this is the thanks I get? I would not be *you* for quids, Lannah.'

I would feel the tension in my jaw creating a toothache. I always had to pretend to agree with his rantings.

The taxi driver would speed up as we neared the milk bar, Dad drunkenly squinting ahead to see if Mum was standing at the back door wielding a poker. He'd forget where he was for a moment when he fell onto the lino floor, Mum standing over him like a demon, waving the poker around. She once hit Dad so hard that blood spurted out into a sack of rotten potatoes, casting them with a rather spectacular red glow.

When they fought, I'd wheel Martin on his wooden trolley of tragedy into the room I shared with my sister. The dinner Mum had been keeping warm for Dad would dribble down the walls while she chain-smoked to the sounds of my father's chronic sentimentality.

'I'm a hopeless father, I'm never going to amount to anything, you poor fucking kids never had a chance, you're right, Aileen. I'm a failure.'

My sister and I would sit together on the lino to watch the final act: Mum surveying the damage, her shoulders frozen, her mouth tight, her eyes spitting fire at her landowner/lord/husband/future prime minister. Dad had been wounded many times by Mum's wicked taunts, laid low by her unnatural talent for reducing him to a wretch before our very eyes.

'You're a FAILURE, Jimmy. A two-bob snob, a FAILURE to everyone. I hope you rot in hell.'

On the 'fighting' nights, my sister and I would huddle into each other. Dad would fall to his knees and crawl toward us like a giant bald baby, bawling to us how we were mongrels, and it was a shame we had been born. Mum, her mouth tight, would nod at me with a solidarity that made me love her a little bit.

I remember thinking that if this was love, a father's love for his daughter, I'd better bloody lap it up, as I needed his love to survive.

I wish I had felt nothing but happiness to see Dad showing his love for me, but with his head buried in my lap, and my hands forced to stroke his face, it didn't feel how I imagined love from a father should feel. He would stay crouched for too long, his hands grabbing my legs, his head buried, forgetting I was his daughter.

When I heard the slap of Mum's hand across the back of my father's head, I would move fast. I'd run inside the milk bar and take all the money, including the coins. I would grab ten packets of cigarettes and a box of matches for Mum, a bag of lollies and a choc wedge ice-cream for me. I'd throw a nightie of Mum's into a suitcase, along with her good slacks, her good jumper and the car keys. I'd toss them into the car parked beneath the harsh light of a Penguin street lamp. Mum wouldn't say a word. I wouldn't say a word. The night would be still and silent as we escaped into the gloom and mist like two jailbirds.

I'd feel safe in the Holden (even though Mum didn't understand reverse wasn't a gear change), drawing further and further away from the milk bar, safe from my father, my siblings, from the Coke bottles lined up along the hallway and the butcher's knife jammed in the milk bar doors. The butcher's knife was to stop me from entering at night and eating *all* the profits!

Once, in the middle of the night, me and my pillowcase crept past my parents' bedroom and, like a mother filling a Christmas stocking, I filled my pillowcase with Samboy chips, mixed lollies and a small assortment of more expensive treats: Golden Roughs, Mint Patties, Milky Bars and Choo Choo licorice bars. And just like Santa Claus I handed out my stolen loot to the most popular kids, hoping it would buy me some friends. A Choo Choo bar for Wendie, a Mint Pattie for Tracee, Samboy chips for Trudy. You're not popular, so *nothing* for you, I'm afraid!

One morning Andrew Smith, the most popular boy in my grade, asked me to add a packet of Champion Ruby tobacco to the gift situation.

But my father caught me red-handed, Champions in my guilty hand. He clipped me behind the ears and treated my 'pillowcase theft' as if it made me a deranged Tasmanian devil – a devil who had committed a mortal sin against him. Dad lodged a large carving knife with a wooden handle across the entrance to the milk bar so that I couldn't 'break in' *ever* again.

My pillowcase theft hadn't even worked – I was still friendless! There was a knife lodged in the milk bar door to remind me.

I wondered afterward if God knew I was going straight to hell and had given up on me. I didn't understand why I'd never had any friends. On cockier days, I'd convince myself it was because I was a fast runner. On lonelier days I'd convince myself it was because I was ugly and my family had a bad reputation.

'Not long to go now, Lan. Not long to go now, dear … we'll be at Nan's soon. Don't tell Nan about your father … she'll only worry. Good girl, Lan, you're a good girl, aren't you, Lan?'

Driving down that dark concrete highway where nothing made sense, I'd feel Mum's hand touching mine, her fingers trying to grab my shaking wrists. I couldn't look at her for I thought I might split open. This was our sacred moment, my most intimate memory wrapped up in hope. Mum would squeeze my hand, whispering words under her breath, words that I never did quite hear. The squeeze on my wretched little church hands still haunts me.

I would train both my eyes on the concrete highway, my mouth full of illicit lollies, my heart singing along with the radio station Mum allowed me to have on, the one that Dad would never let me listen to. For five hours we'd drive to the safety of my nan's dark, clean, silent flat in Elboden Street, South Hobart. She had been living there alone since Pop died of pancreatic cancer.

I watched Mum and Nan closely after Pop died. I watched them become even closer. Apparently after Pop's funeral, Mum walked silently into her bedroom and closed the door on the world. She cried and slept for an entire week. Mum always told me how much she missed her father and how fiercely she'd loved him. Her disappointment when my father refused to help her with the dishes on the eve of their honeymoon was the beginning of the end of their marriage, Mum told me.

It would be almost dawn as we neared Hobart town, and even though I could sense my mum was a little calmer, I could also see the hollow of her chest, feel the emptiness pressing down on her bruised heart.

'Nearly there now, Lan. Nearly there. Be a good girl now, Lan, and go straight to bed, won't you?'

'I will, Mum. I'll go straight to bed. Can I have a bath at Nan's?'

Mum would nod, watching the winding highway ahead, tapping her hand on my knee, lost in a distant memory.

I would listen to Mum and Nan nattering for hours. Their conversation was often so intense it seemed they didn't stop to draw breath. I could hear the familiar sound of a teaspoon spinning in one of Nan's 'good china' teacups and the sound of a match lighting their only comfort, cigarettes. Nan and Mum would soothe each other as they both agreed that Mum's marriage was a gigantic mistake.

'I warned you, dear Aileen … I warned you, Aileen, dear.'

It was always a shock when I saw Mum out from behind the milk bar counter. She was less shouty, less teary and maybe a little happier. Nan fussed over Mum's nerves and fears, and they'd pray, repeating the Hail Mary with Nan's blessed-by-the-Pope rosary beads. There was always much discussion on how the milk bar would trade without Mum around, and who would open the milk bar for the bread man at 5.30 am.[7]

7 Nobody got out of bed for the bread man when Mum wasn't there.

And just as I was getting settled into a routine of daytime Hobart TV and being allowed to visit the South Hobart op shop on my own, Mum would announce in a flood of tears that we were driving back immediately. Martin was young and Dad wasn't managing.

After a few stern words on how I had to look after Mum and to try to be a good girl, Nan would wave us goodbye with a clean handkerchief. Mum could barely breathe after we pulled out of Nan's safe, leafy street. I have never seen her cry harder and for longer than after a visit with Nan, and we'd often have to stop so that Mum could pull herself back together.

My mood would quickly sour on the long drive back from Hobart to Penguin. I'd be angry with Mum for leaving so quickly after the comfort of fleeing.

It seemed that nobody ever noticed the great fleeing, they all just floated off into their own small worlds again. It was almost as if the great fleeing never happened.

6

A-Grade

Mrs Stephenson was my favourite teacher at primary school; she'd given me six As and a B+ on my grade 6 report. I worried myself sick that she would step onto the lino floor, heralded by the tinkle of the milk bar bell, and spy me sitting behind the counter in my scorched-pink dressing gown.

She'd told Mum and the entire school that I was clever, and that I had a wonderful, vivid imagination. I believe these were my first ever compliments, and I held on to them like a child holding a sparkly rattle. Mrs Stephenson told Mum that my essay about a rag doll in a pram was excellent work.

'But Judith, JUDITH! What are you TALKING about? Lannah doesn't have a doll!' I heard her tell Mrs Stephenson.

'Oh, that makes it even more extraordinary, as Alannah's story was so vivid and so full of imagination. She's a very good student.'

The truth is, there was so much my mum didn't know about me: I had to believe that Mum was too busy in the milk bar to understand my school achievements.

I was competitive, a true Aries, throwing myself into English essays, completing all the work before anybody else, speed reading, being a good girl to try to impress my parents. I wanted to prove myself at Penguin state school, to prove that I was no longer an unjoined shadow doll.

When I was in grade 6, Bernadette and I were both chosen to play in the Tasmanian State Junior North-West basketball team. I'd thrown myself furiously into the game, fleet of foot and often too quick to choose where next to hurl that hard, pot scourer–surfaced brown ball of thrilling doom! I was given an orange shirt with a number on the back and a pair of black shorts. Bernadette was given the same. She was number 5 and I was number 8.

Bernadette could shoot goals from the centre of the court. She'd line up the ball, aim it at the back of the ring, and whoooosh, straight into the basket. I was a guard, a quick-running one, which meant I was permitted to roam all over the basketball court. The point guards were often called hoggers.

'Don't *hog* the ball, Hill! She's hogging the ball again, get her *off the court*. She's hogging the ball!'

Bernadette confirmed I was a hogger.

She also confirmed that all I did was run wild around the basketball court, bouncing up and down, looking for attention.

I auditioned for the primary school play, a giddy pantomime of nonsense and foolery. Mrs Stephenson gave me a script and said, 'You're going to be Frosty the Snowman.' I played the starring role, performing a tap dance. I don't think anybody in my family knew I was learning how to tap dance, but some Saturday mornings I would attend the tap dancing lessons held in the Penguin Scout Hall. I'd tap, tap, tap away with a graceful shuffle over endless afternoons of desperate boredom at home, tapping my way into a new technicolour reality. Not a soul at school knew I had the special power of tap, so quite a scene ensued when I broke into a tap routine at our next rehearsal, fully robed in my snow-white Frosty costume.

I looked forward to the gala premiere at the Penguin Scout Hall and my debut upon the stage. But when it came, I could see the seats marked *Mr & Mrs Hill* were both empty. No matter how hard I sang, tap-danced and acted upon the stage, I couldn't stop the growing emptiness I felt.

After the show, the entire cast was presented with an award. Mrs Stephenson congratulated me, and other girls came up to me with kind words, but I couldn't hear a word that was said, only the circuitous questions spinning through my mind. *Where were they? Why couldn't they come? Why were they never there? Why didn't they care?*

7

Girl on a Train

Sometimes I wanted to be a nun, a lovely, wicked, *adorable* nun. But something happened to me when I was around twelve years old that changed me in ways I still don't completely understand and I expect I never really will. The guilt and shame that followed this event shattered my faith and trust in people. I became disillusioned with life and whatever was left of my childhood disappeared.

I was off to visit Nan, for a one-week holiday. Bernadette wasn't coming with me on this trip so I felt *very* special and privileged. My brother Joseph was travelling with me to Hobart and then going on to Geeveston, where my father's brother, Hayden, owned a butcher shop. Joseph and I barely spoke to each other – I cannot recall a single conversation we'd ever had. I disliked him and he disliked me. I avoided him and he avoided me.

My mother didn't see my brother for a week after he was born. In 1959, if you didn't see your baby for days after the birth, it meant something had gone wrong, often with no real explanation. Joseph was handed back to Mum when he was seven days old, and she was simply told that he had been born in a 'shocked condition' and had needed extra oxygen. My father was unable to hide his disappointment at siring a son who was born in a shocked condition.

When Joseph was around three years old, he knocked the handle on a pot that was boiling on Nan's stove. The boiling water spilled all over his naked skin and he lay in a 'burns cot' for six weeks in the Hobart hospital with burns to 60 per cent of his body. He was left alone there, with his hands and feet tied to the ends of a hospital bed.

Mum and Dad did not visit Joseph. They said they were too busy, and Mum was pregnant with me, and so Joseph lay alone for six weeks, tossing from side to side, side to side, in his tiny burns cot. It was often hard for me not to feel a bit sorry for the little boy Joseph, and his grim start in life.

But growing up, I didn't like being around him because his manner was perverse and unpredictable. So I stayed silent on the platform with him as we watched the famous Tasman Limited luxury train slowly roll in, the colossal fear of living the only thing we had in common.

I remember the smoothness of my train ticket in my hand, and my mum's runaway brown suitcase by my side, held together with a pair of brown pantyhose. The name on the tag read *Aileen Hill, Penguin*, and I made a little note to myself to rub out the 'ileen' and just leave the 'A'.

A Hill, Penguin.

The journey from Penguin to Hobart was eight hours. I climbed aboard first, not speaking to or looking at Joseph. I looked for a seat away from him but our tickets were numbered and stamped, so we had to sit together, although I instinctively made sure my brown suitcase separated us.

The train cut through the countryside of the Tasmanian Midlands. Outside I could see miles and miles of lush green pastures, with giant sloping trees shielding the vast cattle estates in the picturesque townships of Ross and Campbell Town from Tasmania's harsh winter. Pretty spring flowers had begun to grow along the train tracks and at one stage I even saw a kangaroo. The train rocked wildly but I stared down at my hands, counting the ever-multiplying freckles on the back of them. A red lollipop got stuck in my hair and I couldn't get it out.

Coral, the beaming ruddy-faced mistress of the Tasman Limited, mentioned how lucky we were to have so much privacy – our carriage car was almost empty. She brought me an Enid Blyton book to read. Soon after, Coral informed the train over her PA system that she would be resting for two hours and if we wanted a drink or more lollipops to wander through to the cafe carriage between 3 and 4 pm.

I was very busy pretending to be asleep so that I didn't have to *look at* or *speak to* my brother. He was staring ahead at nothing.

Time was moving very slowly for me that day. I listened to the regular bump of the carriage wheels and the clatter of dishes as the lunch trays were being washed and dried in the restaurant carriage. The sun slanted through the windows of the moving train and my pretend dozing finally worked because I fell into a Tasman Limited sleep.

And then, suddenly, I was *wide* awake. I woke to heavy frantic breathing and something being pushed inside me.

Wide awake, confused and horrified.

I knew in that same moment I wanted to die – I wanted to die forever and ever. I felt the sharp pain from something being pushed into my private girl parts. I remember wondering why my brother wasn't helping me and then I realised it was him.

The tartan coat he'd been wearing that day was covering my body, so nobody could see what he was doing. He told me to stay quiet and be still, to just lie there while he continued to push his fingers deep inside me, pushing and squeezing my girl parts until I wondered how I was going to keep breathing. He told me I would like what he was doing, and asked me questions about what two fingers felt like, what three fingers felt like … he asked me to tell him how much I liked it. He told me not to talk about what had happened with anyone. I would be in big trouble with everyone if I did.

I wanted to throw up my Vegemite sandwich. I wanted the past to start all over again. I wanted him to stop, but for every painful second that passed on the train that afternoon, I became more and more desperate with myself. *Why can't I move away from him? Why can't I just get up and slap him?*

But I was trapped. Frozen. I didn't know how to make him stop.

I held my Catholic breath and imagined leaving mist on the train's window, so I could write the words *help me*, but I didn't do any of that. I just lay there, completely still and horrified, as station after station passed by.

I didn't want to open my eyes to see how the world had changed.

Limp and broken, I felt like a throwaway doll that could never be put back together. By the time the train finally pulled into Hobart Station, I was not the same girl any longer. I was a shadow person, and I felt like a monster.

My dear nan was waiting on the cold, empty platform, her new op-shop purchase, a glittering tiara, placed perfectly on her seventy-year-old violet-permed head. Nan's wrinkled hands were outstretched to me and she immediately asked of my mother.

'How is your poor mother, Lan? How is your poor, poor mother? I hope you're being a good girl, Lan. I hope you're looking after her. You're working in the milk bar after school, aren't you, Lan? You're helping her with the Sunday bread orders, aren't you, Lan? And going to confession down at the church, aren't you, Lan? And Joe! Joseph dear, come here, give your old nan a kiss! Oh, you have grown, Joe! You're a giant! How old are you? Fifteen? Isn't he a giant, Lan? You must have had a lovely trip down together. Did you natter and play cards? Did you eat anything, Joe, you look tired.'

My heart was breaking. I was screaming but no one could hear me.

Look at me, Nan. Look *at me! I am ruined ... Can't you see? Mum is fine. I am not fine. Look at what just happened to me, Nan. Please help me. Get him away from me. I can't breathe or speak, Nan. I will never be the same ever again, Nan. I am ruined, I will not recover from this ...*

We caught a taxi to Nan's flat and I had to sit there with him at Nan's tiny kitchen table wondering when the local priest would deliver me into hell, burning me alive for the rest of my life.

'Why didn't you stop him?' I heard God ask.

'Why didn't *you* stop him?' I heard myself asking God.

I remember Nan asking why I wasn't eating my favourite meal, arrowroot biscuits with warm milk and four spoonfuls of sugar. I wanted to throw Nan's meal against the wall but instead I was mute. Silent. I'd never felt uglier. I listened to the sound of Nan nattering over the ABC news, all the while hating myself.

I hid in the toilet and threw my dancing-daisy panties into the flushing water. I remember the green daisies laughing at me as they drowned just like it was yesterday.

'Come on, Lan, dear, *Young Talent Time* is about to start ... Did you wash your hair today, Lan? The *Young Talent Time* girls wash their hair with Velvet soap, that's why their hair is always so shiny ...'

Later, Nan ran a bath for me. I found some pink calamine lotion in the cupboard and poured it over myself to stop the hurting.

Nan wasn't the easygoing-nan type. She was getting old and wanted her privacy. I wanted *no privacy* and needed to be near her, so I crept into her room when she was asleep and lay beside her in the dark.

At the time, I didn't tell anyone what had happened because I had no words and no clue how to make any kind of sense of it. It was only a year or so later that, embarrassed, I told my sister. I had to tell someone in the milk bar why I couldn't be around my brother. Afterwards, we both just stared ahead at the Penguin Oval, 9 metres away from our milk bar. We didn't know what to say, or what to think.

I already thought of myself as a little mongrel basdard, and so I believed that's what happened to girls like me. I knew my hair would never shine like the girls on *Young Talent Time* and I blamed myself, I lost my confidence for a long time, and I felt like all the butterflies in the world had died.

Mum would often say, 'Joe's SO good with his hands, Lan, isn't he? He's a BORN carpenter, just like Jesus was! Look at how GOOD he is with his hands, Lan.'

The thought of Joseph's hands doing anything good left me in a state of total darkness. I refused to look at him, refused to speak to him, refused to be near him.

To tell somebody what had happened meant that I would have to remember it all over again; giving a voice to what he did would make it too real, and my feelings of helplessness around him made me feel angry and abnormal. It took everything I had left to carry on with life.

Fifteen years later the secret came out. I was in Tasmania on my annual three-day Christmas visit. My brother Mark's wife, Maureen, confided in me one evening, even though we were not close. She told me she didn't like her two children being around Joseph. She wondered why she didn't feel comfortable around him either, and thought he seemed emotionally gutted, stunted. She asked if there was something wrong with him. I confided back and told her my childhood secret. I trusted her not to tell my mother.

As soon as I arrived home to Melbourne, I received an ear-piercingly shrill call from Mum, informing me that I was a liar, and how *dare* I bring down the family name by telling lies about poor old Joe …

'How DARE you gossip to that MAUREEN that you were molested? How DARE you! The gossip will be ALL over town, Lannaaaaah.'

We wouldn't talk about what happened on that train in any meaningful way until I was nearly fifty and Mum was nearly dead.

I understand that for Joseph it was a moment in time, a moment in time that was wrong. I understand why he still can't face me. I do not blame my brother, dear reader, but it would have helped to have somebody I could trust in the days, the months, the years that followed.

One of the most damaging things you can do to an abused girl is to *not* believe her. For me, to not be believed was worse than what happened on the train. Sometimes this can set a different train in motion, a runaway, nightmare train filled with teenage girls and a driver with no intention of stopping.

8

Death by Lawnmower

After the train incident, I went right off the Tasman Limited rails. I didn't know where I was going and I didn't know how to get used to my new *off the rails* self. I built a very tall fence around my heart – nobody was *ever* going to get in, and nobody was *ever* going to get out.

It felt like I had died and all my dreams of becoming a somebody had vanished into the whirring wheels of my runaway childhood. I threw away the clothes I had been wearing on the train that day. I threw away any last threads of trust. I could not laugh, or hide. I couldn't talk properly. A scared tip-rat, I cried at the drop of a scream. And I could not be in the same room as Joseph.

No one in my family took any notice of my new personality.

Looking back, I think I was in shock, afflicted by a convulsion of memories I was trying hard to forget. I shook my head a thousand times a day trying to wish what had happened away. But in the end, I did what girls who often feel ashamed, guilty and sad do: I diminished. I watched my school grades decline and I didn't care. I couldn't keep friends and I didn't care. I became both louder and more introverted. I believed I was dirty and so I went looking for a new family that I thought might understand me: a family I'd spied scavenging from the Penguin tip.

In every small rural town there is at least one house, one family, one situation that is 'special'. Special because the house is haunted, or because of some berserk act of violence or horror so profound that not a living soul speaks of it – maybe a squad of mad communists or a religious sex cult. A house of ill repute. A fop house! All children, good and bad, know the story of the special house; they even help circulate the rumours that build its myth.

If Penguin had a Special House, it was most definitely the one five doors away from our milk bar – the house that we all believed to be a front for some unholy activity, very likely of a treacherous nature, a house inhabited by a family called the Williamses.

The Williams house was pale asbestos and whenever it rained it turned from a dull nunnery grey to a mottled Bible black. The water stains on its outer walls suggested demonic faces, witch-burnings and various blasphemies in unknown languages. The windows were dark mirrors that distorted our reflections and prevented us from solving the mystery of the Williamses. The wild daisies straggling across the front garden seemed dangerously different to any daisy that I'd ever seen, and I believed the tortured bushes held poisonous seedlings that, if inhaled, would immediately infect you with a Williams virus that would kill you dead within a week.

Usually, a Special House family would have fallen on hard times from a supremely dizzy height for reasons beyond their control, but the Williamses had managed to achieve their notoriety without any particular effort. The Williamses were simply one of those families cursed by something untoward in their DNA. And in my confused, abused state,

I was drawn to them like a butterfly to a rotting flower. I became obsessed with all their comings and goings, carefully monitoring each tip trip, on alert for the sounds of their falling-apart blue truck. I would spy the truck coughing past the milk bar, overflowing with tyres, old cupboards, a set of swings and once even a small car. My mum was curious as to why I was so curious about the tip family.

'You LOVE the Williams, don't you, Lan?'

'Mum, they're crazy, they terrify me! When I'm at the tip looking for cats and prams they're *always* there, they seem to *live* on the tip, Mum, they're always staring at me in their dirty rag clothing. I hate that Robert Williams. He flashed his thing at me once when I walked past the Williams house. Flashed it at me, Mum! I don't like what Jane and Robert Williams do together at the creek and —'

'What DID you SAY, Lan? What do you MEAN? What does Robert Williams do to Jane Williams? What do they do, Lan? You said it so now you better SPIT IT OUT, LAN, what does ROBERT do to JANE Williams?'

'I think he touches her up, Mum.'

'He WHAT?'

'He touches her up.'

I had to be quick here, dear reader. I could see Mum's mind mulling over my Williams news, her Catholic self appalled and disgusted by the thought of anyone touching anyone, let alone a Williams touching a Williams. Uninvited, shame crept into my own heart and took up residence. I absorbed everything I felt in its entirety and allowed it to sink into the centre of my being until it became part of my identity. I was now part of the Robert-and-Jane-Williams-touching-up reality and I could see it made Mum angry.

By the time my path crossed with the Williamses', the entire family had regressed into a state of irredeemable decay. The Williams children – Jane,

Robert and Susie – had a feral air of unpredictability, rarely attended school and seemed almost entirely unsupervised. The Williams parents were never seen except as smudged silhouettes, heard only as distant, muffled voices, with an aura of unreality.

We were all warned to turn away from them and to shun the asbestos house. What the parents of Penguin didn't know was that Robert and Jane Williams (who *may* have been twins) had contrived a medieval sideshow for reasons of their own that lured me and a handful of others to a damp and unloved gully in some rough bush creek beyond Penguin's outer limits to witness forbidden acts.

Jane and Robert would put on their sad show for the five bored teens in Penguin, sexing each other beneath a towering ghost gum. I was always very disturbed and yet terribly curious, sitting on a little rock watching Jane and Robert having *real-life* actual sex. The desolate Penguin creek formed the backdrop to the dismal scene of Jane and Robert Williams as they seemed to float toward each other and at the same time float away from each other, like islands in the stream of their own squalid universe. We five gruesome locals would sit watching patiently. Not a word was said, not a blackbird cawed. God had been distracted by something else.

One autumn afternoon in the middle of Jane and Robert Williams' performance, a freezing Sunkist ice block burning blisters into my fingers, I became overwrought, upset and, for reasons I cannot understand, I stood up. This was against the rules of the Jane and Robert Williams Show. I threw all of Jane's clothes in the Penguin creek, *knowing* she'd have nothing to wear home. Perhaps it was my way of pushing someone to do something about this crime, or maybe it was a subconscious urge to drown out the desperation I felt – the red-and-white spotted cotton dress, a stained white man's cardigan, her brother's socks and sandals, each sandal a different size and colour.

Years later I would see woodcut images from long ago of naked peasants cavorting with the devil by moonlight in unlovely covert locations, images of the Inquisition, witchcraft, a parallel reality – and I would feel the same endless falling vertigo I experienced in the hopelessly sad sideshow of the young Williamses and their travesty of love.

All this was before the fateful evening.

Sitting on my small stool behind the counter in the milk bar, I heard the shop bell's little tinkle of doom telling me a customer was *actually* inside the milk bar. I was immediately annoyed and presumed it would be a small child trading their Coca-Cola bottle for five cents' worth of mixed lollies. I had painted my mouth with Mum's lipstick, drawing over the lines of my lips with a dark Avon pencil to give me the ghoulish appearance of the Joker. I was ready to scowl but the customer was not a child trader – it was a Williams! Susie Williams.

The many mutating legends of the Williamses and their ghastly lives flashed through my mind in a rapidly unwinding horror movie. I noticed Susie Williams circling her own shadow, her grey eyes shifting from misery to despair in a micro-second. Susie seemed ill at ease and the dark circles under her eyes made them look bigger and wilder still. She had recently cut her hair short – it was very straight and brown and came to a point over each ear, with her eyebrows plucked away to nothing. In their place Susie had drawn in dark-green texta the shape of a semicircle. If you stood a little away from Susie, her head resembled a question mark.

Whenever Susie sloped in to buy half a loaf of bread in the darkened glow of our milk bar, her eyes would shimmer, her gaze never settling on anything solid. I wondered what it was that haunted her so.

I looked up into her eyes and witnessed more terror, more pain and more unhappiness than I ever thought possible from a fourteen-year-old girl.

'What is it, Susie? What's happened? What can I … ?'

Her voice was strangely alien. She didn't scream, she didn't yell, she didn't even raise her voice. 'It's Mum. I don't know, I can't wake her up – I can't pull her out of the bath – she's too big and she's lying on top of a lawnmower anyway. Dad keeps the mower in the bath.'

I was *beside* myself.

I became even more beside myself than anyone beside me could *ever* hope to be. A *dead* Williams mother? Apparently *in* a bath on top of a lawnmower? I loved a drama, big or small. And this drama appeared to be not small at all – far from it!

'Dead? You think your mum's dead, Susie? Should we ring someone? This is *very* serious. Susie? Where's Jane? Robert? Your dad? Where are they?'

Susie was a statue of fear. Her hands were black and I could see tear stains on her face – the police must be called.

'Susie, I'll run next door and get them to call the police,' I said with a singsong twist to reassure Susie that everything would be alright. I screamed at our neighbour Mr Butcher to call the bloody police or bloody anybody. Mrs Williams was *dead in a bath.* He withered before my eyes, rolling drunk amid the litter of twenty tins of Boag's, a pack of cards, and cold takeaway fish and chips, incapable of telephoning anybody.

I hurled myself back into the milk bar to find Susie in exactly the same position as when I left, her eyes darting toward mine as though looking for some kind of miracle.

'Susie, it will be alright, love.' I began to fib. 'The ambulance is coming, the fire brigade is coming, the scoutmaster is coming, they're *all* coming for your mum, Susie. Everything will be alright – here, have a raspberry or a Cobber, actually take the whole box with you – you want to stay here with me or go see how your mum is doing, love?'

'She's not waking up. Someone pushed her and she hit her head. Mum hit her head and there's blood and —'

'Blood? Someone pushed her? That is *murder*, Susie. I watched that on *The Waltons* last week. Like *real* blood? Do you think we should walk down to the *house* and have a bit of a look?'

Susie stared straight ahead, sucking on a Cobber. She didn't suck on it like a normal person; rather, she moved the Cobber around her mouth and licked it with her tongue. I stared in wonder at this new phenomenon while Susie whimpered before my black-kohled eyes.

'I can't eat lollies properly, I got no teeth … Mama's asleep in the bath and Jane's pregnant! Robert got her pregnant and me dad found out and Mum fell into the bath …'

I grabbed Susie's hand in mine and pulled her back to her own shadow-house. Jane and Robert Williams were lying in each other's arms on the dirt floor, weeping loudly, which made me weep also.

Mrs Williams was draped across a rusty lawnmower in the bath and Mr Williams was nowhere to be seen. My chest suddenly felt hollow; it felt like there was a giant hole, and at the bottom of this hole a heavy weight was pressing down onto my stomach. I couldn't stand to see that much sadness in the world; I couldn't look at life's hopelessness any longer. Pregnant fifteen-year-old Jane lay on the floor like an overgrown child next to her brother, the father of the innocent baby inside her belly with the wrong DNA, the wrong life, the wrong parents. The wrongness of this God-awful mess seared my soul.

It was the last I ever saw of the Williams family.

In the front paddock, a litter of kittens was living on the front seat of a decaying car, meowing their pitiful little cries to nobody and nothing – I could see no sign of the mother cat so I took those motherless kittens and hid them underneath my bed. They lived with me for eighteen hours until my father discovered them. He hated cats. He hated animals. I knew as soon as I arrived home from school the next day that my kittens were gone.

I peered under my bed hoping

hoping

hoping

hoping.

But my family of kittens was all gone.

I was too frightened to ask where they were. I knew the answer would destroy me. I lay down on the floor beside my unmade single bed and cried into my platform school shoes.

9

Mushroom Perm

Mum was sent urgently to hospital and we were told all her insides were coming out in a three-hour operation. It was what Mum called 'her hysteria', a hysterectomy. After two whole weeks in the hospital, an angrier, more impatient version of Mum returned home.

She was instructed to rest in her bedroom for three weeks, but with Dad selling superannuation plans as well as life insurance schemes, Mum was back behind the counter in less than four days. She soon had something called a prolapse and had to go back to the hospital. Nan came up on the train and looked after us, and I heard her talking to my father in a voice I hadn't heard before – a serious, stern and determined voice, telling my father that the milk bar was killing Mum and we had to sell up and move away. For Mum's sake. I furiously agreed as I eavesdropped.

After Mum recovered from her 'hysteria' and prolapse, we swapped our milk bar for a house in Ulverstone. On the same day, the Hansons moved into our milk bar and we moved into their house in Queen Street. A perfect swap. I walked the 1.5 kilometres to school every day on my own in my platform shoes and black tights.

All through grades 9 and 10, I purchased the popular girls' lunches from the school canteen. The popular girls were caramel brown and they all had boyfriends. They were not only beautiful but they played sport, had loving families and money for lunch.

I took the popular girls' orders, nodding in agreement at their choices of sugar-filled canteen food, lost in my private horror – how the *hell* did I let this happen? *Get your own effing lunches*, I thought to myself. But outwardly I high-schooled along in this demented situation, the high-pitched demands of the popular girls ringing in my ears:

'I want *three* cream buns!'

'I want a *pie*!'

'I want a *cold* drink! Cold, not warm.'

'I want a salad roll with *no* beetroot, *no* tomato, *no* ham, *no* lettuce and *no* butter – you got that? *No butter*!'

'You better hurry cos we're *all starving*! Starving! Go, Wardrobe,[8] go!'

These beautiful girls, who glowed and shone in the shower of heavenly rose petals that fell inside their elite area, would hand me their money and I'd set off dutifully to fulfil all their insane lunch orders,[9] often bumping into my sister, who ghosted around the school corridors with three mysterious library-type girls. She wouldn't look at me or speak to me, and her three library friends were also instructed not to.

Sometimes Mr Fox, the bored yet slightly caring maths teacher, would spot me in the quadrangle, nervous perspiration on my upper lip, my brow creased and freckled hands fumbling the girls' change.

'You alright there, Alannah?'

I saw in his face what I found impossible to hide. Water began welling up in my eyes. He regarded me rather sadly, the raspberry jam from a cream bun dripping onto my op-shop clothes.

'Everything OK at home, Alannah?'

---

8 My nickname was Wardrobe or Mushroom Head. My dark hair had acquired, courtesy of Mum, a pensioner's perm – a knotted mess of over-curled, over-dried, over-cooked permed hair, which adorned my head more like a mushroom than a halo.

9 I also purchased the recess snacks.

I scurried away from Mr Fox and his brown lace-up shoes and corduroy pants. I was becoming aware of a new and *very* alarming situation about myself: if anyone showed me any kindness or warmth or real concern, I had to control every nerve, every neuro-nerve, every cell in my body not to fall into their arms and rest a while. If I didn't run when I felt the tears welling up, I'd never be able to look myself in the eye again. I couldn't allow any kind of comfort from strangers. Not even Mr Fox.

Paradoxically, I also didn't want to look or be like everybody else. I often found myself on a cold wooden plank outside the headmaster's office, waiting for a dressing down for having dared to wear platform shoes, black tights and a too-short pleated skirt, with no hint of the dull grey school uniform. This was frowned upon by the school. My defiant dress code, along with all the make-up I was wearing to school and my mushroom perm, was apparently considered untoward. Five attempts to telephone my parents to inform them of my misdemeanours had gone unanswered.

Another strategy I discovered to *not* be at home was to join the Girl Guides. The Girl Guides of Penguin town accepted me as a Girl Guide for one week. With two other girls, I would knock on strange doors selling our stale Girl Guide biscuits and fulfilling my natural compulsion to peek into other people's houses in the hope of discovering different realities to my own. The Girl Guide uniform was too expensive for my parents and so very, very creatively (I thought) I began to make the patches and badges of Girl Guide achievement from loose scraps I found, purloined or scrounged from the Penguin tip. My attempt to replicate the uniform and its attendant honours was dimly viewed by the Girl Guide leadership group. A team leader with baggy skin from a thousand and one bush hikes told me I didn't have the right outlook to become a real Girl Guide and it was decided I could 'pop in' to the Girl Guide hall but I would not be able to call myself a Girl Guide. I could not go on any trips, play any of the games or sell the biscuits at strangers' doors.

I was crushed. Unjoined. I couldn't fit in anywhere. I crushed up a packet of Girl Guide biscuits and stomped on them in an act of rebellious hurt.

Then one day, a slow-moving carnie gang crept into Ulverstone via the Old Coast Road, passing right in front of our Queen Street porch, their garish caravans decorated in various gypsy colours, a mangy tranquillised tiger trapped in a small cage beside four sleeping (possibly dead) monkeys. I threw myself up into the air hoping a dead monkey might catch me. This was the break I'd been after!

'Mum! The circus is in town. I think they're heading for the showgrounds? I could get a job in the circus, Mum, with my dance moves! You know I'll be leaving home to go and live with them, don't you, Mum? You do know that, don't you, Mum? I am going to be a circus performer! What do you think about that then, Mum? Are you thrilled for me, Mum?'

Mum didn't seem to be thrilled about anything – her voice was flat; her hair was flat.

'Off you go then, Lan. Off you go to join the circus, dear. Your father will like that. You can tell him you're going to travel around Australia with a circus.'

'I'm going now, Mum. Aren't you worried about me, Mum? I'm going to be a carnie girl, Mum, riding elephants and doing all sorts of —'

'Off you go then, Lan. Do they sell show bags down there, Lan, dear?'

I stared at my mother but she didn't stare back. I left Mum in her kitchen smoking corner and ran away to join the circus.

The carnie life, unfortunately, was not a life for a girl like me. This was made quite apparent to my naive self by an oversized, overzealous, somewhat crazed man wearing a leather patch over one of his black eyes and cracking a well-cracked whip. He was the ringmaster, the manager, the only clown, the tamer of the animals, the *killer* of the animals. He told me I'd be sleeping in the yellow caravan with the jailbird chef, who I'd spied out of the corner of my eye carving up a freshly killed kangaroo, placing pieces of it into a small esky.

I spent two hours sewing sequins onto costumes.

I cleaned out the monkey cages.

I rode an elephant.

I tried to sleep in the chef's caravan but by 6.30 the next morning I decided I would run away back home to Mum in Queen Street. There was nowhere else to go.

Mum didn't seem to have noticed I'd been gone.

10

Where Did She Go?

I sat on a grey steel bench in the school quadrangle, my black-stockinged legs crisscrossed, my stained skirt perfectly pleated. It was the last day of high school and I was dying for the day to end. My report card up until grade 8 had displayed the first letter of my first name, but my grade 10 results proved to be rather damning. I comforted myself with the knowledge that nobody would care.

Across the quadrangle the popular girls were huddled together, weeping into handkerchiefs and scribbling emotional goodbyes to high school in patterned autograph books. I had overheard my schoolfriends discussing their plans to attend Devonport Technical College or Burnie Matriculation College and I was slightly alarmed. I realised my parents had never discussed my education with me, how I was going or where I wanted to go in the world.

Dad had encouraged Bernadette to attend Devonport Technical College with her straight As in typing, shorthand and taking dictation with 99 per cent accuracy. If she was going to be secretary to the Prime Minister of Australia, Bernadette must attend college to receive a framed certificate of excellence for secretarial skills. She caught a bus to the college each morning and within a year would receive her certificate.

On my last day of school, my father announced into the air and to nobody in particular that I was to be a hairdresser at Maria's Hair Shoppe in Ulverstone. 'This is the kind of job that can really take you places. You start on Monday, Alannah, and for God's sake, Aileen, tell Alannah not to let me down.'

I let my father down.

My hairdressing apprenticeship lasted six months. It was just me and a lady called Maria. Maria sat out the back in a tiny sectioned-off hallway stirring mugs of coffee, writing letters and breaking up with her second husband. I sat out the front stirring nothing and not breaking up with anybody, except for Maria. We didn't have many hair customers (or *clientele*) and I was forced to attend hairdressing school in Devonport one day a week. I got into trouble for setting the timers of all the hairdryers at trade school so they'd go off at the same time, and Maria received a handwritten letter from the trade school executives. I resigned from Maria's Hair Shoppe a few days after the letter arrived.

By this time, Bernadette had completely stopped talking to me. She didn't look my way any longer, and I didn't know if I cared, if I was hurt or angry. She then crept away in the middle of the night. One minute Bernadette was sleeping in the bed next to me, the next, she'd completely vanished from my world. I missed Bernadette's presence, knowing she was by my side in our small bedroom with our matching orange chenille bedspreads. I felt unsafe without her.

Mum informed me, after I'd combed her hair, made three cups of instant coffee and rubbed her tired, aching feet, that Bernadette had taken flight to live with a girlfriend from high school in Perth. She was working as a stenographer in a law office.

'Why is she ignoring me, Mum?'

Mum stared at me, juggling two lit cigarettes and three cups of cold coffee, a defiant, gleeful look on her face. She told me Bernadette didn't like ambitious, show-off girls, and apparently I fell headfirst into this category. She didn't like my unruly attention-seeking foolette behaviour.

Mark, my eldest brother, also vanished. Riding a black Harley-Davidson motorbike, black leather jacket flapping in the wind, he disappeared into the night. According to Mum, Mark was going straight to hell, moving and shaking with a new form of heathen, a Tasmanian biker gang whose leader promised Mark that he'd be anointed into the club just like a baptism. I was desperate to attend, but Mum assured me bikers would not understand me and I should stay away from my brother.

Mum had trained all of us to be nervous in Mark's presence, alarmed by his dark, obsessive temper, his angry shouting outbursts and his blatant disregard for authority. But Mark, my stranger brother, had a secret talent. My angry brother was a teenage poet! And in his own way, he spoke the truth of our past.

I am twelve years old and running late as I fearfully sneak through the gate
Silently slide through the rain, grimace at the impending pain
He snarls and strikes and I take the blow, the plaster cracks and down I go
'But, Dad, I won a trophy, Dad, aren't you proud?!' another blow and now he's ranting loud
It's hard to breathe here on the floor, more kicks and punches until I'm out the door
The wind is howling and it's raining hard, the door is locked and I'm in the yard
I sit and cry in an abandoned shed but to go back in fills me with dread
I know he's drunk and doesn't mean it and I try to live in between it
He was sent away at age eleven to a place with priests who spoke of heaven

What happened there in those years, did they hurt him and fill him with fear?
Is that the reason, could that be it so when he drinks he kicks and hits?
I don't know, I'm just cold and wet, three hours now and no rescue yet
Mum can't help, she's just too scared and tomorrow he won't know or care
My face is swollen and my legs are shaking, I fear tomorrow I fear his wakening
It never changes it's always the same and he makes me feel like I'm the one to blame[10]

With Bernadette and Mark having fled, I was living with Mum, Dad, Joseph and Martin – my family of glaring strangers. Being around Joseph caused me to breathe differently: I didn't know whether to hold my breath, or lose my breath completely. I decided I was going to leave home, this time for real.

But before I ran away for good, I turned myself inside out, upside down. Deciding that the love I craved could be won only by magnetically attracting it to myself, I began to reinvent everything I could find into dress-ups and costumes to make myself more lovable. I locked myself in the bathroom, draping my mother's polyester lace curtains around my body. I fashioned a startling Vaseline-styled '30s hairdo. I covered my face in beige foundation, lipstick, bright-blue eye shadow. I was determined not a single beam of light would ever shine through my impenetrable suit of armour.

I announced to Mum that I'd now be wearing make-up for the rest of my life. She told me I looked ridiculous and to take some 'layers' of her foundation off. I told her I'd be wearing more layers of eye shadow, more layers of lipstick, more layers of everything, and that nobody would ever see me without make-up, a costume or a hairdo *ever* again. Mum agreed that it was probably a good idea.

I op-shopped for my costumes, climbing over counters, over would-be competitors, over grandmothers, over small children, over anybody in my

10 Mark's dream was to become a songwriter or a band manager. As I write this Mark is living alone in a shed. He is divorced, with two grown children. He has stage-four liver cancer.

quest to get my hands on a fur muff or a black lace '60s frock. I tore up old clothes, refashioning them into outfits. I made myself a scarf from op-shop tea towels. I hitchhiked to Launceston, which had 'secret' op shops displaying signs like *New Arrivals* and *LayBy Now*. I was learning how to apply Dolly Cover Girl Make-Up and How to Make Your Stringy Hair Shiny.

I felt like a different person. I was transformed. No longer an abused little mongrel basdard, I understood the power of make-up and clothing. I was becoming the girl I'd always imagined I could be. Deep in my make-up world, a strange new reflection stared back from the bathroom mirror. My reinvention became my weapon to deal with the world. They say with any reinvention comes great power, and I held on to this belief like a Catholic girl's Bible, never letting it out of my sight.

My belief worked! A guardian angel performed a miracle – my sister needed me! Mum told me how Perth wasn't right for Bernadette and that she was living in a boarding house in Hobart. She had asked Mum if I would hitchhike to Battery Point to actually live with her.

I couldn't believe it when she told Mum she was ready for me.

The morning I hitchhiked the eight hours to Hobart, Mum was wrapped in one of her leopard-print dressing gowns. I climbed into a giant Golden Fleece petrol tanker with a stranger named King before turning and looking for Mum on the street, waving frantically. To nobody.

Mum had already gone back inside to bed.

11

Tantallon Boarding House

King, my Golden Fleece truck driver, dropped me in Macquarie Street outside the National Mutual building. I found a taxi that took me to my new room at Tantallon Boarding House. My taxi driver, unlike the silent King, took great delight in telling me the sad tale of Mr Charlesworth, who had lived out most of his eighty-four years at Tantallon. He caught alight from a small fire he'd built in the grate of his spartan room while he sat in front of a transistor radio listening to the greyhound races at the Glenorchy Showgrounds.

This grim little tale gave me some forewarning of what was to come.

Tantallon Boarding House was a derelict, decaying mansion on Mona Street, Battery Point, hiding itself in shame despite the views of the magnificent Derwent River below; it was a sad, lonesome, falling-down haunted house, estranged from all other houses in the world – almost as if its soul was rotting with boredom.[11]

---

11 I would find out later that the surrounding local residents had complained of the 'vagabond types' the boarding house seemed to attract – disenchanted taxi drivers, peculiar vagrants, ex-prisoners from Risdon Prison – and of the smell of petrol seeping from the front lawn and the little fires that seemed to start and finish with a match and a puff of smoke. The local council maintained it was an eyesore and threatened to close the place down.

Out the front was a handmade sign covered in spider webs:

Tant oardin ouse.

Complete with a full stop after the 'e'.

The once majestic hallway of Tantallon Boarding House was filled with ghostly spirit creatures. I could feel them. Hear them. It was impossible to ignore them. I stood silently in the doorway among the ghosts as the gloomy evening light slowly eclipsed my own frail shadow, and the rain tumbled from the gutters, forming petite lakes around my feet.

It was June 1977.

My battered $8 suitcase was held together with one fiercely knotted black stocking to protect the costumes that lay hidden within it in plastic bags. The little locks had been broken years before – they no longer clicked or even pretended they ever had. My hair had been newly fashioned – cut by myself. My old-lady mushroom perm had fantastically disappeared, replaced by a black bob with hot-pink cooking jelly smeared on one side. Eight pale-blue ribbons were loosely tied around the ends, and my mouth was smeared with black lipstick I'd borrowed from an op shop. Suddenly, I felt pale and afraid; what was I was doing here in the decrepit grandeur of Tantallon Boarding House, surrounded by ghosts and the obnoxious smell of burnt cabbage and kangaroo meat, mixed in with the familiar smell from a thousand cigarettes?

At the end of the hallway, a small sign printed with the words *DINING OOM* in a faded gothic font hovered above a dingy doorway. I wandered into the dining oom and sat down to rest my weary legs.

I sat like a ghost at one of the four shabby dining tables in the dining oom, staring into the eyes of four taxi drivers. They had put down their knives and forks to take a good look at the new resident. I took a good look back and attempted a smile. One of them smiled back and I looked quickly away. Despite this I could feel a sense of new-found freedom and wonder with the world. A silent tear sneaked out of one eye and floated down onto my rouged, freckled cheeks.

'Hello! You must be Alainaar? Are you Alainaar?' A booming voice startled my falling tear.

'I am!' I heard myself say. 'I am Alannah. Alannah Hill. I've come to Hobart to make my fortune!'

The largest person I had ever seen beamed down on me with an intelligent, bored gaze. She was wearing what looked like a brown chenille eiderdown. I could never *ever* remember her real name and from that first day I simply called her Eider Down. She never corrected me, and everybody else came to refer to her as Eider Down too.

'Do you want a cuppa, dear? Or some water? Maybe a little shandy? I've got some Arnott's bickies if you'd like one? And don't let those silly taxi men worry you, they're on their afternoon shift, so they'll *all* be gone soon and they won't be back until supper time. *Norman!* You drink too much and you're a fool!'

I madly, fearfully, read the rules and regulations on a board hooked to the wall by a brightly coloured ball of wool. They read like the Ten Commandments:

DINING ROOM RULES.

1. *Breakfast – 7.00 am until 7.30 am*
2. *No eating in your room*
3. *You can smoke in your room*
4. *No music allowed at any time*
5. *Tea – 6.00 pm until 6.30 pm*
6. *No foreign guests allowed on Tantallon property*
7. *No guns/knives allowed*
8. *Showers/toilet/bathroom time = ten minutes each guest*
9. *No entertaining other guests in your room*
10. *Respect others – shiftworkers asleep*

It slowly dawned on me that the boarding house had but one bathroom and one toilet to share among fifteen people. Out of the corner of my eye, I spied Eider Down rumbling toward me holding a huge dinner plate, two Arnott's biscuits resting disdainfully upon it.

'Take one, dear. Take one! Eat it now. I hope you're not the snobby type? You have to share the bathroom and the toilet with the other guests and study those rules, young lady, or else you will miss meal times. What's all that muck on your face for? Are you relishing that biscuit? I do hope you're not a snob.'

I shook my head, tasting the stale Arnott's biscuit as it tried to glide down my throat. 'No, oh *no*, I'm not a snob – I'm no *snob*. I've got nothing to be a snob about …'

My voice trailed off as Eider Down continued talking wildly. It seemed my sister had left a certain impression on the residents of Tantallon, and I was beginning to wonder when I'd be shown to my shared room, a gnawing hunger making me jig a little in my shoes.

Eider Down would not shut up!

'I *don't like* guests eating in their rooms. I just *don't* like it! I always insist that guests do not entertain. This is a fine establishment – a *five-star* establishment. It's very hard to get a room here now … what's wrong with the biscuit? You might be a *snob*, and you just don't know it yet?'

Eider Down finally stopped talking, but only for a moment. She handed me a key ring with two keys held together by an elastic band. She told me to wait quietly in room 2DW (room two, Derwent River side).

'You wait quietly in there for your sister to get home. She's *never* late, always on the knocker at six o'clock, it's her homecoming time. Now don't you forget, young lady, tea time is six o'clock sharp. I do *not* serve tea at six ten. I do not serve tea at six twenty. I serve tea at six o'clock, so don't be late or you won't get fed.'

I grabbed the keys, walked very quickly and quietly to room 2DW, and waited. The room housed a double bed and a small radiator. There was no toilet, no bathroom and no cupboards. The complete lack of privacy seemed like further proof that my sister and I were not quite good enough to be separate people.

We were like a set of bookends, twin-like and yet un-twinny in every way. I began to wonder if we had *anything* in common. I tried to push my panic away and pulled out my hand mirror to check my make-up. I picked up a lipstick I found near the bed and covered my lips in its bright berry shade. I popped it in my bag. I wondered if Bernadette would notice a stray lipstick was missing.

My sister had been explaining to Mum and me for years how she'd been born in the wrong era, that she should have been born in 1905 and not 1961. She was drawn to enigmatic stars such as Greta Garbo and Marlene Dietrich. She'd read both of their biographies, over and over again. Looking around my sister's room in the soft afternoon light, I realised the room was set-dressed exactly like an image from one of Bernadette's black-and-white Marlene Dietrich biographies. There were several framed photographs of Garbo placed on two doilies atop a dark-stained bookcase. A larger image of Dietrich hung crookedly on the coffee-coloured wall and three more biographies were sloping to one side, floral bookmarks poking from the pages. Paisley flannelette sheets were folded in a corner. There were several velvet coverlets, cream lace throws and a small wooden bedside table holding an assortment of delicate ordiments.[12] Priceless little ordiments. Ordiments I wanted. Ordiments I needed.

Bernadette seemed to be in possession of at least ten beautiful and rarefied *personal* things. I didn't possess any personal or rarefied things but I made a note to *get cracking* and begin collecting antique spoons or clocks.[13] Mum often told me that Bernadette had a special talent,

---

12 Ordiments! Barry Humphries coined this superb word from the real word 'ornaments'. I have been using the ordiment vibe for as long as I can remember.

13 A decade later I began to collect religious pictures, bottles of holy water, plastic angels, doilies, canisters, bakelite objects and perfume bottles from the '50s.

that she possessed Mum's gene for priceless antiques and chipped Royal Doulton ordiments.

The room was still with expectation. I heard the key in the lock and out of habit I immediately jumped off the unmade bed. 'Bernadette! Bernadette! Bernadette, I'm here! Look at me, I have arrived! You've made the place look so old-fashioned. I love it … it's going to be all *so* marvellous and cosy, isn't it?'

'Lan, shh, keep your voice down, we don't want people listening.'

Understanding I was too loud for my sister, I acted out an awkward, dumbed-down version of myself. Apparently, I was an alarmer of people.

Bernadette was wearing clothing I hadn't seen before. She had a brand-new hairdo and I wasn't certain if she was pleased to see me. She had transformed into a proper grown-up person during the months since we'd last laid eyes on each other. She had two jobs – legal secretary to five lawyers and an evening waitress at Dirty Dick's Steakhouse. Dad was so proud of Fair Bernadette with her two careers, that for our birthdays one time he drove to Hobart. At Dirty Dick's on my birthday night, Dad and I watched how well Bernadette waitressed, never missing an order, bringing out dessert at exactly the right time and giving the correct change. My father and I did not speak. Dad watched my sister waitress and I watched my father eating bloodied rump steak and boiled potatoes.

12

Jicky Parfum

I was fearless yet frightened, and full of vim as I set about making myself into a little starlet in Hobart town. I wandered alone up and down empty streets, homesick for places I'd never known, homesick for the only place I had known.

I fed ducks bread and lollies in the botanical gardens and borrowed sixty roses to sell on the streets to lovebirds. I sat in the Hobart library and pretended I was a librarian, handing out books to strangers, daring myself not to be caught. I discovered new op shops and vintage stores, visited Nan, ate sugary lunches, dressed up in various-sized garbage bags and hitchhiked while speaking a made-up French-like language to strangers.

Every Sunday afternoon, Bernadette and I would catch the bus from Davey Street to Nan's pensioner bedsit in North Hobart. Even though Nan had been living alone since Pop had passed away ten years earlier, I didn't have to worry about her being lonely. Four of Nan's sisters lived in the same block, almost on top of her, and Mum told me they all kept great company with constant bickering, sisterly love and cups of tea. Uncle Bob, the Catholic priest and their God-like brother, would often pop in and check on them all.

Nan's sisters, Brenda, Joan, Jean and Sherry, all had dead husbands except for Auntie Sherry, who of course was married to God. Being a good Catholic nun, Auntie Sherry was still the talk of the town with her roaring, sherry-fuelled drinking. Mum told me it had been a full-time job trying to hide Auntie Sherry's drinking from the Church and the other nuns. Eventually she was found out, and kicked out of the convent.

I would always buy a cake for Nan and me from the Cat and Fiddle Arcade, along with three bags of chips, five Eskimo Pie ice-creams, one dollar's worth of mixed lollies and some liquorice for Nan.

Nan's hair was set every Tuesday at 11 am into lilac permed waves, and she wore a headscarf to bed so her hair wouldn't flop. She also wore the headscarf to the butcher's, the grocery store and to church – one of Nan's fears was that her lilac permed hair *could and would* flop anywhere, anytime.[14]

Bernadette and I would sit in Nan's bedsit nattering over Cat and Fiddle Arcade cake and ice-cream. We'd gossip about Catholic priests, witches, homosexuals, lesbians, Nan's sisters, and her two sons, Will and Francis Manton. Nan told me Will and Francis were snobs and their wives were to blame.

Somehow, we understood we were Nan's favourite grandchildren. Uncle Will and Uncle Francis both had children but we saw them rarely. Nan told me her family disliked being around us Hills because we were tainted, second class, and they did not like Dad. They didn't want their children playing with us in case the tainting was catching, like measles. I wanted to taint, scorn and mock our three cousins but Nan wouldn't let me. I wanted to give them the measles.

We'd talk about how I wanted to be an acting star and whether I'd *ever* magically appear on *Young Talent Time*, but we'd always end up

---

14 Hilariously, it's now one of my fears, the flopping of my wavy hair!

speaking about Mum and how terrible her life was. Nan encouraged us to telephone Mum whenever we visited. I knew she'd told Mum how much she worried about me and that Nan didn't know what was going to become of me. Bernadette had stenographer skills but I was skill-less after leaving my hairdressing apprenticeship in Ulverstone.

'What are you going to turn into, Lan?' Nan would ask in a worried voice.

'An actress, Nan, a *famous famous* actress.'

'But you can't act, Lan. You haven't been trained, has she, Bernadette?'

'I don't need to be trained, Nan … I'm a natural. I won the most sustained character prize in the school play in Deloraine, I won that herb kit, remember?'[15]

'Everyone needs to be trained, dear, look at Rita Hayworth and Marilyn Monroe, both trained, Lan, dear, trained actresses. I don't know why you left your lovely hairdressing apprenticeship in Ulverstone. You had it *made*, Lan, with that little job; everyone needs a set and a perm, Lan.

'Lan, dear! Lan! *Listen* to me, Lan, dear. Why don't you send your school certificate to one of the airlines, dear, TAA or Ansett … you could apply for a job. Couldn't she, Bernadette? You'd be a good little air hostess. Bernadette, wouldn't Lan make a good little air hostess?'

'An air hostess? Lan has to be eighteen and she needs to have matriculated.'

'I don't want to be an air hostess for TAA. I heard Dad telling Bernadette that air hostesses are just glorified waitresses. Is that right, Nan?'

'Well, your father's got a point there, Lan, from what I hear about

---

15 In grade 10 I auditioned for the end-of-year Ulverstone High School play and won the role of the mad drunk character. The drama teacher told me after rehearsals one day that I was very good. He often asked me to his flat after school to rehearse but I felt uncomfortable being alone with him. The school play went on tour to Deloraine and this is where I won the award.

that kind of world, he may be right. Auntie Joan's been on an aeroplane, you could ask her, dear, I've never been on an aeroplane, Lan, so I don't know, I can't help you there, Lan.'

Bernadette would be smiling at me with laughing blue eyes – she'd even had a lick of the ice-cream. It made me curiously happy that I had the power to make Bernadette smile.

'Show us, Lan. Come on! Show Nan how you'd act if you *did* get a job being an air hostess for TAA. Watch her, Nan, she's funny, and don't forget to be spontaneous, Alannah. Start acting like you're on the plane and you're flying from Penguin to Hobart. Start acting now. One, two, three … ACT!'

With a cup of tea poised, Nan watched me closely. 'You can't be shy, Lan, if you want to sing on *Young Talent Time*, don't forget to act confident and play along nicely, Lan. Oh dear, your hair would be shining if you were a real air hostess … off you go, Lan, off you go.'

And off I'd go. With my banged-up confidence, I'd parade about wearing a costume I'd thrown together from one of Nan's drawers. Bernadette was in charge of the imaginary red velvet curtain I had instructed her to pull to one side for my big air hostess reveal …

'Hellooooooo, mongrels! My name is Sherry and I'm a nun, but I'm Sister Sherry O'Brien to you lot. I am *not* honoured to be your air hostess today, so don't sit back, don't relax, but allow me to drizzle God's blood over each and every one of you. You all need a nip of good Catholic sherry and because I'm God's legal bride, I get to tell you demonic, sinning heathens what to do. Repeat after me, "I am a sinner and I must be punished. I am a *sinner and I want to be punished.*" Do not get up. Do not go to the toilet. Do not laugh. Do not smile. Do not breathe and do *not* eat. God is watching and he doesn't like you, you're all going to hell. And if anyone has any alcohol on board … *give* it to me. God wants it. He's thirsty!'

Bernadette, Nan and I laughed until we cried, all at the expense of Auntie Sherry. I wanted her to be caught drinking by the priests, I wanted her to faint for around twenty years. I wanted to slap her legs in a dark room and tell her that God wasn't very pleased with her either, that she was meant to be a Catholic nun and help people. She wasn't helping anyone and I wanted to let her know that God knew all about her.

Nan was very protective of Auntie Sherry and I knew when to stop making fun of her. We'd laugh our guilty hearts out with Nan peering nervously from her ground-floor unit window making sure our racket wasn't overheard. Nan was always worried I was going to embarrass her in front of the other pensioners.

Bernadette and I would catch the bus back to our room at Tantallon and prepare for our evening. Our preparation included 'how to avoid all the other boarders and Eider Down's inedible tea at six sharp'. Eider Down was trialling a new menu: liver stew and no dessert. It seemed all desserts were off the menu, and dessert was the only reason I ever attended 'tea at six sharp' and so I stopped going. Bernadette agreed skipping dessert was a good idea for me because blancmange had 300 calories, calories I could not afford on my small frame.

After years of trying, I was finding moments of joy and triumph now I was living with my sister. I was learning to survive, and had worked out ways I could feel important. Even if they only lasted a few seconds, it was something for me to believe in and something to cling to.

I was curiously upbeat about my future, a future I'd secretly mapped out inside my head, a head that according to my whip-sharp mum was far too small for my body – the size of an apple, a pinhead apparently. My neck was also too short for my body, my hair too thin, and there wasn't enough of it.

I joined something I had never heard of before called the Dole. All I had to do was sign a form, list my dream jobs and the Dole would telephone me to inform me of any interviews, with my dream job as a top priority. I was told not to wear my sailor girl costume to any interviews and to be respectful and diligent at all times. If I had character references, I needed to show them at the interviews.

My first interview was a roaring success and after thirteen minutes I knew luck had come spinning my way – I was to be the junior kitchenhand at Kentucky Fried Chicken on Sandy Bay Road, earning $4 an hour! By the time I turned up to work, I had already invented a different title for myself. Instead of being a *junior kitchenhand*, I was, in fact, the only daughter of the great man himself, Colonel Sanders, and I would be inheriting that little Kentucky Fried Chicken on the Sandy Bay Road in a few years.

Now dear reader, let me explain. I *had* imagined something a little more extravagant for myself, job-wise. My dream job was to become a lady croupier at the casino, greeting people and spinning the blackjack wheel to find their fortune. My second dream job was to work at Cobb and Co in the city, a very fashionable, chic, smart boutique[16] right bang smack in the centre of town. I was not delighted, I was not excited, I wasn't even mildly amused at my kitchenhand job at the Kentucky Fried Chicken on Sandy Bay Road. But I had a job, a little stepping stone to my fantastical future dream world.

I lasted five weeks.

I told a small lie about my nan dying and it grew a little life of its own … she might have been strangled and then had a massive heart attack … anything to *not* go back to the Kentucky Fried Chicken oil slick.

Instead, I returned to the gloomy offices of the Dole where the lady clerk stamped my forms with vengeance and thundering boredom.

I lay on our double bed in the Tantallon Boarding House eating

16 Pronounced *bow teek*.

Peppermint Patties and Cherry Ripes, wondering what was to become of me. Bernadette would appear at 6 pm to change into her Dirty Dick's outfit. She would purse her lips and stare sourly at me, telling me to get off the bed and get a career. She sometimes asked me to work at Dirty Dick's with her if she felt it would be a busy night; I had to do the dishes, wait the tables, take the tips, and I wasn't permitted to eat a thing as I was too fat, apparently. I knew not to flirt or encourage laughter from the customers; I understood my sister didn't like me looking for attention or receiving attention. But my weight, 59 kilograms, was becoming a real problem. For both of us.

'How many calories have you had today Alannah?' she would ask.

'I think I've had eight hundred and ninety thousand, nine thousand nine hundred and ninety-nine.'

'You're really fat. You shouldn't be eating anything, at least for two more weeks. Show some strength of character. Why are you so weak?'

I couldn't tell my tiara-wearing nan that I'd just walked out of the only job a little mongrel like me could possibly hope for. But she found out after she came into the Kentucky Fried Chicken one day.

'How *could you*, Lan!' she cried. 'How could you walk out of such a lovely job? Why didn't you stick it out? You'll never find another job like that, Lan.'

Nan would often ask me to come and visit with a newspaper and a bottle of Jicky perfume. 'Can you bring that newspaper I like, Lan? *The Truth*? Hide it in your bag though, Lan – don't tell *anyone* it's for me. And Lan, dear, if you walk past Myer's, pop in and get me some of that Jicky perfume. Oh, I love that Jicky perfume. It's behind the counter, you know how to get it, just bring your old nan a bottle of the Jicky. It's sixty dollars, Lan, I'm an old pensioner, I can't afford Jicky!'

I think this was Nan's way of asking me to steal her a bottle of the Jicky perfume. But I was too afraid, a guilty Catholic chicken, and I hated myself for not being able to give my nan the elusive Jicky. I'd arrive at her small flat, all girled up with *The Truth* newspaper tucked into my bag. Nan would eye the bag's contents for the perfect bottle of Jicky, peering in with a look of disappointment slowly forming.

'Just the *newspaper* then, Lan, dear?'

I never did steal that bottle of Jicky for my nan – my Catholic guilt was twice-over immersed in Catholic guilt. Instead, on my very first overseas trip with my very first boyfriend about ten years later, I bought Nan a bottle of Jicky duty-free at Heathrow Airport. I wrapped it in gold shiny paper and tied a red bow neatly around it. I also bought a sympathy card as I knew she would like that – slightly religious and slightly mental all at the same time. I posted my marvellous little gift off at the Heathrow Airport post office, my boyfriend Steven becoming impatient with how long I was taking. I wrote all over the gold shiny paper with the words:

ALL THE WAY FROM ENGLAND, NAN.

My perfect bottle of Jicky arrived at Nan's door two days after she died from a heart attack while having her hair set at the local salon.

My nan never received her Jicky.

And my soul lay quiet for a time.

I had the idea that our souls hovered above our heads like a milky little cloud in a fairy story. Nan and her sisters told me that our souls *did not* hover above our heads – instead, they said, our souls were inside us, silent, still and unknown. I would ask where our souls rested and the nuns always pointed to my heart. I was also told that all souls are different and I should stop asking questions.

'The most *important thing*, Lannah, is to *treasure* your soul and not give your soul away! You must keep your soul from harm's way. Hold on to your soul, Lan, because if you don't the devil will take it from you and eat it. In hell, with you.'

I believe that the soul is an essential part of all of us. Our bodies change, they will wither and perish, but our inner core stays true. In our hearts we can blossom and flourish, like spring leaves or flowers on a cherry tree. If we have loved enough, allowed enough exhilaration into our lives, enough elation, enough wonder at the marvel of creation to keep ourselves spiritually alive, our soul will go marching on, long after we have passed. In time, our soul will shine its light on us all over again.

I loved Nan. And she seemed to like me. (Although years later I found a letter Nan had written to my mother about my untoward character, writing that I had a 'certain look in my eye'. A look that dared to stare. She warned that it was *this look* that would get me into trouble in the years to come – it wasn't Catholic, and it wasn't ladylike.) I remember wishing that Nan might whisper that she loved me. They did that in *The Waltons* and I craved to hear those three words, although I'd never uttered them myself.

I'm still not entirely sure where my soul resides, but to my fantastic little nan – I hope your soul is swimming in a sea of Jicky perfume.

13

The Social Poltergeist

My sister and I had been living together in a 10-metre-square room at Tantallon Boarding House for almost six months. One room for two Aries sisters, born two days apart, one year apart.

We shared a double bed, costumes, vintage shoes, op-shop Avon make-up, hairbrushes, combs, bobby pins and ten arty friends from the Hobart subculture scene we'd separately been attempting to infiltrate. We shared the same tights, the same blankets, the same air and the same legacy of childhood trauma. The combination was lethal. The sibling rivalry between Bernadette and me was a silently screaming juggernaut forcing its way through the most vulnerable parts of each other. There was nowhere to hide: our present seemed unreal, no future wanted us and our past lay in wait, beckoning for our return.

I'd noticed (with pangs of fiery jealousy) that Bernadette was looking dainty and slim, and had taken to wearing lace slips, lace petticoats, floating '30s Monet garden prints and perfectly applied make-up. Her hair was bobbed with a long blunt fringe. With my spectacular background in hairdressing, Bernadette trusted me just enough to colour her perfect bob into a glowing halo of strawberry peach with glistening orange hues. She wore a simple black clip to hold her fringe back, and she always carried a clean linen handkerchief.

The few sentences Bernadette spoke to me most days seemed to arrive fully composed. Aloof and mysterious, she had begun reading obscure German books (although she hadn't studied German), and her face had become more angular, giving her a painterly, old-fashioned look.

Bernadette set rules for both of us. She was rule mad-crazy. I was a rule punk!

We were both fastidious about our appearance, to an almost military level of precision, with hours and hours spent preening and unpreening in the small mirror I'd sticky-taped to the wall. One of the arty friends had shown me an image of Siouxsie and the Banshees and I was praying to God, Jesus and St Anthony that one of them would answer my prayers to please turn me into a Siouxsie Banshee. If no one answered my prayers, I planned to turn myself into a Siouxsie Banshee by wearing eye make-up heavy as lead, a white-painted face, dark lipstick, sequined and embellished futuristic shoes, long mohair jumpers and a floral scarf tied into a bow around my neck.

Bernadette wasn't given to making announcements but that's exactly what she did. She made an announcement. She told me it was time to leave our boarding-house room. She told me there was no eleventh commandment that committed us to the term of our natural lives at Tantallon Boarding House. We were both young, and we were both feminists.[17]

The plan was that we would disappear at dawn without giving notice, avoiding the humiliation of our bond not being refunded. Traces of sibling rivalry were visible everywhere on our Tantallon battlefield: black marks on the walls, lipstick stains on every surface imaginable, green jelly glued to the carpet.

---

17 I had no idea what a feminist was, but Bernadette said I had to be one.

Almost immediately, I became a real estate agent.

I decided we needed to find rooms in a Battery Point mansion. My sister was appalled at the gall of me. 'How can girls like us live in a mansion, Lan? They're *mansions*! Look at the size of the doors, they've all got security gates, we'll never get past the gates. We'll have to try something else; people who live in mansions don't have rooms for girls like us!'

Determined to prove her wrong, determined we'd make a life together like proper Grey Gardens girls, I'd march through a mansion's gates with my cocky real estate how-to-live-in-a-mansion-when-you're-not-a-mansion-girl vibe while Bernadette hid behind a pole.

I knocked and I knocked and I knocked on mansion doors. I was rejected and rejected and rejected until we found our Mr and Mrs Sparrow. Mr and Mrs Sparrow hadn't received a visitor for almost twenty years. Mr and Mrs Sparrow had spent their adult lives alone and wealthy, driving an immaculate Jaguar to and from the local supermarket, and they were willing to allow my sister and me into the fully furnished nineteenth-century servants quarters adjacent to their expansive house on Sandy Bay Road.

The flatette miraculously contained all the magic ingredients necessary for my sister to live in the Bloomsbury style she felt she truly deserved.[18] Our servants quarters contained one windowless bedroom, one three-quarter bed with a stained striped mattress too small for its frame, and a wardrobe reeking of mothballs and lavender water, along with several twisted wire hangers and a cobweb-covered pair of gumboots hiding in the corner. Our kitchen parlour was a bleak, dark room with a curio cabinet, a fridge and a chamber-pot. Our fridge was always empty except for ice-cream and cabbage. The bathroom had the marvellous addition of four handrails to assist any sister who dared bathe in the rust-tub of a bath.

---

18 Virginia Woolf was my sister's idol, alongside the black-and-white movie stars of the '30s.

A long silent hallway snaked through to a lounge room too small for a full lounge suite or a table. Mrs Sparrow allowed us to choose between a small couch or a Tim Tam–coloured leatherette chair – we chose a chair for both of us to share. But the crowning glory of our servants quarters was the glorious Vulcan gas heater. I'd often lay my head on a pillow directly in front of the Vulcan's skin-burning heat and watch my sister twirl a small section of orange hair around her fingers as she turned the pages of her library book. If I felt Bernadette hadn't shared the share chair, I'd distract her into the gloomy kitchen, then like a little black vulture I'd throw myself into the share chair, creating havoc on Bernadette's return.

I wanted my sister, I needed her, but somehow, I repelled her. I was too loud, too flirtatious, too emotional, too fat, and what's more, I was socially competitive, and not in a good way. I'd committed the mortal sin of showing off. Bernadette began going out without me, leaving me home alone to brood before the violent rays of the Vulcan. I attempted to follow her to a Sylvia Plath poetry reading in Battery Point Park, but I wasn't welcome. Poetry readings were quiet affairs and I was apparently not a quiet affair. Bernadette was mixing with the crowd we'd both tried to infiltrate but, somehow, Bernadette had won them all over. All of them, all to herself. I wasn't permitted inside the In Crowd: my need for attention was too uncool.

I'd been spending more and more time by myself, and one afternoon I'd discovered Hadley's Orient Hotel while walking through the centre of town desperately searching for a job. The haunted hotel dates back to 1834 and was often frequented by Errol Flynn, Tasmania's homegrown movie star.

Hadley's Orient Hotel was my safe house, my own private oasis, my office.

On a small Art Deco table, I placed a permanent written note:

RESERVED ALL DAY – EVERY DAY – FOR MISS HILL

I spent entire days propped up like a small black poodle in the lounge bar/dining room reading books, ordering lime spiders, bleakly observing the bleary-eyed drunken folk falling in on top of themselves as they ordered Pimm's and lemonade. Strangers would sit opposite, daring me to look at them; I took their dares up frequently – staring them out, staring them in, blocking them out, blocking myself in.

I was rapidly arriving at the unpleasant realisation that I was deeply troubled about my place in the world. In my heart, I knew my recently acquired two-day-a-week job at the jeweller might soon be coming to a catastrophic end.

I had accidentally pierced a six-year-old girl's cheek instead of her two ears. My little piercing handgun had a shiny silver point attached but it missed the little girl's ears by a millisecond and I was faced with the sounds of two cheek-piercing screams, one from the mother and the other from the little girl herself. The mum slapped me hard on the wrist and told me I needed to go back to wherever it was I had come from.

I was to be reported, deported!

A telegram from my boss, Harry Hart, arrived that same afternoon informing me that he wanted to see me. I was to bring my first aid certificate along with references I had assured him were stored in a security box at the post office.

There were no certificates.

There were no references.

There was no security box.

There was, however, a homemade Certificate of Science. I had typed it out myself. It stated that my name was Alannah Hill and that I had studied Science at Hobart University.

I sat opposite Harry Hart in his fluorescent-lit office, the telegram sweating in my tight-fisted hands.

'You do realise I am going to be sacking you, don't you, Alannah?'

'Yes. Yes, I do realise you are sacking me, but I —'

'Don't embarrass yourself with any more talk, Alannah. If you need a reference just make one up yourself and I'll sign it.'

Harry Hart walked over to my carefully made-up self and stroked my face, drawing his hands down the front of my dress, feeling my frightened breasts, his breath hot on my skin, his body slowly pushing itself into me.

'You've got quite a figure on you, Alannah. Ever thought of doing any escort work?'

'Escort work? I can't drive an Escort, I haven't even learnt to drive! Or do you mean the cigarettes? Escort cigarettes? We used to sell them in the milk bar!'[19]

The air around me seemed to change into an opaque mist of disappointment and failure. The siren in my head rapidly amplified to a loud scream. I pushed Harry Hart's hands away from my dress with a dramatically nervous gesture, picked up my bag and walked out of his squalid office.

And just like that, my short-lived career as an ear piercer was over.

Bernadette's and my fights became vindictive and violent. We tore the servants quarters apart ducking and weaving objects we threw at each other's brains. My sister was much stronger than me so I'd retaliate with words. Cruel, cut-throat, barbed words. Lamps were broken, a window smashed, clothing hidden so the other couldn't go out. I realised we were crossing over to the dark side but we couldn't stop. We knew there were certain parts of ourselves that were off limits, and yet we broke every rule imaginable. Bernadette knew exactly how to destroy me. I knew exactly how to destroy her. I cut pieces of her hair in the middle of the night while she slept. I froze her make-up by hiding it in the

---

19 Escort cigarettes had been the biggest-selling cigarettes in our milk bar. There was also an Escort car, a little like a Torana.

freezer. I filled the green jelly Bernadette prepared before she went to bed with green Palmolive dishwashing liquid.

Mrs Sparrow, our busybody landlady, knocked on our front door once a day to ensure the two fighting Catholic sisters, her tenants, weren't turning her fully furnished flatette into a ruin. She'd heard screaming and crying coming from our flat when she was hanging out her washing in her private garden. The crying seemed to come from the bedroom, she said, and the yelling was constant.

I didn't see the end of the war coming, although we'd been fighting for months. The flatette was in tatters and we'd broken everything we could lay our hands on. I was feeling the sting of Bernadette's independence, her desire to rid me from her life, teasing me to breaking point.

And so I snapped, dear reader. I snapped!

Bernadette had bought a pair of new shoes; she'd saved up for them for two months. I was exhausted by lists of how I could make her like me, how I could make her take me out to the poetry readings, how I could hurt her for ignoring me. And so I did it. I threw Bernadette's brand-new shoes onto the Sandy Bay Road. Then I cowered near the Vulcan's fiery rumble watching her look for them, knowing I'd gone too far, waiting for the consequences, for my punishment.

'Alannah, what have you done with my fucking shoes? They're gone! If you threw them out I will fucking kill you. I am starting to hate you. Hate Hate Hate.'

I didn't like the three 'hate's, sitting ducks all in a row.

'You're the little bitch, Bernadette. You just love that ignoring game, don't you? You *just love* that boring old ignoring game and anyway, I'm sick to *death* of you treating me like an imposter, like I don't belong in your arty scene – what's wrong with me anyway? The arty people like me, I know they do.'

'You *are* a social embarrassment. A social poltergeist! You're wearing garbage bags for God's sake, *garbage* bags!'

'You're always ignoring me, you won't even let me eat, you keep telling me I'm fat. Why don't you and Dad go and live together and watch ABC, you're his favourite and you're only his favourite because you —'

I felt the slap. I deserved that slap. The air was filled with a horrified silence. Bernadette was crying. I hadn't seen her cry for a long time. We both sat glaring at each other in the cracked gloom. I'd broken something and I didn't know how to fix it. The noise around me was deafening. For Bernadette, perhaps the silence without me calmed the chaos I'd brought to her life.

I arrived home to our Art Deco flat the next day and my sister was gone. She had packed up all her precious things and left. I was broken. I didn't know how to fix myself. I couldn't manage life without her. The mornings lost their light, the twilight lost its darkness, and my evenings lost their sheen – after Bernadette left there were just endless lonely moments in time. I remember the grief of lost sibling rivalry aching inside me as I drifted through the empty streets, the blue convict buildings of Hobart that threatened to bury me alive.

14

Glory Box of Angst

Hobart was bleak without my sister. She had disappeared without a trace after the shoe incident. Despite knocking on every door in Hobart, I couldn't find her. Mum wouldn't tell me where she was, not even Nan would tell me where she was. Mrs Sparrow claimed she was under strict instructions *not* to divulge private information about my sister to me. Mrs Sparrow asked me how I was going to pay the rent now that I was living alone. There was only one bedroom and I had never had a boyfriend. I wasn't interested in having a boyfriend, but Mrs Sparrow said the only way I could afford the flat was to get myself a husband of some sort.

I went looking for a husband of some sort.

Wednesday evening was the evening of *all* evenings in Hobart in 1978.

You may wonder, dear reader, how a simple Wednesday evening could provoke such glittering diamond memories. But please allow me to carry on a little about the marvellous Hadley's Orient Hotel.

Every Wednesday evening, Hadley's held an Extravaganza night. Nothing in this world could smother the electrifyingly dangerous gaiety beating in my heart in anticipation; sleep would not touch my eyes, not while my head pounded with Donna Summer beats and my body writhed, possessed by artfully choreographed dance routines featuring more twists and turns and ballet/jazz/modern steps than are humanly possible.

I'd hit the dance floor in Hadley's grand ballroom at 11 pm and wouldn't stop my self-choreographed routines until the doors finally closed – I was always the last dancer on the tiny dance floor. I didn't drink. I didn't smoke. Driven by a need to move and to watch others move, I drank red cordial to keep my spark alight long into the morning.

The bar served champagne and punch for $2 a pop, while misty fog from hidden smoke machines filled the room.

Hadley's Hotel felt as if it was struggling to breathe, struggling for life. Yet its faded opulence distracted anyone who entered – for a few hours they could escape into a world of pure magic, their troubles and their aching sadness forgotten. The great legend of Hadley's ghost fascinated me. Hadley's held a beautiful white ghost, seen to linger on the staircase that led into the magnificent ballroom. I often imagined I could see her in every corner.

A very small disco ball had been left to hang in the middle of the dance floor, re-creating the scene from the new hit movie *Saturday Night Fever*. The very small disco ball didn't *spark up* as it should; its frantic beaming multicoloured lights seemed to be on strike, quietly disgusted with having to shine their precious photons on thirty-nine New Wave dancing, prancing iconoclasts, skating to Blondie, Boney M., Chic, ABBA and the soundtrack to *Grease*.

But thanks to Hadley's Hotel I now had a girl gang, something I felt my sister would not have permitted. A girl gang of three ghastly little show-offs!

Each Wednesday evening my new girl gang and I dollied ourselves up to dance our little hearts inside out and upside down at Hadley's Orient Hotel. I had taken to wearing bright-red rollerskates and ribboned-and-bowed garbage bags – I wore them to the shops, to the park, to the fish-and-chip shop and to Hadley's, all to the disgust of Albert, the ninety-eight-year-old doorman.[20]

'Leave! You have to leave! Coming in here dressed in a garbage bag. No respect. No damned respect from you *young* people these days!'

My girl gang – Daisy and Emily – always 'got ourselves up' in Hobart's coolest hairdressing salon, Garbo's, before our Wednesday evening gang-of-three disco stampede. Daisy worked as a stylist in the salon. We stared at ourselves in the long narrow mirrors that were placed against a yellow velvet–covered wall. As we stared, we smiled wildly into each other's eyes, contemplating our costumes, nodding and flashing our beguiling smiles from perfectly painted cherry-red lips.

My new Hobart vintage starlets were my first real girl gang and we all had mad crushes on each other. I was pretending to be in love with Emily, Daisy was pretending to be in love with me, Emily was pretending to be in love with Daisy, and when the clock struck midnight we *all* pretended we were in love with each other.

Of course we didn't have a clue who we really were or what the hell we were doing with our odd little waterfall lives, but for now, staring at ourselves in the mirrors of Garbo's Hairdressing Salon was the only thing that mattered.

I had met Daisy at the salon when I'd had my hair professionally dyed for the very first time. My chosen colour was cyclamen pink. Daisy also sported the same pink colour. Oh my, oh my, oh my, Daisy, with her creamy alabaster skin, her perfect lipstick pout and piercing grey eyes that, when she stared at you long enough, turned almost violet in their hue.

---

20 I was rather fond of Albert in a berserk kind of way. I found it absurd, comical and yet very sad that he claimed to be *the* doorman and yet he was in a wheelchair, unable to hold anybody back from entering the night of all nights.

'Oh, hello! And what's your name, *lover* girl?'

Startled alight with girl-spark wonder, I looked up into her eyes and saw beautiful, eccentric Daisy. She had placed a glittering heart-shaped brooch onto her dress that sparkled in tune with her violet eyes. She was by far the most beautiful girl I had ever seen.

Daisy's excitable, unforgettable voice hovered in rooms long after she had left them; she was my girl crush and we often used to kiss passionately in the street, smearing our lipsticks together.

Daisy, Emily and I dressed up in the finest garbage bags known to mankind and descended on innocent Albert at 11 pm every Wednesday evening. Our moods were high, our youth an irreverent act proclaiming that we didn't have a care in the world. I kept a notebook in my bag, which I often looked at intently – I had written myself a little love poem:

Don't forget to love her, Alannah girl

The little girl you used to be

Remember she lay inside of you

Untucked, Unstuck,

Is she sleeping peacefully?

Our girl gang was at full throttle, each of us desperate to outdo the others. We did this in every way possible – more eye shadow, more lipstick, wilder hair, pinker than fuchsia, blush plummier than plum mouths.

'Daisy, oh Daisy, you're incredible, I miss you even when I'm looking at you!' I heard myself say.

Daisy pulled my pink-bowed green garbage bag over my head, her voice quiet and sad. Her perfect upturned lips floated toward me, her breath falling soft on my skin, her face full of curiosity. I wasn't sure what was expected of me. I wondered if Daisy knew what was expected of her.

It was almost as if we had cast ourselves in our own play, my girl gang the ensemble cast of beauties destined for a ghastly fall from grace.

Emily, our *mysterious* Emily, enjoyed chopping up travel sickness tablets; they were long and cream with the letters 'TS' inscribed on each one. Emily would sell up to twenty pills a night at the bar for a dollar each. My new girl gang and I had a little ritual of snorting the travel sickness pills and washing them down with my nan's nerve drink, Fishaphos.

Nan had been drinking Fishaphos all her life.[21] I kept my personal Nan drink in a small clear flask superglued to a garbage bag I'd fashioned into a frock by sewing on tiny pale-pink ribbons. My special drink reeked but I sipped on it anyway, washing it down with raspberry cordial and milk bottle lollies. My righteous fear of the world was slung aside; the Good Girl me watched the new me from the sidelines, a melancholic air of morbid sympathy on her paradoxical face.

Daisy, Emily and I would sleep together in my bed after our Wednesday evenings – my bedroom was empty and cold and I craved comfort. We'd lie together silently. Doll in a doll in a doll. Hand in a hand in a hand. Eyes locked. Hearts beating fast.

In hindsight, it seems that Emily and I were both suffering – suffering from a sense of utter loneliness, like little empty vessels that nothing was able to fill; and the most painfully sharp point occurred at the most abstract moment in time.

I cannot place when it happened or how it happened: Daisy was away visiting her parents, leaving Emily and I to discover ourselves in Emily's North Hobart bedsit, which she called 'Dead Room'. Her Dead Room was almost collapsing into the drycleaner's that nestled below.

'Come visit me, Alannah, my beauty. Come visit me before I kill myself, and bring pizza and ice-cream. Please? Be a darling, darling, and let's read poetry together – we shall *read Shakespeare*!'

Oh dear. Shakespeare?

---

21 This was a drink made with homoeopathic household remedy called Fishaphos Nerve Tonic.

I decided instead to bring my new op-shop book, *Valley of the Dolls*. It was the only book I possessed since Bernadette had taken all the precious things with her that fateful afternoon. I took the bus route 78 to Emily's, bringing pizza and ice-cream, which I placed on the floor as Emily's Dead Room bedsit held no furniture except for a large hospital bed. Her clothing, strewn across the wooden floor, suggested the tantrum of a small child possessed by a passion for pink tulle.

Emily chopped up sheets of travel sickness tablets and crushed the powder into several Coke bottles, which we both naively imbibed. We drank our car-sick drinks with liquid kisses, tentatively licking the sweet Coca-Cola off each other's lips, our mouths searching for a version of love that we had never known and could barely imagine.

We teased out each other's painful past secret by secret, our restless girl bodies interleaved in the hazy gloom of the Dead Room bedsit. Emily's slender body was long and straight with small sleepless breasts, her eerily translucent skin crisscrossed by blue bloodlines all leading straight to her heart. Her feigned toughness masked a vulnerable child's soul. Although she could smile and love with a heart-rending tenderness, an unnamed terror lurked just out of sight. I felt her race against time, her need to flee her own soul, and I understood why it had to be this way, as I too was followed by demons from the slipstream of my own childhood.

Emily's power of pulling me into her own sorrow, a sorrow I couldn't afford to wallow in, threatened to suffocate me. Gently, I drew away from her, leaving part of my young-girl soul in that stuffy, fear-smudged, collapsing single Dead Room. In the first light of morning, Emily waved me goodbye from her window, smiling and calling out to me that I was her girl.

It was the last time I saw her alive.

Emily's lithe, lifeless body was found slumped on the floor in her room above the drycleaner in North Hobart, eighty-six packets of travel tablets strewn among the tantrum of clothing she left behind.

And I mourned my girl Emily, dear reader. Her sorrow and death haunted me.

I always struggled to imagine her last thoughts before she took her lethal dose. I replayed how she had died over and over in my own suicidal mind. Emily and I had spoken about suicide and how she'd tried to kill herself twice before. Stricken and sad, I wondered if it was anything I'd said, something I'd done or hadn't done.

It didn't make any difference. Emily was gone. And I was angry with her. She could have been so many things, and yet she chose to be shaped by the past, fractured by it. Emily grew up believing that she didn't deserve a life with any joy in it.

Dear reader, there are gala nights to remember, but there are also gala nights to forget, paranormal nights that have the power to change who we are or what we thought we ever could be. There is one story I have not yet shared with you, a story that has been too overwhelming to speak, let alone write about.

Drinking red cordial and skating to and from Hadley's ballroom in a bowed-up garbage-bag frock, I noticed two uniformed policemen drinking at the bar, muttering sly talk and watching everything with reptilian eyes. Daisy had occasionally been sleeping with one of the policemen, or so she said.

While I talked my wild talk, one of the policemen cupped my chin, held my mouth open and placed a tiny piece of what felt like paper on my tongue. The little white ticket tasted sour and I swallowed it, laughing, unknowing. Daisy said she'd had the white paper too but was starting to feel sick.

'What was it, Daisy?'

'LSD.'

'LSD? What's LSD? It is drugs? What *is* it, Daisy? Will it make me feel sick? I can't take drugs like that, Daisy! Why did they give it to us?'

Daisy attempted to calm my worries.

'Just go with it, don't fight it … have a good triiiiiiippppp.'

And suddenly, alarmingly, I was walking alone along Sandy Bay Road barefoot, clutching one rollerskate. I didn't know how I'd come to be there alone on the street, but my head felt like it was growing into a ghastly Halloween pumpkin, my heart was outside my body, and the cars driving past me beckoned me to run into their sequined, starry headlights. I stumbled. I fell. I walked into poles. I saw buildings stretched to unbelievable heights threatening to fall on top of me, and I remember screaming silently, wordlessly, for someone to help.

My face seemed to be crumbling from within. The very substance of me was crumbling, crumbling like a papier-mâché roof collapsing in a downpour of sorrow. The full force of the fluorescent acid trip had set me ablaze with fear, cruising through my bloodstream like a huge submarine.

Where the hell am I?

Who am I with?

Where is my handbag?

Why am I carrying only one rollerskate?

Am I dead or alive?

I lay down on the Sandy Bay Road footpath in the hope that I might be dreaming. Yes, I actually lay down on that cold concrete footpath in the hope and expectation that it was my own warm, cosy bed; I was magically thinking that if I lay my crumbling body down on the unflinching ground, my double bed would somehow materialise and I'd be safely home.

A late-night reveller wearing a black beanie walked slowly past me, staring at the sight of a girl in a garbage-bag dress, a single rollerskate in her hand, rolling madly on the footpath.

'Don't *touch* me,' I cried out, shocked to hear my own voice so childishly high-pitched. 'Don't you *dare* do anything as the police will be here soon! Yes, the police are coming. I have a special alarm attached to the bow in my hair and it is vibrating like a lightning rod!'

'Do you like my dress?' I heard myself whisper. 'Do you think I'm ugly?'

I looked up toward the dark, unreadable eyes of the lion-headed man, only to discover he was no longer there. I sat alone at a freezing bus stop. Catching sight of my reflection in the bus-shelter window, I didn't know who I was any longer. Red lipstick was smeared all over my white, alien face, and my pink-bowed garbage-bag dress had slipped from a frock into a skirt – I was semi-naked, except for a pink-lace bra with its flame-red flowers embossed on the cups.

Somehow, I managed to find my way home to my flat. Shattered, kaleidoscopic memories of the psychedelic night kept flashing back through my mind, and my single rollerskate haunted me; like me, it was somehow mislaid and useless without its other half.

As I slipped into my op-shop slip, I wondered what had become of my lovely girlfriend Daisy. I lay on the double bed, tormented by twisted memories of the last few hours. I knew I'd never touch acid trips ever again. I hated every second the tab snaked through my girl body.

Suddenly, I heard a loud bang. Had the world turned into an exploding sun? Or was it my head exploding with light?

And then, in the early-morning silence, I heard the front door close. I was sure I had locked the front door when I let myself in. But *had* I locked it? I heard the sound of men's voices erupting in the hallway and torchlight shone onto my bed. And there they stood. The two policemen from Hadley's, smirking and twirling their batons.

I struggled and screamed and fought. I was flabbergasted, devastated and out of my mind, my fingers bleeding as they scratched against the wall in a hopeless attempt to escape.

I kicked one of them in the mouth. The other one picked me up and hurled me against the wardrobe before his crooked partner handcuffed me to the bed. I said I was pregnant, but it made no difference – I was cornered. I tried to train my mind into oblivion, an oblivion I had to either embrace or allow to destroy my mind. I couldn't fight off two drunken cops. I suspended thought, stopped my heart from beating, my eyes from seeing and my ears from hearing.

But young-girl Alannah, who I'd tried so hard to protect despite my naivety and mystic faith in other people, what about her?

Let me tell you, dear reader, my head was a slaughterhouse of raging anger and sorrow. I remember wondering if I should kill myself as soon as the pain left my body or, alternatively, simply wash myself, fix my hair and dress up in my Sunday best and keep going.

I didn't leave the flat for two weeks. I forced myself to take endless baths. I locked all the doors. I pulled all the blinds and lived in the dark. I shook and cried all the time. I didn't know how to pull myself out of the excruciating blame and shame I put upon myself.

I sometimes think deeply about what happened to me on that Wednesday night – I do not talk of the night to many and I am still unclear of the impact it may have had on my soul and future.

I tried to keep it secret and I never reported it. I wonder if I was a coward. I couldn't face what I knew would be too many questions, questions that I didn't have good enough answers for. I knew enough to know that if I reported the rapist policemen, it would be revealed I had taken the acid and left my door unlocked. I understood how this might appear to unsympathetic eyes in '70s Tasmania.

I pushed the memories away and my heart grew black with sorrow.

I forced my mind to forget, to regroup and rewire, burying the pain of what happened.

You may be wondering why I've chosen to share this story with you.

What happened in my lonely flat on Sandy Bay Road left me struggling to breathe.

Struggling to stay alive.

I had a choice whether I could live or die.

I chose to live.

To live on, to live large, to truly live my dreams; because our dreams are the one thing that cannot be taken from us in this life, no matter how dark the days might become. Our dreams, dear reader, connect us to the universe, to the greater reality beyond our powers of understanding, to our supernatural selves that no one and nothing can spoil, ruin or steal away from us. That is our power: to defeat violence and rape as an act of revenge and defiance. To not let them win.

15

Live and Let Live

No longer could I live at the Art Deco flat.

When you want to live a new life, how do you start that new life, where do you live, who do you know, where do you go? After what had happened to me in Hobart, I was a stranger to myself, darkness threading through me like a venomous spider web. Mrs Sparrow evicted me for not paying rent; with a shrug of her shoulders she told me to pack up my things, tidy the flat and leave. I stared into her glassy eyes and half of me begged my other half to tell her. But I didn't. I also didn't pack up my things or tidy the flat; I just left. I caught the Greyhound bus from Hobart to Ulverstone, leaving Hobart and all my precious things behind.

I moved back home.

Back home to Mum, Dad, Martin and Joseph.

Each morning Mum's voice would build to a crescendo of high-pitched questions thrown at me. I felt a hole burning in my soul while Mum butted her cigarettes out on an ashtray that was already overflowing.

'WHAT are you GOING to DO with the rest of your life, Lannah?'

I had no answer.

My new Alannah reinvention was going to be a daring, lonely, extravagant experiment that would often become so harrowing that I'd feel a certain ache – my heart was like a bomb, constantly ticking inside me, barely allowing me to breathe. The reinvention of a girl such as me would, perhaps, become the very death of me.

Throughout my bewildering childhood, I'd often fantasise that somewhere out there, in the big wide world of life, there lay a new world of wonder, and I was utterly determined to find it. I wondered about my destiny. I wondered if I was doomed. Once again, I was without a plan, without a friend, and without a future.

Ever since we had swapped our milk bar for a normal house in Queen Street, Ulverstone, Mum had had time on her hands. Spending time with a mother such as mine *with time on her hands* was a dangerous and rather alarming ordeal, but sit through it I did, as I had nothing better to do. I was captive. My dreams of jetsetting to an unknown land were becoming more and more remote.

I only half-listened to Mum while she puff-puff-puffed on cigarettes, one after the other after the other. Mum's advice was often spoken into cigarette air. I knew Mum's advice like the sound of my own heartbeat.

NO point in living, NO point in having children, NO point in walking down the street, NO point in having friends, NO point in having hobbies, NO point in listening to music, NO point in travelling, NO point in dreaming, NO point in having a boyfriend, NO point to LOVE, NO point in getting married and for God's sake, Lannah, get that muck off your face. And always the final stinging bite, the chorus:

'WHAT are you GOING to DO with the rest of your life, Lannah?'

I'd shuffle around nervously by the overheating radiator as it scorched the back of my legs. It was maddening to have to listen to Mum; I wanted to plead and beg her to be a little more hopeful.

But my mother's voice was strong, holding all of her dark 'truths', her wild exaggerations, her invented storms. Mum had created a new game for herself: she played the negative, concerned, histrionic mother hunting down her prey. I often wonder if she had *any* idea of the long-lasting damage her spectacular negativity was having on her daughter. Somehow her smash-up hobby appeared to calm her reckless mind. I sometimes saw what looked to be a moment of contrition as her mouth went quiet and she thought she might have gone too far.

'WHAT have you done to your HAIR, Lan?'

'Oh, I just curled it a little bit with the curling iron. I like it, Mum, it sort of makes my head look a little bigger – you can see that, can't you, Mum?'

'It's not going to STAY curled, Lan, it's going to FLOP! Your hair is SHOCKING, Lan, it's so fine, SOOOOOO wispy and it's never going to stay wavy, Lan. The best thing you can do this afternoon is to go and get yourself a nice expensive perm. Ohhh LOOK – here comes Joe! Good old JOE! Why don't you take Lannah down the street, Joe – she's bored.'

Mum made strong instant coffee while she spoke of all the other car trips that Joseph could make with me in his green Falcon, which he would detail to Virgo perfection every day. Sometimes twice a day. Sometimes *three* times a day. He came and went from the house in the green Falcon with its 3-metre-high antenna swaying from the roof.

My mother's story was that Joseph had acquired a CB radio that he used to keep in touch with all the truck drivers travelling along the

North West Coast's empty, silent freeways. I had seen him burning up and down Queen Street, Status Quo blaring from his cassette player, the CB radio terrifying stray dogs and nervous teenagers. Joseph was also using a police siren that *apparently* he'd bought from the police.

'That's a big ten-four, sir! Yep! That's a BIG ten-FOUR and there are four slut YLs[22] in front of me now and I'm gunna mow them all down!'

Joseph's stuttering words were on loud volume as his CB-radio freak show shrank small dogs to ants, withered newly planted daffodils to weeds and tore autumn leaves off all the trees on Queen Street.

Joseph kept his comings and goings to himself – he would often come home from CB-radio hell telling outrageous stories of his whereabouts:

'I've been working all day with a bricklayer I met and he gave me $50,000.'

'I went for two job interviews and got them, and they want me to start at six in the morning, and I have to work five days straight.'

'I'm going to live in America to shoot wild animals.'

'The council asked me to sweep the beach and I'm getting a bravery award.'

'I saved four kids from drowning and then met a guy who I punched in the head. I tried to drown him.'

'I was at the pub last night with four blokes. Two of them asked me to move in with them but I told them to get fucked. They don't like dogs.'

'The Dole are giving me two Doles because I asked for two Doles.'

On and on he'd go. There was no way I was getting in a car with him to go anywhere.

Joseph would glare at me.

I'd glare at the stained floor, my mind burning, my body yearning to walk down my own path, at my own pace; my sheared-off pain,

---

22 Young Ladies

my raw wounds, my anger and bitterness not yet at peace. I knew if I stayed inside 49 Queen Street with Mum and Joseph, I would never be able to find my own peace. Both of them had built the road I was now walking on.

I knew my very own mum had a power that could hold me back, with all her negative, thoughtless and yet *occasionally* wise words. I didn't know if Mum loved me, or disliked me, if I *really* was her favourite or if she was perhaps a little envious that I was sixteen, daring to have a dream that she had never dared to.

If Mum saw me slip even for a moment, if she saw I needed her or showed any weakness, she had the startling ability to weaken my vim. With my voice shaking and a lump the size of three sugar cubes in my throat I would try to stay calm, to defend myself and offer Mum some insight into who I really was. I was becoming desperate for her to hear me.

'Mum! I *don't* want to be a failure. I *have* to have hope, Mum, without it I can't go on living! Nobody in this damned house has dared to have *any* hope, Mum, no one has dared to have a dream because *how could you* in this fucked-up house? But Mum, I'm sick to death of this self of mine, I need a *new* self, Mum! I've lived in the dark for so long that I reckon I'll be buried alive if I stay here. There are things I've *never* told you, Mum, things that have happened that have hurt me, but I don't tell you because you're mental! I am just fucking pretending, Mum! I pretend to you all the time.'

Mum lit another cigarette and stared straight ahead at the oven, which was covered in small dabs of sticky dried meat.

I could feel myself becoming exhausted from the game, the charade of being the Good Girl. I was struggling to not cry, to not give in, to *not give in*. I felt madness running through me, day after day, but I had a small inkling that there were some positive aspects of my character left that I could cobble together to make a real live person – not a shadow girl but a real girl with a heart and a soul and a future.

'I have to go, Mum. I *have to* try it. I have to *do something* with my life!'

Mum's composure was short-lived. 'Oh GO ON with you, Lannah! Take your BED over there then! Take YOUR BED to Melbourne and lie in it on your OWN and see JUST how quickly you run back here to Ulverstone! Go ON! Nobody EVER rings for you. Why's THAT, Lan? Why doesn't anyone ring for you? Maybe it's your get-up and the way you STICKYBEAK into other people's business. You're such a stickybeak, Lan, and people DON'T LIKE a stickybeak.'

She spoke her truths, she smoked her ash, she queried again and again what my future would hold – as it surely wasn't able to hold much. I was deeply puzzled and I wondered if the pounding of my heart was a sign that something grand or even murderous was about to happen.

I had heard 'WHAT are you GOING to DO with the rest of your life, Lannah?' *so many times* during the few months I was back home, I couldn't bear it any longer. I heard words streaming from my mouth, words with purpose, more than I knew I had.

'I am moving to Melbourne, Mum. I *am* getting out of Tasmania. I'm going to live in a far-off land all by myself to see the world.'

There. I'd said it.

'I'll tell you what's going to happen to you, young lady! You'll end up in a shallow grave. DEAD. Did you hear me, Lan? A shallow grave. DEAD! That's all that will happen to you, Lan, you're not TRAINED, dear, for life!'

In my imaginary world of 'How to stand up to your mother', I had a vision of myself spitting my words of Catholic wrath while my mother shed rosary beads that flew around the ceiling then fell like small pops of sugar.

But in the real world, I just blurted.

'Well! Mum! *Mum!* You *should* have trained me for *life* and given me the gift of how to live properly. You let me do anything I wanted, you didn't care what I did or where I went – you *even* let me leave school early and I didn't get to go to technical college or learn how to be a librarian or play the piano or anything. You and Dad bought *Bernadette* a piano to learn, but she didn't like it so you sent it back. I would have *loved* to learn to play the piano but you didn't care, *Mum*! You didn't even come to *Frosty the Snowman* or a basketball game or *anything*! Nothing *happens* here but despair and by the way, Mum – *by the way* – your and Dad's seats were *empty*! I saw them! They were *empty*! I was the *star of that show*.'

Silence.

Cold, silent air filled the room.

'ME? Where WAS I?? Where WAS I??? For a PATHETIC little show at the town hall about a bloody snowman? Why should I GO to anything that you're showing yourself off in? I was LOOKING after a MILK BAR with five rotten kids and a rotten husband. You wait, girl, YOU WAIT until you have children – GOD forbid you DO – but YOU wait, JUST YOU WAIT, LANNAH! And Melbourne? You'll be eaten alive, Lannah. Eaten ALIVE!'

'Well, I'm going to go and find my fortune! In Melbourne!'

I often wonder about the look that crossed my face at this point in time, for this was the time that I knew I had to leave. I stared hard into Mum's hurt brown eyes, glazed with cigarette smoke. She stared back at me, daring me to leave.

I bought a copy of *The Age* and circled all the jobs that were perfect for me.

Part-time Actresses Wanted

Escort Girls Needed. Part-time and Full-time Positions Available

Acting Lessons – Females Only – References Not Required
Do You Want to be a Star? Phone Bob Now!

Mum occasionally hobbled out from her corner in the kitchen with a staged limp, cigarette in hand, only to laugh uproariously at me. But not a soul in the house was even vaguely interested in what I was doing. I'd saved enough money from my jobs: dog walking, babysitting, waitressing and selling Avon make-up door to door.

I scribbled notes on the back of my hand and paid for a bedsit in a place called Windsor for a month. I headed to the local op shop and bought eight suitcases. I needed eight for all my costumes, make-up and op-shop trinkets.

'Mum! I'm *all* packed! I've put everything I need in the suitcases from the op shop, I've booked my ticket, I have two job interviews and I even have a bedsit to live in, in a place called *Windsor*! What do you bloody well *think* about that then, *Mum*?'

Mum stood frozen with her coffee cup poised at her lips. Her voice was thin and not her own – her face a sight to behold – and she smiled crookedly at me.

'You're really going, Lan? You're leaving me to live in Melbourne? Nothing's going to happen there, dear. Windsor? What's Windsor? That's where the Queen lives, Lannah. You're not going to London, Lannah, and you're not going to stay alive if you live in Melbourne in this Windy-sor area. What IS Windsor?'

I couldn't understand. Did she want me to stay? Did she want me to go? What did she *really* mean? Her voice was almost that of a small child, pained and stricken.

Two days later, Mum drove me to the tiny little airport in Devonport for my huge international flight to Melbourne, TAA flight 107 departing at 1 pm. Mum and I put *The Best of ABBA* on the little cassette player and I checked my Glomesh purse for the hundredth time. We sat like two frightened children watching the empty grey highways disappear as we veered toward the shed that was Devonport Airport. It was the morning rush hour for bird life – perky sparrows gathered above the car, flying recklessly through the trees, escaping from the blue winter skies. I closed my eyes to the sounds of ABBA's 'SOS', a song in which every word that ABBA breathed lay hidden a secret message that I clung to for dear life. I'd sing the words loudly to Mum hoping she'd hear me, daring her to understand that I had an SOS dream not to end up like her.

I was dressed in a sailor girl outfit with perfect white pleats – shiny blue buttons dazzled on the double-breasted front of the dress. The sailor girl outfit had dark-blue contrast stitching that matched the dazzling buttons, and I was rather thrilled about this.[23] When we left the house, I heard Mum mutter to the dusty pictures nailed on the stained walls, 'She's NOT a sailor. Why IS she wearing a SAILOR GIRL outfit? Queer little thing she is. Queer little thing, that girl!'

Dad did not say goodbye – he was somewhere on the north west coast playing in a golf tournament. I don't remember the boys waving me off – they were simply nowhere in sight.

I sat with Mum in that tiny airport, half-listening as she spoke to nobody in particular. She was clutching her brown purse, which never held any money in it, just a card for her licence and one single 50-cent piece.

'Well! We're here, LAN! We're at the DROME! You're OFF to Melbourne then. You're off to Melbourne! OFF TO MELBOURNE – Lan is OFF to Melbourne! Little Lan is OFF to Melbourne to MAKE her fortune!'

---

23 I've always loved a contrast stitch with a matching button!

Mum was talking to herself, trying to understand that I was indeed *off to Melbourne*!

We sat on small plastic chairs with a plastic table between us. I was eating two fried dim sims, a packet of potato chips and a dollar's worth of mixed lollies. Mum stared solemnly ahead, telling me how disappointed she was, while she reached around the table searching for my hands. I was sweating and worried as Mum and I had never touched, hugged or embraced, and I was yet to hear the words 'I love you' from anybody.

I waited, counting the seconds until I could start my brand-new reinvention in Melbourne, barely able to contain my excitement as I shivered in the midday chill of the bitter winds at the Devonport drome. I couldn't look at Mum for I didn't know what I'd see.

If she looked glad I would be sad.

If she looked glib I would be sad.

If she looked sad I would be sad.

If she looked happy I would be sad.

I stole a glance at Mum and felt her trying to love me. Why I couldn't tell Mum I loved her will always remain a mystery. Her op-shop coat was too small and her stained brown purse filled me with a sense of deep sorrow along with the desire to flee in equal measure. I was hoping my mum might say the three words.[24]

I felt Mum slipping something onto my dim sim–greasy finger, and as I slowly looked down my heart threw itself into an ABBA song. It was Mum's golden wedding ring, the ring that held no love. She held the tears of a mother in her eyes and yet I knew a part of Mum was hidden away from herself – almost like a crescent moon. Mum told me to look after the ring and if I ever got into trouble, to sell it.

Mum's tears fell onto my sailor girl outfit. 'Lan! The plane's going to leave without you! You better run, dear, you BETTER RUN before that PLANE flies off on you, Lan.'

---

24 When I finally did hear these words spoken for the very first time, I had to go to the bathroom with stomach pains so acute that I thought I was having a stomach heart attack.

I couldn't say goodbye to Mum. I faltered for a moment and felt the cracking of my skin, the tearing-up of my girl-self as I ran toward the plane, the engines' roaring drowning out my feelings. Throwing myself into seat 26B, I could see Mum through the window, standing on the tarmac only metres away – shaking her fingers at me and mouthing the words, 'Don't you DARE get pregnant, and don't STARE at people with those wayward eyes of yours – don't you DARE ...'

A lady strapped me into my seat and told me that tea and coffee would be served after we had reached 30,000 feet. There were only four other people on the plane and I could not believe we had our very own butler serving us. I took one more look out the window and saw Mum slowly limping off into the car park with her too-small op-shop coat huddled around her shoulders. As I felt the wedding ring on my finger, I didn't know if I was disappointing my mum or being brave, or simply abandoning her in Ulverstone to live out the rest of a life I would soon know little about.

I held my tears until the nice butler lady said, 'You going on a holiday, Miss Hill?'

I blubbered that I was *actually* going to Melbourne to make my fortune, and I didn't know a soul and not a soul knew me!

'Good for you, Miss Hill.'

Every cell in my body knew I was doing the right thing, escaping to a new land of reinvention with the '80s just around the corner. New Wave music and fashion were exploding into a kaleidoscope of technicolour chaos and brilliant white light.

And so I flew like a young sparrow at full speed into the blinding light of the future, staring in wonder from my window seat at the marshmallow clouds of a brand-new world.

MELBOURNE

1980–2001

'There is a life and there is a death and there are beauty and melancholy between.'

ALBERT CAMUS

16

Good Luck, Sailor Girl

My heart flip-flopped. I was aghast and thrilled at Melbourne's Tullamarine Airport, a virtual suburb filled with newsagencies, milk bars and hundreds of well-dressed men and women wearing business slacks, long lace skirts and make-up out of a *Cleo* magazine. What's more, I didn't spy one *single* mushroom perm. Not one! These new aliens, who I dared not stare at, were moving and talking at a very fast pace. Busy. Everybody was busy.

I decided to behave as if I too were very busy – and very beautiful; I had read about this little trick of behaving as if you were very, very beautiful. Apparently, it was the secret for God's charming, unjoined girls – believe you are beautiful, and people may *just* find you charming. Believe you are very, *very* beautiful and people may warm to you. My new trick to life was going to be the trick of self-delusion.

I finally secured a taxi big enough to house my eight suitcases of costumes – nurse, flapper, cowboy, policeman, schoolgirl and marching girl – in the folding-down back seats. The driver of the yellow taxi asked if I was a real-life showgirl, with all my suitcases filled with showbiz garb. Or was I perhaps a make-up sales rep for Avon? I informed the taxi driver that I was a sales rep for Avon and that my name, in fact, was Avon – Avon Avon from Penguin, Tasmania. Random shafts of afternoon sun bounced off the suburban sprawl, burning my eyes as we roared along the Tullamarine Freeway to my new home, a little bedsit room to call my own.

I watched the scenery speeding by, the tone quickly changing to charcoal as a vast and heavy veil of black clouds threatened to unleash their tears on my very first day in Melbourne. Suddenly, there wasn't a lot of colour to be seen anywhere, in place of the sun a terrible burning grey eye projecting gloom and judgement with only the briefest glimpses of blue and gold shining through.

I made a deal with the driver for my taxi trip. I had only $30 to spare. My taxi man was grand enough to tell me that he would drive me as far as $30 would allow. He turned around to look at me as we waited for the lights to turn green. He told me we might end up in Prahran, or we might not – it would depend on the traffic. He asked me why I was staying at a flophouse, and that I should be careful in places like that.

A flophouse? My magical bedsit?

My thoughts were interrupted by the sudden braking of the yellow taxi cab. We were here – or rather, we were twelve blocks away from my flophouse, which was as far as my thirty bucks was going to take me.

'How far is twelve blocks?' I asked him nervously. I felt the first pangs of the staggering feeling of being utterly alone in an unknown city, where I didn't know a soul and not a soul knew me. Cars roared up and down the incredible Chapel Street, a street that appeared to be endless, full of people and shops.

'Well … could you help me with my suitcases, please – I'll carry them to my boarding house, my FLOPhouse … I just need a bit of help getting them onto the street.'

'Oh, *Jesus*. Fuck! Now I have to get out and help you? That's gunna cost ya extra.'

I handed him my single $50 note, the only money I had in the world. Huffing like a cartoon gorilla, he dumped my suitcases on the footpath, beeped his horn five times, gave me the finger and yelled as he drove away, 'Good luck, Sailor Girl, ya gunna need it!'

I imagined his yellow car of hell bursting into red-hot flames.

Magical Chapel Street of 1979 fell into focus around me with sudden clarity – or maybe it was that I fell into it, like an extra on the movie set of *Alice in Wonderland*.

The tattered terraces hummed and whispered their sordid boom-and-bust histories; the slow-moving green trams tangled with delivery trucks and taxis; people ran and walked in all directions, some occasionally giving me a curious look, which for some unknown reason made me feel witty, enigmatic, invincible.

Perched on the sturdiest of my suitcases I nervously glanced around, immediately noticing a posh bow teek opposite with eight gorgeous mannequins lined up in spectacular fashion in the window. I looked down at my suitcases tied together with several old pairs of beige pantyhose. They seemed shabby and out of order on this glamorous street. My shoes glared at me, scuffed and worn. My sailor girl dress was stained with Sunny Boy juice and my hair had started to flop. I was concerned with how I was going to carry eight suitcases twelve blocks. How?

I eventually decided to carry two at a time for around three metres. I'd go back to collect two more. I'd carry them to the waiting two. I'd go back and collect two more. I'd carry them back to the waiting four. I'd go back and get two more. I'd carry them back to the waiting six. I'd go back and get two more. I'd carry them back – until eight suitcases surrounded me once again.

All around me was a citified pandemonium – the trams shook and rumbled and the cars gunned their engines and everyone seemed obsessed with the furious pace of their own city lives. I continued my ludicrous carry-on of the carrying of the suitcases for twelve whole blocks until, utterly exhausted, I finally reached my new bedsit: a 1970s situation containing 6999 blocks of burnt-orange bricks. My glamour bedsit was no more than a jail compound, a misplaced toilet block, or perhaps just a very large garage.

Blinking quickly to cover my nerves, I called out into the still evening.

'I'm Alannah. Alannah Hill from Tasmania. I'm five hours late, you see ... I was meant to meet a caretaker ... I'm late because of my suitcases, but can you help me now?'

A bright torchlight appeared from nowhere, a man lurking behind it. I sensed danger, smelt danger, I could feel *the danger* lurking.

'Hello, miss? I can offer you my services. I'll show you to your room, and you'll be very grateful because I know *everything* about everything.'

A small flagon of wine crept out of his pocket and made its way to his lips where he took giant gulps as if vanquishing a terrible thirst, only stopping for a moment to drag on a cigarette. Sporting pale denim jeans, huge Adidas runners, a cheap bright blue T-shirt and a short leather jacket,[25] this porter made me feel quite uneasy as he proffered the unlabelled bottle.

I followed the stone-washed danger up three flights of concrete stairs; he was tall and commanding and he had magicked the key to my bedsit from somewhere.

'*Nice* room they gave you. Ya don't need proper windows anyway, no one can look at ya and ya can't look at no one either, fair's fair if ya know what me drift is. What are you doing in Melbourne? You're on ya own, aren't ya? Aren't cha?'

---

25 I realise now it was actually a leatherette jacket. And stone-washed!

'Yes. I am alone. I don't have much money left, I had to pay the taxi driver.' This was my first Melbourne mistake.

'The taxi driver? He woulda ripped you off. He woulda seen you coming … Fuck, you need caretaking and someone to porter you. What's your name anyway?'

'Alannah.'

'Alannah? An Alannah girl alone in the big bad city with no money. Ripped off by a taxi driver … What you going to do without money?'

I could feel the uncomfortable truth of his question hanging in anticipation in my new bedsit room. I wondered if the world still shimmered outside under the darkening sky, its jellied stillness quivering to the first mutters of a thunderstorm. I thought I could hear water, water rushing at me; I could either sink or swim.

'The girl livin' here before you topped herself, ya know, she cut her wrists wide open. You can still see the blood on the mirror there. See? Can ya see the red blood? Some dickhead tried to clean it but blood don't come outta concrete. Dickhead!'

My new bedsit was beginning to feel not so special. The room was wall-to-wall bright orange brick, the floor a putrid mustard-coloured carpet, mould clung to the bricks, the fluorescent light was switched on twenty-four hours a day. No light could shine in, no darkness could escape.

A single bed was thrust into a corner, not a blanket or sheet in sight, a tea-stained pillow stuffed underneath. A dwarf-sized wardrobe sloped against the wall. The shower was hidden behind a piece of fabric, a fabric I've not *seen* or felt since – it wasn't polyester, nor was it a shower curtain. A yellow plastic duck lay abandoned on the floor. The kitchen was not actually a proper kitchen, not like the kitchen I had read about in *The Age* newspaper – *LUXURY STYLE BEDSITS / KITCHENETTE / SHOWER / WINDSOR AREA*. Instead, it was a hotplate sitting alongside a small sink. The atmosphere was stale and flat and it sheltered an air of supreme nothingness.

'Well, I'll let you settle in then. I'm right across the hall from you, so give me a knock-knock-knockity-knock whenever you like, I am the *man* to help you. I know all about jealousy, money, politics, petty crims, cops, time, I'm a bloody *encyclopedia*. I know about freedom as well. You've run away from home, haven't you? You don't know what you're *doing*, do you? No money in your purse and all dressed up like a cartoon girl. You'll be knocking, I know you will, so don't be shy, *Alannah*! Knock-knock-knockity-knock!'

His hand grabbed his crotch and he gave me a look of urgency. I knew this look. The look of sex and power. I was a girl blinded in the headlights of naivety, a baby rabbit frozen.

As soon as I was alone, the reality started to sink in. I had no clock. No telephone. No licence. No ID. And *no money*.

I got cracking: I needed to reinvent this room! Suitcases turned into tables, the towel I'd brought with me turned itself into a mat, my costumes were draped in various shapes and degrees of separation on the walls. I owned one bottle of perfume, Tabu, that I placed on a little shelf I'd made from the lining of the suitcase. I found a milk bottle in a dusty, musty cupboard and filled it with water, then emptied my lavender hair dye into it to make a spectacular lilac bottle of old-fashioned lavender. I'd brought a single candle with me, and placed it behind the lavender water, giving a lilac-mauve air of gracefulness to the dead stillness.

I lay across my sloping single bed. Eyes wide open, I watched a spider on the ceiling weave a web. I hoped my stomach would forget it was starving. I can still see myself lying half-awake on that single bed trying to remember where I was, who I was – it seemed I'd been half-asleep for the last million years, lying in wait for this moment.

A scratching sound was gnawing its way into my thoughts, nagging my attention inside the bedsit. *A mouse?* I thought. The door to my room was vibrating and I could hear no birdlike tweets, no trams or cars. The fathomless Melbourne night faintly echoed like one of my favourite songs, Simon and Garfunkel's 'The Sound of Silence'.

The slippery, scratching sound at my door had turned itself into a drunken growl. This was no mouse gnawing through my frightened door. Porter Man, I thought. Porter Man! I fumbled and stumbled in the dark for my vintage dressing gown.

The danger had somehow ghosted himself into my room. As porter, he said, he was in charge of all the spare keys.

'Get up. It's late. Ya hungry? I'll take you to Coles … show you how to get free food. Hurry up and get a coat, it's cold outside and Coles doesn't stay open all bloody night just for you!'

As if in a dream, I found my coat in one of the suitcases and followed him outside. He tried to grab my hand and we walked in a frozen silence to Coles, my heart beating so fast I forgot to breathe. Porter Man directed me to follow his commands and, despite the rattling and humming of knowing it all felt terribly wrong, I went along with his commands.

'Here, take this jumper and shove it down your skirt. You have to look pregnant. Follow me around the aisles and act normal, speak *only* if I speak to ya and don't go talking to anyone or telling anyone anything … ya got that?'

'Why? I don't under—'

'You're *pregnant*, right? Preggers! Don't ask me fucking stupid questions, you're like a bloody cop! You're preggers! Do what I tell ya, I'm trained for this sort of shit so keep that jumper folded down ya skirt like that and don't let it slip cos I'll be real fucking angry if ya fuck this up. Hey, see that cardboard box? Jesus, hurry up. Grab the fucking box, will ya?'

I told myself this was theatre, that I was preparing for a career on a Melbourne stage, nodding and smiling occasionally as I wandered fluorescent aisles stacked high with grocery items I'd never seen or heard about – avocados, anchovies, canned olives, coffee in packets, spaghetti, milk called 'soy' in a carton. This huge supermarket even had an aisle to itself for biscuits and another two aisles just for shampoo and make-up … but my favourite item in the supermarket was a broom.

I love to sweep, you see, dear reader, I just love to sweep.

I'd learnt I could ease my anxiety with gentle sweeping motions, sweeping away the broken parts of me as they fell.

Porter Man placed the grocery items inside the cardboard box, cans of Melbourne Bitter, a bottle of something called Southern Comfort, lighter fluid, potatoes, fish fingers, cans of Coke, tea towels, a packet of soup, Spam, bread and a tin of sardines. Porter Man never explained why he wanted me to hide the groceries inside the box and I didn't ask why. He was a twisted question mark of a man with a hawk-like face that once upon a time may have been handsome but was now blotched and tarnished by depravity and sleeping rough. White bubbles flecked the corner of his mouth and his eyes seemed blacker and more dangerous in the stark glare of supermarket lighting. Glaring into my wide-awake eyes, he pointed his finger in a gun-like motion at my head and told me to get ready to run.

'When I say run, *run*. OK?'

I was about to open my squawk-box mouth to inform Porter Man I had won the 100-metre dash at Penguin High School the year before, but he was already on the move.

'Outta our way, the baby's coming, *my wife is having a baby*! The waters are *broken*, now get outta our way, excuse me, miss, yes, my wife is having a baby and I've got to get her to the hospital … *for fuck's sake*, outta our way before she goes into labour.'

Porter Man pushed me and the box of groceries through the supermarket door and into the asphalt car park, shouting with absurd confidence and conviction, and the bored, curious checkout staff believed every word he said. Even I began to believe I was pregnant. This was a man who not only knew how to live a lie but could convince everyone around him of the truth of his lies as well.

The next day I shoplifted a hammer.

17

Shallow Grave

In those early days in Melbourne, fantastical news bulletins looped through my mind, constantly whispering ghastly untruths into my ear. I would visualise helicopters hung with 7000-watt globes searching for me all night long, police cars wailing their screams of desperate urgency roaring along desolate highways while a cast of hundreds joined hands like one giant gumbooted family, holding their torches aloft in the faint hope of finding me alive. I'd imagine the very worst trouble I could possibly attract, the most heinous people stalking or trying to kill me. My wild scenarios would distract me for hours, little snuff-loops of horror recording my ravaged cadaver being exhumed from a shallow grave in the middle of nowhere.

I'd always be found dead.

A forgotten, unjoined dead girl, with a family who didn't care to look for me. No matter how hard I tried to conjure up the image, my family were never part of the search party – I could never picture them in my movie-length fantasy of death and survival.

Maybe these thoughts were exacerbated by the madman across

the hallway, who was never far away. I wasn't strong enough to tell him to just get lost. I heard him gurgling my name through closed doors, through open doors.

'Alaaaaaaaaannaaaaaah, Alaaaaaannnaaaahhhh, I've got the most *enormous* erection, ya better come and get it. I made it big just for you. Ya never seen anything like this before in ya entire life and you're having my baby anyway, so open up ya door.'

This announcement, followed by a bear-like growl morphing into a hyena's howl, sent shivers all through me. I would grab my shiny shoplifted hammer.

'*Alannah*, I've left somethin' under ya door for ya ... ya gunna get it good, me big fella's as big as a tree.'

And then I saw them. Five small packets in a neat row with writing scrawled across each. Condoms. My special drunken delivery was five condoms.

The bluebird of luck had flown away from me for a moment's rest.

'Come on, I'm just joking ya!' said Porter Man, his voice muffled, as if his tongue were made from blotting paper.

I pulled my dressing gown across my body and slowly opened the door. I checked the corridor, but all the lights were out in the pre-dawn gloom and so I went back inside, closing the door with a heavy sigh.

I owned one plate, one spoon, one fork, one bowl and a tin of Milo. My ritual was to stack four scoops of sloppy vanilla ice-cream[26] into a bowl and drizzle the Milo over the ice-cream, thrilled with the sensation of ice-cream and Milo stuck together like Siamese twins. It was in these ice-cream moments I'd plan my day in my new land of freedom. Melbourne.

I scooped four teaspoons of ice-cream into my mouth, and then I heard the speaking of the madman as he opened my door. 'I'm here darlin', I'm here! Hide and seek time, little Bo-Peeeeep!' He sat like a

---

26 Because I didn't have a fridge I would rest the ice-cream in the sink in cold water.

prisoner on my single bed, and picked up my mother's wedding ring. It rest dangerously in his shaking hands as his eyes slid around the room. I could feel words forming in my throat. I wanted to roar at him, 'Why are you even here? You can't be in here, this is *my* room … *get out*!'

But I was the girl on a train again. I couldn't move or speak.

'Ya gotta hammer, have ya, love? Huh! You're a real country girl, aren't ya, standing there in that old thing ya wearin'. Young girl dressed up like a grandmother with a hammer. Whatcha gunna do with ya hammer, eh, Nanna? So what are you up to today, Hammer Nanna? What you going to do for money today?'

This strange man seemed to be inviting me into his hotchpotch of a life like a lonely traveller who meets another traveller in a pretty beach town in summertime. But this was no beach town in summertime, this was my brick bedsit and he was sitting on my bed. An uneasy doubt fell around me, the air in the room thick and sticky. I could see him manhandling my mother's wedding ring, which lay awaiting its fate in his stained hands.

'Come on! Get dressed! I'll wait for you outside while you get changed. I'll take you to a special place, and we'll take the ring to a pawn shop so you can have some moolah, so hurry up, we gotta lot to do today.'

Alarmingly willing to go along with his wretched plan, I dressed in my Sunday best. I'd noticed a subversive fashion situation where girls were adopting a schoolgirl look. I called it the Kindergarten Whore Girl. My Sunday best for that dismal Wednesday was a school uniform I'd picked up in an op shop in Penguin for a dollar.

I was also trying out punky, absurd looks with my make-up, feeling like a movie star one second and Bette Davis as the ghoulish, hilariously wrong sister in *Whatever Happened to Baby Jane?* the next. My eye shadow was bright canary yellow, my lips pillar-box red, and I'd taken to drawing over my freckles with black texta. I was wildly hoping I looked interesting and a little bit like Siouxsie Sioux or one of her Banshees!

He was waiting for me outside the door, the whiskey flask glued to his lips. I walked two steps behind him until we came to the pawn shop. He told me to wait outside and he'd get the best money he could for my mum's wedding ring. I wanted to run as fast as I could back up Chapel Street to collect my ordiments, my doilies and costumes and find a new bedsit but I was stuck, stuck for this moment in time; my running legs seemed broken, unable to skip, hop or kick.

'Here! Take ya fifty bucks, I keep forty for doin' the trade and you keep fifty. Ring was shit quality, ya know, ya dad didn't spend much on ya mum's wedding ring, did he?'

His voice had begun to bubble at me again but I was barely listening. I allowed him to seat me in what could only be described as an unkempt, deserted, broken-down hut at the back of a block of red-brick flats in Wellington Street, St Kilda. Green cordial crates were our wine stools, twenty-eight bottles of beer seemed to be the wine, our guest was another Porter Man type, a deep red sore festering on the left side of his face. Both he and the other Porter Man snorted line after line of white powder up their thick noses.

'Go on, snort yaself a line,' one said very quickly.

'No, I actually have to go in a minute or two. I have a job appointment I forgot about. I have a job appointment, an actual real job interview, you know, for a secretarial job in South Melbourne.'

They didn't seem to hear a word I said. I knew enough to sip the beer offered to me. I also knew enough to pretend I wasn't against their criminal activity, which was becoming more obvious by the second. Their drug-addled state had them jumping in square circles, a wad of cash and a gun handed back and forth like a game of chess, talk of stealing a mate called Dicko's motorbike, chatter about cooking up something called bathtub speed.

I knew I must escape the garish wine bar/garage without either of them noticing, but where could I go? Listening to their chatter, I began to realise Porter Man thought that I was older than I really was and assumed that I could be swayed into becoming his partner in crime. In hindsight, I understood what he'd seen in me, the cracked broken parts of me, my curious nature and blatant naivety.[27]

But this was the New Me: the new girl Alannah, with a brand-new hammer, dressed up as a nanna. I was ready, more willing and more able to slay anyone who dared touch or look at me like the two policemen in Hobart had – I made a vow to never put myself in such a vulnerable position ever again.

27 Little did I know, dear reader, that very soon, both of these dangerous crims would crash to a brutal end, with policemen dragging them into police cars on the street right opposite my room.

18

I Did a Bad, Bad Thing

Without money, stenography skills or a second language, I was having a spot of trouble finding a real job. I felt desperate. I knew I was slipping. And then I slipped up, and like all splendid slip-ups, my fall from grace brought enlightenment in its wake.

I was down to the nib of my Black Tulip lipliner and they were $6 each, $6 I didn't have. I could not be seen outside or inside without lipstick, so I did a bad, bad thing. Idling through the aisles of a chemist in Prahran, I saw hundreds of items I needed – hair shampoos, nail varnishes, soaps and small containers filled with unknown pleasures. I stared at the beckoning lipliners and wondered if anybody would notice that one was missing. Surely not. The lipliners had been beckoning only me. I slipped one of the beckoning Black Tulip lipliners into the sleeve of my tight cardigan and tried to stand unnoticed in the queue. I had $5 and wanted to pay for a chocolate Freddo Frog I'd already beheaded in aisle 4. Suddenly a firm hand gripped my shoulder and pushed me toward the back of the store. A whippet-thin lady with a face too small for her head told me to sit down. She took my details while I asked her what seemed to be the problem. She told me to shut up. And then she called the police.

'You're a professional thief, and I'm sick of you little punks coming in here pinching things *that are not yours*! You can tell the police what you did. I'm handcuffing you to this chair until they come. You've done this before, haven't you? And then you all run, don't cha? You *all* run. Bunch of cowards. Well, you can't run now, can you? The police are coming for you!'

I hated the police. I thought they were all rapists. I folded in on myself, waiting for the sirens to take me to jail or to hell. Soon a female and a male policeman were standing over my handcuffed self; I hoped the right words would come out of my mouth.

'Name, please?'

And I didn't think twice: 'Sister Sherry O'Brien.'

'That your real name?'

'Yes, that's my real name.'

I thought this might help my situation. I'd been raised a good Catholic girl. I wanted to blame something or someone, so I immediately thought of Auntie Sherry.

'You've been caught stealing? Do you understand what that means, Miss O—' The man stopped mid-sentence when he saw my handcuffed hands and the trickle of wee trailing down my legs.

The policewoman said, 'Un-handcuff this poor girl, she's shaking like a leaf!'

I loved that policewoman.

She turned to look at the Chemist Nazi and then at the other officer, and then they both did something remarkable – the police let me go! They told me never to shoplift again and that I was banned from *that* particular chemist. I was so grateful I wanted to hug them. The chemist lady scowled, and with the body of the headless, unpaid Freddo melting in my hands, I ventured back out onto Chapel Street, a shrunken, humiliated version of myself.

I was waiting, waiting for the feeling of freedom. I had thought living on my own in a city where nobody knew me would make me happy, but I didn't feel as happy or free as I'd dreamt. I came to understand that I'd always been free. I didn't have to be home at a certain time; in fact, I didn't have to be home at all, I didn't have to do any homework, I could come and go as I wanted just as long as I was a good girl and looked after my poor, ailing, sick mother.

I wasn't quite at ease in my new world where money was hard to find and my one friend was a petty crim. And now I was a petty criminal as well; it was contagious.

I was doubting my move to Melbourne, doubting everything. It felt like something disturbingly false was at the core of it all, as if I had forced myself into a city where I didn't know how to survive. I struggled with the colossal burden of how I was going to continue to live in the bedsit. I was resilient, independent, and I knew I couldn't attach myself to another person in the hope they'd provide me with *their* money or throw *their* happiness over me like holy water. I couldn't rely on anyone for anything – I had to get a real job.

I walked into every store on Chapel Street, leaving my name and a reference I'd written myself, stating ten skills I did not have, one of them being stenography.

I said I could type ninety-nine words per minute with 100 per cent accuracy, and with all my experience in the stenography world I had in my possession a reference on National Mutual letterhead (borrowed from my father's briefcase). My reference boldly stated that I held a happy disposition and worked diligently and effectively. I was job crazy. I caught trams or hitchhiked, sometimes turning up to four interviews in one day and not getting *one of them*!

19

Lan, Dear, Where Are You?

The city of Melbourne was a locked fortress, a secret world that didn't seem to take too kindly to smashed-up girls from smashed-up Tasmanian milk bars. I was alone but I held a special gift: the gift of desperation. I was ready to climb but I still hadn't met a single soul ready to climb with me.

I was naturally a rather shy girl.[28] I'd ride the Melbourne trams, squinting into the sun, killing time, making time, watching the time, catching endless trams all the way down the line to deep suburban terminuses. It was a novelty – in Tasmania I would rollerskate, hitchhike or walk, but Melbourne city sprawled out into thousands of suburbs: Balwyn, Glen Iris, Sunshine, Moonee Ponds, Elsternwick, Windsor, Camberwell … Endless blocks of perfect middle-class homes with trimly clipped hedges and two posh European cars in the driveway. I wondered how the hell I was going to climb out of my deep and total anonymity into the intoxicating oxygen of self-realisation on that twisted ladder's topmost rung.

My all-time favourite name for a suburb was St Kilda. I loved it due to my Catholic upbringing, my nan's wish for me to become a nun,

---

28 I spent years trying to help people understand I was shy. Nobody believes it to be true. I think it's true.

my fear of not getting into heaven, and my ongoing deal with the devil: Saint Kill Daaaaaar – I loved saying these holy words out loud.

Most Sunday evenings I'd call Mum from a nearby phone box. I was always nervous before making the phone call. If Joseph answered the phone, we would both immediately hang up. If Dad answered the phone, the silence was deadly, until I heard him mumble, 'I'll just get your mother.' I remember the hurt hurtling its way through the telephone cord.

'Lan, dear, where ARE you?'

'Oh, Mum, I'm in a place called Saint Kill Daaaaaaar – and there's a *crystal ballroom*, Mum! A crystal *ballroom*! I haven't been inside it yet, Mum, but it's apparently a giant *ballroom*, made entirely out of crystals!'

'Lannaaaaaah! LANNAAAAAAH! You're going to end up in that shallow grave talking like that, dear. Is there a Catholic church in Saint Kill Daaaaaaar, Lan? Have you got a JOB yet, dear? What do you DOOOOO all day, Lannaaaaah? You better get back on the plane and come back here, you're not going to make it over there on your own, Lan. Oh you're NOT managing are you, dear? I KNOW you, Lannaaaaah, and I know you'd be giving the men that untoward look you carry around with you, you're GIVING MEN THE LOOK, aren't you, LAN? HANG on a minute, dear, I'm just getting a cigarette!'

'Are you thinking of coming to Melbourne soon, Mum, to see me?'

'No – NO – NO – No – No – No – Nooooooooo!'

Our last words were often about my missing sister.

'Have you heard from her yet, Mum?'

'Lan, I TOLD you I can't tell you WHERE she is, dear, she's very VERY angry with you, Lan, she's not going to speak to you ever again, dear, I CAN'T tell you where she is. I PROMISED her, Lan!

I PROMISED her! She's staying with a group of girls in North Hobart and they're ALL feminists!'

Our phone call would always be brief. I would hear my father shouting in the background about the cost of calls, especially reverse-charge ones from Melbourne. I could hear him telling Mum to get me off the phone, it must be costing him a *fucking fortune*!

And before I could say goodbye, I would hear the sudden click of the phone hanging up.

I had hoped by leaving Tasmania, it would magically make me popular and I'd finally be reading from the Bible of Inclusion. I was learning how to use my pretend bold, confident, eccentric exterior to gatecrash the utter indifference to my existence that I felt the world had for me. I was an outsider searching for a way to break into a barricaded punky-rocky world that I sensed existed but had never seen – a place where fey and floppy arty types could find a door to knock on, a platform to stand on, a microphone, a spotlight, to signify something beyond the broken asphalt reality of my everyday life.

20

Indigo Bow Teek

The pearly rays from a new spring sun flashed across my wide-awake eyes. It was late October 1980. Spring had finally arrived inside my Windsor flophouse. I quite liked the idea of a flophouse although my mum argued it was not a FLOPhouse. It was a FOPhouse. Radiant beams of pure nothingness swirled around my brick horror of a room, embracing my op-shop relics, showing up the cracks, the splits, the chips in my second-hand finery. Spring tattooed its pretty colours onto the streets, banishing the long, cold claws of winter. Pale-lilac wisterias blossomed throughout Melbourne, giant trees thawed and green grass grew. The arrival of spring gave me courage for the future, a little more peace with my past and a fizzy confidence about my present.

With fourteen hot-pink bows bobby pinned through my '60s beehive, I wondered how much longer I'd have to waitress, how much longer I'd have to hustle for jobs I was completely unsuited for. I joined the queues marked 'Desperate' at the Dole office. A nobody standing in line for a food voucher, a cash handout and bedsit rental assistance – when in God's name would I magically turn into a somebody?

I had been working part-time as a punked-up waitress at Chapel Street's Spaghetti Graffiti, Melbourne's first twenty-four-hour spaghetti restaurant. The elderly manager, who insisted his name was Rexie Sexie, sported a bright-orange permed toupee, his face damp with matching orange foundation that was smeared around his bloodshot eyes.

One life-changing day, as I carelessly wiped wine stains off the tables, a beacon of light pierced the panes of glass at Spaghetti Graffiti, iridescent colours transporting me momentarily into my fashion future. The person who brought me the light was Jill Gould, who owned the hippie bow teek opposite Spaghetti.

Jill had a smile that beamed a kind of homecoming. She seemed disarmingly unaware of her prettiness, or how her shiny auburn hair flowed like Farrah Fawcett's. Her shiny hair marked her as clearly a somebody and probably a secret cult member of *Young Talent Time*.

So blinded was I by the light and how Jill's hair shone, I spilt a takeaway coffee all over her perfect tanned hands. Unflappable, she asked if I'd ever worked in retail. My mouth opened and it immediately told a crooked black lie.

'I've worked in retail my entire life! My *entire life*, Jill!'

Jill explained how difficult it was to find kind, intelligent and loyal staff for her bow teek, and how, despite my 'mad little punk look', she was struck by my 'friendly, bold, outgoing personality'. She asked if I'd consider trialling for a day, working as a sales assistant at Indigo. My shoes slipped off my feet with excitement. I immediately said yes to Jill, and she immediately wrote in her diary when my trial would begin.

Jill had opened Indigo on Chapel Street in 1973 selling panelled denim flares, panelled denim jackets, denim shirts and denim shorts.[29] She told me how her business partner, John, was away on an inspirational trip to Afghanistan, India and Nepal, sourcing tribal wedding gowns, tribal headwear, tribal climbing shoes, handwoven ponchos and a new

29 Hence the name Indigo.

scent of Indian incense. She explained he might not be ready for a little punkette like me. I immediately thought I might not be ready for a man who bought fancy-dress costumes from hippie markets and onsold them as actual clothing at bow teeks. I was curious as to what the new Indian incense smelt like. I was curious about John. I was curious about Jill. I was terribly curious about both of them.

On the day of my trial Jill handed me a hippie bell–ringing, mirrored wedding dress.

This was to be my costume for the day, but I didn't care that it wasn't my style. I was on trial with a real-life job. I wondered what my mum would think: her youngest daughter in Melbourne working at a real-life job in a bow teek! *She will* die *when she hears about this*, I thought. Jill gave me a list of what to do and what not to do. No eating in the store; always a friendly, singsong hello to people; no phone calls; no friends to pop in and distract me. I had to remember to never leave more than $40 in the drawer.[30] Jill kindly told me to just 'be myself'.

Just be myself?

Be *myself?*

Before disappearing upstairs to work on Indigo's winter collection (which, Jill told me, included a floor-length patchwork tie-dyed coat with silver coins sewn across the hem), Jill explained that I should try to look busy every second of the day. To a customer, there was nothing worse than a bored shop assistant. She thought customers would respond to my personality.

I reached out to hug her. Jill hugged me back, handing me four sticks of incense to burn in the store for my day trial. She also handed me a record with a large triangle on it. *Tubular Bells*. I was to play that record all day.

I Windexed through the entire bottle of blue fluid, burnt the four sticks of incense, played the *Bells* record, but mostly I tried *not* to look

30 There was no till.

like a bored shop assistant. I served ten customers, disturbing Jill only once to ask if she had other sizes in the bell-ringing wedding gown I was wearing. It seemed I had a little knack for being able to sell the clothes off my back. I sold three of the tribal wedding gowns, a red windcheater, a pair of tribal socks, a tribal hat and four tie-dyed pieces that appeared to be sheets worn as frocks. I mingled with the customers, spinning around with my Windex, spending an hour with a middle-aged lady who had cancer: she was looking for tribal turbans to cover her falling-out hair.

And then … John appeared, back from his Indian trip, like a genie from a musk-oil bottle. I was preparing to finish for the day, happily changing back into my normal punk clothes. Jill had offered me a ride in her fancy royal-blue Mercedes. She was going to give me feedback on how I trialled, but I worried the lingering musk incense and patchouli oil might have turned me into a real hippie. I worried that I might have failed Jill.

John floated toward me like a man walking on water, his incredible heart-stopping face stopping me in my tracks. I don't recall ever seeing anyone as handsomely hippie in my entire life: I was mesmerised by him. He was slightly aghast at me.

'John, this is Alannah Hill – she trialled with us today …'

I saw his cheekbones move slightly. John's angular jaw and tanned skin gave him the look of eternal youth, his eyes an ocean of deep blue flecked with silver. Together, John and Jill looked the perfect couple, unflappable, kind, knowing. I had already fantasised that I was their long-lost daughter.

He stared at Jill, and then he asked me what star sign I was.

I shouted. I don't know why, but shout I did! '*Aries!* I'm an Aries! What star sign are you? Are you an Aries, too? Are you a guru? You're very beautiful. Isn't he beautiful, Jill?'

John stayed silent, his intense eyes staring at something intensely. Jill said John was a Scorpio.

'Lan has been *amazing*, John. I just received a phone call from a woman she spent over an hour with. She told me Lan offered to make her some colourful punk scarves for her head – she's got cancer, John, and Lan made her day …'

The man on water, John, was speaking, 'It's Lan, is it? Good. I like Aries girls; my first girlfriend was an Aries. Jill's got a new boyfriend, haven't you, Jizz – he's a lawyer, or a barrister. Which kind of liar did you choose over me, Jizz – lawyer or barrister? Liar or liar?'

I loved him. Irreverent and jealous with a Scorpio sting, and he had just called Jill Jizz!

'I'm sure you're good with people. Jill's really found herself with Kennedy. Did Jizz tell you he's now an enlightened lying being?'

He glared at Jill and gave me a soft look before heading upstairs. Jill stared at the timber floor. Whatever situation they were entangled in I hoped they'd feel close enough to light ten sticks of incense and tell me everything.

On our drive to the bedsit Jill offered me a full-time job. She told me I was a natural sales assistant and that my perky, confident personality resonated with the customers. Apparently I was 'tuned in' to the mindset of 'groovy' Chapel Street. After gushing all over Jill for giving me a bow teek chance and promising I'd buy a bottle of patchouli oil, I flew upstairs to my bedsit, sat on the single bed and ate an entire tub of Peter's chocolate ice-cream. It tasted just like patchouli oil.

Maybe the first job we love sticks with us like a first love, the first cut being the deepest. Perhaps it's where we give our all and after that we know better. A piece of us remains in the heart of our first job – it holds our innocence, it holds friendship and, with trial and error, it holds our youth.

For me, Indigo was all of that.

Indigo was also my first real family.

21

Don't You Want Me?

I began to frequent night haunts in the heart of the city, hitchhiking to any club I could find as the gathering New Wave phenomenon swept into Melbourne's cobwebbed nightclub world. Dressed as a kindergarten kabuki girl, it was easy for an unjoined girl like me to arrive alone into dimly lit, uber-cool clubs – I had no posse of friends and no real inkling of how to conduct myself in this grown-up nightclub world. I had no driver's licence, no passport, no ID, no tax file number, I was not on any list, I didn't vote and I wasn't wanted by the police. I didn't even have a criminal record. I simply did not exist!

I didn't drink alcohol, I didn't smoke, nor did I partake in the drinking of tea, coffee, Milo, Quik, iced coffee, orange juice, water, beer, vegetable juice, pineapple juice, milk, hot chocolate or any form of cocktail/mocktail, hightail/lowtail. I would drink lemonade with five ice cubes only through a pink-striped straw. The nightclubs of Melbourne didn't quite understand my need for the straw. It held a queenly position in a small section of my handbag and I'd whip it out each time I sipped on my icy lemonade. I learnt how to not smudge my lipstick when drinking through a straw. My lipstick was never *ever* being ruined, smudged, or altered on my mouth. I couldn't drink without a straw. I couldn't. I *wouldn't*.

The first club to really grasp the Significance of the Straw was Swelter. Every Tuesday at 9 pm, Swelter opened its doors to an eager crowd filled with designers, musicians, artists, wannabes, nobodies, somebodies, along with intense fashionistas. Nightclubs like this, key to the Blitz New Wave phenomenon, would open for a month and then

BOOM!

The doors would close, never to be opened again.

I yearned to become one of the vacant-eyed, bored, beautiful, slightly crazed, vain, arrogant Door Girls, for these girls were handpicked, almost as if they'd fallen from heaven. Such chosen mortals held great power, picking and choosing who would be allowed in and who wouldn't. In the '80s, unless you were deemed model-gorgeous, a girl could never, *ever* dream of becoming a Door Girl.

The addictive '80s sugar-pop sounds of Culture Club, Feargal Sharkey, Joy Division, Spandau Ballet, Dexys Midnight Runners and Kraftwerk howled from the high-frequency DJ pod, and if anyone *dared* to hover around the DJ's sound system, you were hollered out of the Sweltering Swelter and told to fuck off.

It was a balmy evening in May 1982 and a wall of '80s noise was pressing down on me as I hung by a quivering thread in the smoking strobe lights of the New Romantic disco room. Human League were *the* electronic New Wave pop band from London and the room was saturated with 'Don't You Want Me?' their giant *Countdown* number-one hit.

I gazed about me through the out-of-focus Swelter ambience, radiating the teased-up hair and make-up vibe that was entirely my own invention, but miraculously had fallen into step with this English trend sweeping the globe.

I noticed a man leaning on the bar, a cowboy hat falling over his face, a pair of silver spurs attached to cowboy boots, a velvet plum coat that was *far* too long slung like a cloak around his shoulders. The coat trailed around his spurred feet, puddling onto the floor. I'd seen him before and had discovered from asking several thousand questions that this person had *quite* the reputation. There was talk of cemeteries, hearses and wild two-day parties where people fell in love, out of love, out of windows and even into swimming pools.

I heard a voice rasping through the holes in the cowboy hat: 'Where's ya other head? You got another inbred head hiding somewhere?'

This, dear reader, was my introduction to David Heeney, the future CEO of Factory X, a company where I would make my fashion career, my new family, my new self and new friends in years to come. We had no idea that our futures would become so entwined that during our seventeen-year partnership it would become impossible for us to understand where one of us began and the other ended.

David almost fell over chortling, laughing and slapping his knees at this Tasmanian joke I'd heard a thousand times before. He had a flute of champagne in each hand, a half-smoked cigarette of ash dangling from his mouth.

I stared at him. One minute he looked shy and handsome and the next he couldn't look me in the eye. He was dancing, talking, drinking, smoking, jiggling. I was dancing, talking, *not* drinking, *not* smoking, jiggling.

I shouted over the music, 'I have heard some preeeeettttteeeee wild tales about you, Cowboy Man. Are you a hairdresser? *Do* you own a cemetery? Have you shrunk yourself in the wash? You're rather short, dear? Do you own an op shop in Fitzroy Street? Do you have a girlfriend?

ABOVE The apple orchard house in Geeveston. Mum used an axe to chop up op-shop furniture for firewood to keep us from freezing in the bitter Tasmanian winters.

TOP RIGHT Nan and Mum.

RIGHT Mum and me in Queen Street, Ulverstone in 1979. My head is ever so slightly turned because I had an eye infection from trying to use black shoe polish instead of eyeliner. Do not attempt this at home, dear reader.

ABOVE The only known photograph of the Hill family ever taken. This was a staged photograph that appeared in the local paper. It was Christmas Day: the only day the milk bar was closed.

ABOVE Steven Jones-Evans and I hand sewed my first ever design, a pinafore. This photo was taken at Melbourne Grammar, where I would often pop in and spook the boarders. One dared to ask me, 'How much do ya charge to haunt houses?' I threw my ice-cream cone at him.

RIGHT Posing for Quentin on the grounds of Illawarra House in Toorak. We'd just finished hanging stray autumn leaves onto the clothes line and planting a herb garden with Salada crackers.

ABOVE Steven and me in his St Kilda apartment in 1993. After Steve moved into the singles apartment and set-dressed me into oblivion, I made sure we saw each other all the blooming time. Note how Steven is in a world of his own. I made that cup of tea for him because I was the quickest cup of tea–maker known to womankind.

LEFT *Dogs In Space* night shoot, 1986. The decadent ivory-lace blouse became mine. Overnight! Just like that!

ABOVE Indigo's Spring Fling, 1983. Here I am looking very neo-prim with three look-alike Alannahs in the window. On the days I was the *manageress* I'd often pose in the window and spook people wandering past.

LEFT The original Indigo girls in the best-selling dress of all time, the D600. For Jill's birthday in 1988 I organised this photoshoot, had all the Indigo girls sign the photo *Happy Birthday, Jill*, and framed it. We loved Jill.

RIGHT I scream, you scream, we all scream for *ice-cream*! My first Alannah Hill campaign (spring/summer 2009) with Georges Antoni and Andrew Majzner from Paper Stone Scissors. I tried to drag the ice-cream cone home; in fact, I tried to drag *all* the props home.

LEFT Photo by Jez Smith. Art directed by Andrew Majzner from Paper Stone Scissors. Taken at the Palazzo Versace hotel in Queensland for the Alannah Hill spring/summer 2010 campaign. I kind of fell in love with model Simone Kerr. Then I fell into the pool fully clothed.

LEFT Look at me go at a flea market in NYC on one of my business trips. Treasure galore! My mum could not understand why I scrounged around flea markets, and firmly believed I was stuck in my 'milk-bar tip days'.

LEFT On a business trip in London for Indigo. I would ask strangers to take my photograph to prove to Mum I was, in fact, in London!

RIGHT E, three weeks old. I didn't know what to do or where to go so I drove to Chadstone Shopping Centre almost every day.

FAR RIGHT E and I at the Westin Hotel, Sydney, in 2005. I had just given him four Freddo Frogs and a promise he could keep the fake fur jacket.

RIGHT This is the day I found out I was pregnant. I could *not* believe it!

BELOW A little boy's love for his mum! I *know*! (I *may* have forced E to hold the image of me for a photo to send to my mum.)

ABOVE Mum, E and Patch in Ulverstone. This was the morning of The Confession and the last time I saw Mum alive.

LEFT Me, E and Karl on a walk. A lady stopped me and commented on what beautiful clothing my little girl was wearing.

LEFT E and I in Gawler, Tasmania. I threw him up in the air and then he vomited all over me.

BELOW Here I am as the Girl in the Cupboard at Dialogue. I popped out to cut a dress from one of Quoc's patterns.

BELOW RIGHT Here I am purchasing fabric at *Premiaaiir Vizeeoon*. I didn't understand francs. Fabric that I believed was $20 a metre was actually $2000 a metre.

ABOVE The Alannah-ettes in Darlinghurst, Sydney. I would fly to Sydney regularly to meet, greet, entertain, offer advice, peruse spreadsheets and shower the staff with gifts and fashion gossip.

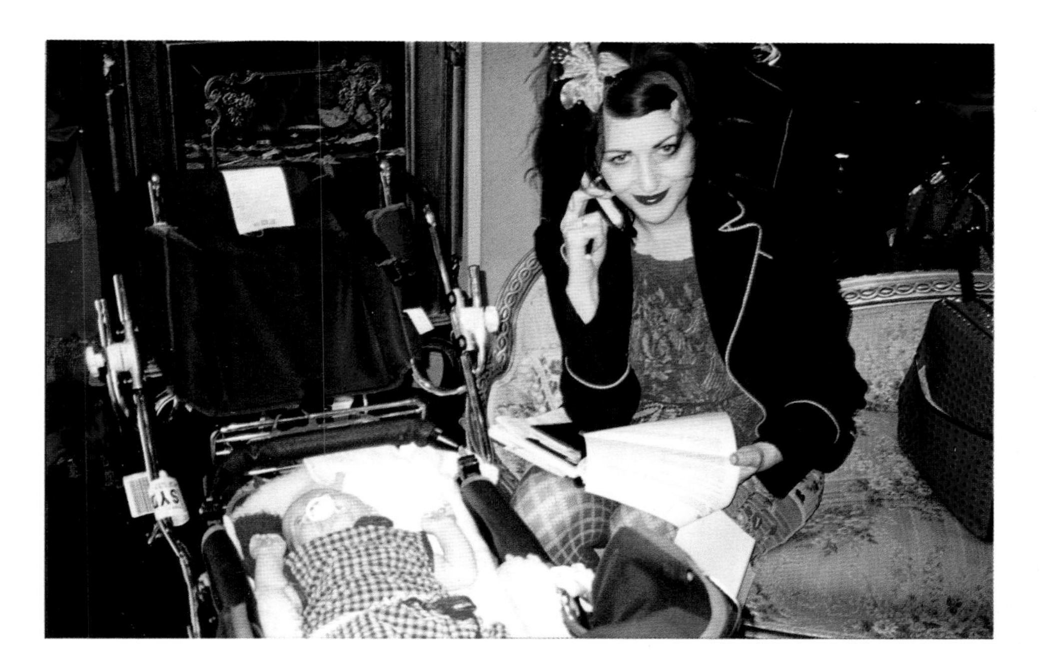

ABOVE E, five months old, at work with me. Mute, silent and angelic he was. That is, until he started shrieking. I had no idea it takes almost 13 months for babies to start nattering. E's first word was 'More?'

LEFT Photo by Georges Antoni for the Alannah Hill spring/summer 2010 campaign. Georges was a dream and Andrew Majzner from Paper Stone Scissors art directed.

BELOW E and I on a business trip to Sydney. I accidentally left E in the David Jones children's wear department.

714

TOP LEFT Henri Bendel on Fifth Avenue in NYC. You can see my gorgeous designs in the window.

ABOVE Photo by Jez Smith for the spring/summer 2010 campaign shoot at Palazzo Versace. My God! How intoxicating is Simone Kerr? She appears to have a headache from my overstyling and intense gaze!

LEFT Photo by Georges Antoni for the Alannah Hill autumn/winter 2010 campaign. The flower wall was utterly spectacular and made with fresh flowers from Flowers Vasette in Fitzroy, one of my all-time favourite florists.

RIGHT Photo by Monty Coles. I was a *cover* girl for *Marie Claire Lifestyle* magazine in 2000! Monty photographed pages and pages of photos in the decadent apartment where I *may* have kicked a certain person for leaving.

ABOVE Photo by Juli Balla for a Louise Love campaign shoot at Crown Casino. The beaded frock is made from blush pink pearls, silk georgette and typhoid. Yes, this is one of the dresses made in India, where I came down with the dreadful typhoid.

ABOVE Hugo and me in Italy, where I lit hundreds of candles in hundreds of churches for Mum.

BELOW From the Louise Love campaign shoot with Juli Balla. I had hoped after five years of only choosing Simone for my campaigns that she *might* finally fall for me. She appears to have covered her eyes with roses to cut out the glare from my unrequited love.

ABOVE By Georges Antoni for the cover of *Sunday Life* in 2014.
The article was to announce the arrival of Louise Love, my new fashion brand,
and to let people know I was no longer part of Alannah Hill.

Are you married? Do you think you will *ever* have children? What are you looking for in life? Love, money or happiness? Which one?'

And I added my new favourite line of enquiry, spoken in a posh English accent: 'And where did you *schooooooooooooool*?'

I kept jiggling. He kept drinking. None of my questions were answered.

And then I saw him. Alone on the wooden dance floor, hands interlaced behind his back, gazing off into some distant dimension only he seemed aware of. I felt a little ripple open in time, a fluttering at the edge of things as if I'd forgotten that this encounter would always happen, that I would always meet this boy in this place. With a gathering sense of wonder, I drifted closer and looked into his eyes, hoping that he would notice how invisible I felt. I skylarked around him performing a tap dance routine, but nothing! He gave me *nothing*. I asked Mildred, a girl I'd met the week before, about the boy dancing alone – this posh boy-person with strawberry hair wearing broken glasses held together by Blu Tack.

Mildred told me his name was Steven Jones Hyphenated Evans and that *she* was sleeping with him and to keep my hands off him. He was extremely mysterious, had been privately schooled in a fine boarding school in Devon, England, and she was in love with him.

I moved closer to him and he backed away.

You see, I had begun to yearn for love. I couldn't hide it, couldn't pretend it wasn't there, this colossal misplaced desire for something I hoped would one day come my way.

'Hello, what's your name and where did you *schooooooooooooool*?'

I noticed the cool-boy flinch at my high-pitched squawk, so I immediately dulled myself down a little. I was shy but I always had to appear larger than life; I knew I wouldn't be seen if I didn't make a scene – I knew instinctively how to spook boys with untoward remarks, curious glances and a need for some kind of attention.

I took another step forward, hoping the sounds of Joy Division would startle him into noticing me.

'I was wondering, I was hoping, you see, I think I could be in *awful* trouble, some kind of mystical trouble. I'm on the wrong track in life; I'm on the wrong bus, the wrong train. I don't really belong anywhere. I was thinking could you *ever* see yourself falling in love with a little mongrel like me, I think I might need looking after, and I've never been in love before. Do you take drugs? I don't like the drugs. Are you European? I'm European. I'm from Tasmania. Would you like to go on a supper date with me?'

My personality was running away from me. I knew I'd asked too many questions without even waiting for his answers.

'I'm here with my brothers. You ask a lot of questions without waiting for answers; it's existential, I guess.'

I had no idea what 'existential, I guess' meant. I presumed it was a way of telling me I asked too many questions.

He backed away slightly so I moved in a little closer. I noted that he hadn't completely backed away so I moved in ever-so-slightly closer …

'I *do*! I ask all kinds of questions and I don't mind if people ask me questions either. In *fact*, I *love* being asked questions. I *love* questions! Ask me *any question* and I'll give you the answer. I can have nine different conversations all at once, my mind works so fast that I can also do ten things at once, I can speed read, tap dance, type ninety-nine words a minute at eighty-six per cent accuracy, I can make chocolate pudding, I can cook takeaway food, I can make tea, I can do the dishes, but would you, *could you*, imagine being in love with a girl like me?'

I couldn't read him. He seemed shut off from the world, shy, silent, expecting nothing and yet wanting so very much. He smiled. I smiled back.

'I have a question for you,' I heard him say.

'Oh! *Ask* away. I *love* being asked questions! Ask me anything you want!'

'Why have you got a nineteen-fifties bakelite tea canister wrapped around your waist with a ribbon?'

'Oh,' I said, looking down at my op-shop tea canister. 'That's my *hand*bag! See? If you press down on the top of it, gentle like, *just* like that, little lollies come out, I've filled it with Smarties! Isn't that marvellous? Press it! Go on – press it and watch the little lollies come out!'

Steven informed me nervously on our very first date that he believed I might have been mad. He thought the Smarties were drugs, that I very well could have been a mental little drug dealer. I made him laugh and he made me feel safe. He had an entire family who eased my soul, a family who took care of me, who seemed to like me. Steven's English mother even bought me a pair of pink towels once for Christmas. His family were arty, middle-class introverts and his four brothers were slightly perverse, intelligent and interesting. There was even a sister who was so startling in her prettiness that I stared at her one Sunday afternoon for six hours straight. She had a halo of shiny auburn hair, and her name was Rae.

Steven Jones Hyphenated Evans and I were inseparable for nine years.

22

Revolt Into Style

By 1983 I no longer felt like a lonely candle flickering inside a Catholic midnight mass. I had discovered new and brighter candles to flicker with, and some might say I was *popping* on the social ladder.

Popping like a thousand champagne corks.

POP

POP

POP!

Bernadette suddenly decided to move to Melbourne to live with Steve and I in our first flat in Adams Street, South Yarra. We had been in one of our good months where we got along, but eventually we started warring over one thing or another and so she moved out, and into a room with a crabby pensioner in Albert Park. Our arty friends and arty scene became Bernadette's arty friends and arty scene, almost immediately.

All around us, the post-punk fashion revolution was gathering momentum, a juggernaut of ambition and creativity gone wild. My nightclub gatherings with friends of friends led to doors opening onto new realities, leaving me spellbound.

Steven's older brother Dale Jones Hyphenated Evans opened one of these doors. He was living with a jewellery designer, a fantastical arty woman, Kate Durham. Kate knew everything about everything art, sculpture and design, was incredibly bright, well-read, a marvellous cook, an arty entertainer; I believe she wore more make-up than myself and she also dressed up to go to bed, just like me! Kate was also an *only child*. How bloody marvellous – I had always wanted to be an only child.

Kate asked me to model some of her fashion-art pieces in her art studio for photographers and artists, and once she even asked me to model in the annual Moomba parade in the city on top of an art float wearing a mermaid's costume made from alfoil, sequins and 20 litres of lilac-hued body paint. I was even on the Channel 9 news, posing here, posing there, posing everywhere, but I was uneasy, apprehensive and felt like I didn't belong, that I wasn't good enough for anybody, let alone appearing in alfoil atop a Moomba float.

The Jones-Evans situation on Malvern Road was very curious. The entire family – Steven and his siblings, Dale, Ashley, Lindsay and Rae, as well as their father, Bruce, and his girlfriend (the cleaner, Beris) – lived in five separate houses right next door to each other, with an art studio built into each house. I had never come across anything like it. A family with a father living with his girlfriend. Where was the real mum, I wondered.

She had met somebody else. They co-owned a health-food store in Lygon Street and lived together in a palace in a rainforest near a town I'd never heard of called Olinda.

My mum told me how the Jones-Evans family planned to take me hostage and perform arty experiments on parts of my body. I didn't know it then but I understand that perhaps Mum was jealous, jealous when I showed any warmth to another mother.

'And what's the MOTHER like? A two-bob snob, Lan? She's not even Catholic, Lannaaah. She wouldn't like you dear, she's only putting up with you. If you start your carrying on and show-offing, they'll soon get rid of you. You don't like the mother anyway, do you?'

'I do a bit, Mum. She's really English and repressed. But she's really kind, Mum, and she doesn't get stressed. I think they're quite posh, Mum.'

'KIND? How is SHE kind? Her husband left her for a cleaner, Lannaaah! A CLEANER! And the MOTHER's probably high on health-food junk. I had a little bit more respect for you than this, Lannaaah. I cannot BELIEVE you think that mother is KIND. She's NOT kind! Did you hear me? She is NOT kind!'

But I drowned Mum's voice out, and began to call her less. I imagined I was part of a staggeringly creative bohemian family, an Evans Hyphenated Hill type of girl.

Any sign of education, artiness or wealth made my confidence shrink. The difference between the way the Jones-Evanses lived and related as a family was a stark contrast to my own family, and in quiet times I listened to the doubts bombing my art-deprived brain.

Why isn't my family like the Jones Hyphenated Evanses?

Why wasn't I given the opportunity to attend a posh private boarding house in Devon, England, with an alcoholic bar?

Why didn't my father build me an art studio inside the milk bar?

Why?

It was becoming clearer to me that it was more than essential for me socially to have knowledge of Pop Art, Low Art, Fine Art, High Art, Renaissance Art, Impressionist Art, Medieval and Byzantine Art, Baroque Art, Neoclassicism, Romanticism, Realism, Cubism, Futurism, Surrealism and Minimalist Art. And then there was the Post-Art situation: Post-Impressionist Art, Post-Baroque Art, Post-Neoclassical Art, Post-Modernism, Post-de-Constructivism Art. I didn't have a clue about any of these art movements and, for one reason or another, took great pride in not having a Byzantine clue about any of them.

I became Steven's polaroid picture model. Steven took hundreds of polaroids, art-directing me into polaroid art-house oblivion. He would scratch a 50-cent coin onto the developing polaroid, making my features almost unrecognisable. Between Steven's arty polaroids, Kate's arty studio shoots and my own forays into the retail fashion scene, I came to be noticed by some very important people.

Robert Pearce was a thinker, a doer, a visionary ahead of his art-designed life. Robert wasn't the usual fey gay man I had become accustomed to; he was buff, gymed, wore scores of silver chains around his body, had his nipples pierced and his hair cut short weekly, had no boyfriends and attended clubs where thrashings and beatings occurred. Thrashings galore, apparently. Beatings not quite as often. I made a note never to dance in the thrashing and beating nightclubs.[31]

I introduced myself to Robert at an art gallery opening one Sunday afternoon. I remember how he slowly looked me up and down, clicked his fingers and moaned, his head tilted back, an unreadable look across his face. He was funny, wildly intelligent, bitchy and wise. And very arty. Robert couldn't live with any form of boredom. He needed to be entertained and he encouraged himself to be entertaining. Whenever I was around Robert, I tried to make sure I was at my most entertaining.

Robert told me he'd spied me a year earlier making a 'tremendous public spectacle' of myself. Confused, I asked him how I'd created such a tremendous public spectacle – I wanted to know how to do it again. Robert said he'd seen me tap dancing and busking outside the Prahran Town Hall on Chapel Street.

'Alannah! I cannot believe this, was that *you* … it was really you? What were you thinking and what were you wearing? Oh my God,

31 Apparently, I didn't have to worry: Robert said girls were not permitted.

Alannah … you're wild, I fucking love you … at the very *least* you're not a crashing bore … or *are* you?'

'Robert, I *am* boring, but you saw me tapping? I love to tap. Was I wearing a pink plastic nineteen-sixties frock? You know, like Pop-Art style, Edie Sedgwick and the Factory and all of that Poppy-Art nonsense? I think that's where War Hole and his mules hung out? Edie Sedgwick acted in an art film that screened for twenty-four days, and she *had* to do everything that the War Hole wanted. That's what art mules are, don't you think?'

I had picked up this marvellous little anecdote from Steven, but apparently I had it all wrong. It was Andy Warhol and his muse, not War Hole and his mules. We laughed about that for years.

In 1983 Robert, Kate Durham and Robert Buckingham launched the Fashion Design Council of Australia. With funding from the Victorian Ministry for the Arts, the FDC promoted the newest and most precocious fashion talent in Australia, and put a spotlight on the role of fashion in a cultural sense.

The FDC was a shining light for girls like me, girls stowed away in whimsical attics hand-sewing sequins onto pairs of black pantyhose or whipping up art smocks made from green leaves or tea leaves. I knew a girl who knew a girl who knew another girl who moved in with her great-grandmother in Kew *just* to have access to a vintage sewing machine.

People such as Kara Baker, with her label Sirens, Martin Grant, Gavin Brown, and Bruce Slorach and Sara Thorn, for Abyss, were all madly slimming waists on frocks, up-styling their wardrobes and ransacking vintage clothing from their grandparents' deceased estate wardrobes. Firestorms of creativity were in the air I breathed, everywhere I seemed to be, everywhere I wanted to be. As far as the eye could see, ruling energies were all around inspiring our hearts.

But the FDC was not the only game in town. Other movers and shakers from the sprawling suburbs of Melbourne were starting up their own arty, kooky cults.

Philip Brophy and Maria Kozic had been crowned king and queen of three new art movements. There isn't a soul alive who can remember why the 'crowning' of Brophy and Kozic occurred, but make *no mistake* about it, Maria and Phil were Art-House Royalty. They were so cool that even the Jones-Evanses *burned* if a 'Philip' or a 'Maria' appeared alongside them at a gallery, an art event or a punk-music evening.

Maria and Phil were expanding their arty empire to Pop-Art smocks screen-printed with a single garden vegetable. You could either have a potato, a carrot or a vegetable called a squash. The squash was bright yellow.

The smock dress cost $500, enough money to buy a new car. Steven loved the vegetable dresses, he just *loved* those vegetable dresses, and he thought I could adopt a more intelligent social demeanour by adopting the vegetable-smock look. One afternoon we made the journey north in Steven's Wolseley car to the castle of culture, the Clifton Hill Community Centre, where the carrot dress was ready and waiting to *vegetablise* me ...

I didn't want to be vegetablised into wearing a shapeless smock with an oversized carrot on the front but in those days (and the many that followed) one of my goals in life was assisting Steven with happiness – even if he didn't want my assistance, it was always there. I felt obliged to wear my Pop-Art smock to every art event and I became known as 'Carrot' until, mysteriously, my arty carrot dress shrunk to the size of a real carrot in a laundromat.

My style chopped and changed, but I always returned to 'codge granny'. Codge granny wasn't just a *look*, it was a lifestyle. Steven loved the codge-granny look, which was excellent news for girls (and boys) like me who were afraid of sex, intimacy and love. My Steven-approved wardrobe consisted of two tartan pleated skirts, three neo-prim white blouses with Peter Pan collars, two codge-textured skirts, a nurse's costume, a school uniform and four mohair cardigans. I felt safe and cosy in my chic granny look, but I was ready to try a new reinvention. I didn't have the confidence to look overtly sexual until I was asked to model at FDC's first major fashion event, Fashion 84. (I modelled for anyone who asked me, and anyone who didn't, though this was not seen as real modelling. You just had to learn to throw yourself down a catwalk, prancing and dancing and jigging in time with the tunes.)

I discussed my new sexy metamorphosis with my friend, Vanessa. We had met on a dance floor years earlier and, in a halo of Final Net hairspray, we instantly became friends. Vanessa was sassy and intelligent. She could sing, sew, and she even knew how to dance! She lived in Camberwell with a posh family and her life seemed perfect to me. She knew everything there was to know about how to change from a codge to a real-life sex starlet – she was coquettish and beguiling and had the come-hither look down pat. Men fainted into whatever they were drinking when Vanessa blitzed past in extravagant homemade cream silk costumes. There was no fainting of men into drinks when I stampeded past.

I needed to step out with my new look and I needed to do it fast, especially after my sexless affair with the carrot dress. Vanessa told me I needed a figure-hugging tube skirt, just like the one worn by Kate Garner from the British pop group Haysi Fantayzee. The tube skirt was a simple idea made from stretch polyester, not a zipper to be seen, no buttons required – it was simply a slimline tube that hugged your body. Tightly. We made the skirt together from fabric we found at the Camberwell Market. One metre of purple stretch polyester with an elastic waistband hand-sewn by me and overlocked by Vanessa.

My first outing showing my transition from 'codge granny' to 'sexy chic' was at something called 'brunch' at the Banff in Fitzroy Street. I huddled myself in Steven's car parked near the cafe and watched my freckled hands sweat onto my gorgeous homemade tube. I urged myself to hurry up and climb out of the car instead of trying to socially asphyxiate inside, but I felt surprisingly flat, with feelings resembling shame clouding any show-off thoughts.

'Ta-daaaaaaar!' I heard myself yelping at the table where our friends sat. 'Ta-daaaaaaarrrrr … your tuuuuuuuuuube skirt girl has arriveeeeed!'

Steven looked away. I burned with his brush-off.

Dale and his friend Randal whistled, and Dale made a figure-eight shape in the air. Steven kept looking away and Randal asked why I'd been covering my 'gorgeous body' for so long, tut-tutting Steven for encouraging the codge-granny look. I began to turn and spin, spinning and turning on thin air, and practically doing cartwheels on the Banff tables with the realisation that I too could be sexy if I chose to be … I wondered if I'd managed to disguise my burning shame by showing sensuality. Steven knew the real me, and he knew I was trying to be something I was not. It was why he looked away. I knew he would be disappointed that I wanted to be a Vanessa clone, wearing figure-hugging tube skirts in an attempt to look sexy and be like everybody else. Where the hell were my codge clothes, he asked.

I rediscovered the power of clothing and dressing up when I made the tube. I saw how a sexy tube skirt could be a silver machete in my hands, a machete to slash and burn away the weeds of self-doubt blotting my true self.

23

Dinner Party as an Idea

When I was the effervescent girlfriend of Steven Jones Hyphenated Evans, we would attend any arty opening that was deemed cool, underground or punk.

Steven's brother Dale was an architect and becoming a little famous with his collaborators from BiltModerne.[32] Dale and Kate were often the toast of the entire Melbourne art scene. I wondered when *they* were going to be crowned king and queen.

Dale informed us one afternoon at a soulless gallery opening that he'd had a 'really interesting idea'. It was called 'dinner-party-as-an-idea'. Dinner party as an idea? I didn't quite understand how a dinner party could be an idea, especially after it had already been invented … I didn't care for a dinner party, they were too intimate for me.

A handwritten dinner party invitation was delivered by a courier service to our gently spinning circle of arty friends. Written on modern, stiff, peculiarly purple paper and sealed with Dale Jones-Evans's

---

32 BiltModerne was an avant-garde architecture firm founded in 1983 by Dale Jones-Evans, Randal Marsh and Roger Wood. By 1985 it was all over, with Dale leaving BiltModerne to set up an architecture firm in Sydney under his own name. Randal Marsh and Roger Wood went on to become Wood Marsh architects.

personal wax seal, it was a dinner party bomb. A new subculture.

One arty couple were nominated to host dinner-party-as-an-idea at their own private home. The dinner party could *only* be held during the week. Weekend dinner parties were apparently not arty! The food was to be interesting and minimal; dessert was considered gauche. The wine was to be a pinot from the Loire Valley. Rare and never-heard-before classical music was to be played on a Bose sound system.

This was a very sudden cultural change for my delicate sensibilities. I was accustomed to fish fingers, chocolate, ice-cream and milk arrowroot biscuits. I knew nothing about wine, cigars, entertaining, menus or real food. Holding the elegant invitation in my ivory fingers, I wondered if this would be a fascinating education in culinary graces or a thousand deaths by public humiliation.

I attended two dinner-party-as-an-ideas, shunning the inedible food in favour of a picnic pack I brought to please myself – red cordial, packets of Smarties, salt and vinegar chips and a box of Cadbury Dairy Milk Chocolates. I questioned everyone seated around the dinner-party-as-an-idea table on exactly how a dinner party could possibly be conceived as a cultural movement.

Mind-blowing conversations flew around the room, as fast as the fallout from Pandora's box – famous philosophers such as Karl Marx, Voltaire, Simone de Beauvoir and Friedrich Nietzsche were discussed, dissected and often discarded between courses. More mind-blowing conversations, amplified by a succession of serious cheeses, would touch on political activists, photographers,[33] the orientation of character, the philosophy of religion and the theory of emotion. I believe everyone seated at the dinner-party-as-an-idea – except me – had (or was in the middle of acquiring) an arts degree from a university I'd never heard of. Picasso, Renoir, Keith Haring, Pop Art, Warhol, Caravaggio, the study of how to look at a painting correctly, the study of how to walk through

---

33 Bill Henson was always mentioned.

a gallery without appearing bored, the study of emotional responses to art, low art, high art … the list of topics open for discussion at the dinner-party-as-an-idea were often so unspeakably boring that I'd revert to asking personal questions, something I had been warned about by Steven. Apparently it was not an arty thing to do and nobody liked it.

I listened to everyone and everything. I picked up information floating around the room to recycle for social camouflage, in the hope I wouldn't be suddenly exposed as a common milk-bar girl, a girl with an inferior education and no arts degree. The way I put the two words 'high school' together seemed to excite the art crowd. They asked me whether I meant High Art School or Low Art School? I told them it was just a high school.

My job was to pretend I knew all about art, politics and social change, but I often felt like the uneducated, street-smart girlfriend Steven had collected from his local op shop. But I had always been good at assuming a new persona to disguise my mongrel self; this was my ultimate art challenge. I'd casually drop lines like, 'I think Keith Haring's graphic art has a sublime and unique texture – but do you think it's really art, Randal? Is graffiti low or high art? High School or Low School? And do you *feel* that Jean Baudrillard's theory about technological progress affects social change?'

My little bombs of wisdom either fell flat or they rose from the ground with artistic fury. On the nights they fell flat, I concentrated on my FBI work which, for me, seemed more intriguing than dissecting art movements. I would ask personal questions, entertaining everyone with wild stories from my past and disappearing into the host's bathroom to ensure there was nothing in there that was 'mine'. Drawers magically opened and levers sprung forth while I sprayed obscure French parfum on my wrists and maybe used the host's make-up in an attempt to turn myself into an idea. A complete idea. Not just a dinner idea.

And then it was Steven's and my turn to host.

Steven was working as a set dresser at Crawford Productions. Unfortunately, he couldn't make it home in time for the selection of the French wine and obscure classical music, the preparation of the fine food or the enforcement of the no-dessert rule. I promised Steven a dinner party that would be talked about for years, and promised I'd deliver all the arty requirements – I was not to be untoward or rebellious; I had to follow his long list of instructions on where to buy the correct food, source the new music and how to set the table (Steven had prepared a drawing for me). I wasn't permitted to wear the tube.

I reinforced the promise that I would be superb. I would not let him down. I promised that I might even curate our one piece of artwork by hanging it on a thin wire from the ceiling with several lights attached to make it look even artier. Steven did not take the curation news well and told me to leave the art piece as it was.

The dinner-party-as-an-idea invitations for dinner at Steven and Alannah's had been delivered. Guests were to arrive at our small flat in Adams Street, South Yarra, at 8 pm. Steven would be late but I'd be saving the day with all my arty values and virtues.

But

unfortunately

very unfortunately

on the special day of the dinner-party-as-an-idea, I lay down at three in the afternoon with a head-banging migraine. I woke three hours later with nothing prepared for the dinner party, except for my costume. My head was spinning. I had no time to source the thirty-five items on the list, each one marked with an anxiety-inducing blue dot.

But I knew *exactly* what to do.

I flew to the supermarket, purchasing lemonade, jelly crystals, packets of Allen's confectionery, candy cane–coloured straws and other arty delicatessen favourites. My God, I was a good problem-solver. The next problem was also easily solved – our small flat wasn't clean enough for Steven's taste nor that of our architecturally enlightened friends, and so I broke into the empty apartment next door, immediately high on the Unbearable Artiness of Being because this vacant apartment was existentially empty!

It was a *real* art gallery. Silent. Arty. Like the Louvre.

With pizza subs in the oven, fire-engine-red saveloys on the boil, fish fingers spluttering in sunflower oil and forty-five party pies ready to be served lip-smackingly cold, I knuckled down to a minimalist aesthetic – the vacant apartment held no furniture of its own to host our guests, so the table setting was arranged on the floor. *Japanese style*, I told myself, just like Kurosawa's *Seven Samurai*. Borrowing flowers from the neighbours' weed garden, I placed them thoughtfully around each guest's position like a delicate little Shinto peace offering.

And then disaster struck.

I was carrying the record player from our apartment into the dinner-party-as-an-idea gallery and it slipped right out of my hands and smashed into a million little pieces. No music! Being clever and canny as you like, I knocked on our neighbours' door. The neighbours allowed me to borrow their portable cassette player, which I was thrilled with. I owned one cassette.

The Best of ABBA

Perfect.

I slipped the cassette into the little Panasonic cradle and pressed play. It was arty in its own way, especially in an existentially empty, illegally entered apartment masquerading as a countercultural art gallery. Confident that I was engaged in a classic Joseph Beuys parody of Situationalist fine dining, I was ready to usher our arty guests into my multi-levelled performance art agenda.

In my attempts to be queen of all dinner parties, I'd forgotten the most important thing. Lighting. With no electricity in this broken-down, broken-in apartment, I once again used my canny smarts by knocking on another neighbour's door and asking for five or ten battery-powered torches. They gave me three.

Our guests, arriving to the splendid sounds of 'Waterloo' by ABBA, arranged themselves on the floor, the borrowed torches shining 150 watts of white light into arty eyes and shadowing faces into Vincent Price horror-movie masks. Looking back, I realise I *might* have mistaken the arty looks of horror for looks of amazement at my version of dinner-party-as-an-idea but I soldiered on while ABBA played on. I brought out tray after plastic tray filled with pizza subs, tomato sauce, party pies and Cheezels, along with several bottles of lemonade that I poured delicately into plastic white cups.

'Isn't this arty?' I exclaimed to everyone.

Silence. Not a word. 'Waterloo' was caught in its own Waterloo cassette horror, the beautiful voices of ABBA tape-twisting into long devilish growls, becoming more distorted each time the word 'Waterloo' was sung, until ABBA's sugary-sweet sounds morphed into the soundtrack from *The Exorcist*.

'Are you playing ABBA, Lan?'

Oh my, an arty voice had spoken, the dream had been broken! Preparing to be crowned queen of dinner-party-as-an-idea, the implicit criticism came as a gloomy, sinking shock. I turned to see Steven silhouetted in the doorway. His face was cast with shadows, but I detected a glint in his eye, and hoped it would contain a new and rarefied love for his milk-bar girlfriend on a creative adventure, even as the circle of borrowed torchlight around us appeared to be losing its glow.

'What have you done, Lan?'

'I *know*, Steve! I know! I did this all by myself! I am kitsch queen … just take a look at the pizza subs in the oven, I even added herbs and spices like they do in Italy. I bought a packet of Tim Tams for dessert and —'

At the sound of the forbidden and deeply gauche 'dessert', the atmosphere changed – arty guests were making excuses to leave my broken-into art gallery of broken dreams and, what's more, I could hear them sniggering. I could spot a snigger from forty-four dinner parties away. They left quickly, two by two, slipping away from my dinner-party-as-an-idea to the sounds of ABBA from *The Exorcist*!

Steven glared straight through my well-ironed costume. The room was silent, the pizza subs cold. The tomato sauce had fallen off its perch and was drizzling itself into the plastic cups, the cold party pies were inedible and the hors d'oeuvres I'd prepared earlier were wilting and soggy on their bed of Salada biscuits.

Steven looked up to the ceiling. I could feel his chronic disappointment in me; I felt the same chronic disappointment in myself. We turned at exactly the same time and looked into each other's eyes. I saw his flame flickering and I held on to him like a Catholic crucifix.

24

Uncool

The word was out. The casting call for a mysterious new movie in the making had set the grapevine alight, and Melbourne was bathed in a nervous punk fever with '80s relics wandering mournful as a flock of seagulls in search of a place to shine. Suddenly everybody was talking about this new punk film that was being made in Melbourne. Not just a handful of people, *everybody* was talking about it. A gritty, atmospheric, hedonistic film set against the backdrop of Melbourne's punk scene in 1979. It was written and directed by an arty-filmy type: Richard Lowenstein.

Dogs in Space was a rebellious, hopeless love story, set in a subculture populated by pale, half-starved New Romantics who shot up drugs, snorted speed and played obnoxious music very loudly and very badly.

If you were not in this film, or part of this film, the social ladder you had spent years climbing would disintegrate before your very own eyes. Rung by brutal rung. Step by blooming step.

Anybody who had ever been *anybody* had to be cast in *Dogs in Space*.

If you were not part of the elite *Dogs in Space* film club, you had to die a lingering *Dogs in Space* social death.

I became the manageress of Indigo bow teek when Jill and John departed on their eastern travels to discover new markets in India, Afghanistan and Paris. I'd sell up a storm in my bell-ringing, musky garb, planning my first fashion collection, which I imagined would be launched at Chasers Nightclub on Chapel Street. My favourite days at Indigo were spent fantasising about a creative future for myself. Long after the store closed, I'd fossick about upstairs in the design area changing the buttons on garments and attaching lace pockets to everything in sight.

For two phantasmal weeks I was more than just a shop girl. I was free to run the bow teek how I imagined it could be run, opening the store a little earlier, and closing even later. I would take lunch breaks, and swap my Windex for lipstick.

You see, dear reader, I was in the middle of an emotional conundrum. I didn't care for people who admitted they were bored, and yet I felt the wings of boredom flapping, dying to rest awhile inside my perfectly bored dancing-girl cage. I was bored with myself, bored with my customers, bored with my need to please, bored with my need to tease. I'd pounce on unsuspecting customers in the hope that at least one of us could alleviate my chronic boredom. As much as I loved Jill and John, I felt we were slipping into two different worlds, worlds apart from each other.

It was becoming clear to me that everybody I came into contact with thought of me not as 'Cool girl Alannah Hill' but 'Uncool girl Alannah Hill' – a dated '80s Blitz girl, a pretend punk. An uncool shop girl from Tasmania.

A list of uncool endeavours gave me the title 'Uncool Alannah Hill':

- Dreaming of home ownership: specifically, purchasing an Art Deco flat.
- Working in a hippie bow teek.
- Secretly wearing musk oil.
- Not indulging in drugs or alcohol.
- Lacking knowledge about the music magazine *NME*.
- Being uneducated on left-wing politics, right-wing politics, and indeed any wings from any political power.
- Secretly listening to ABBA.
- Being emotionally weak.
- Asking too many uncool personal questions.

Nick Cave and his Bad Seeds had been seen by other cool seedlings at the Jump Club on Smith Street, Collingwood, throwing toilet paper dipped into jugs of beer at my over-teased, overdone head. I had committed the unforgivable and mortal sin of robot dancing to an uncool song by an uncool band, 'Computer Games' by Mi-Sex. Nick's seedlings had been watching my fully choreographed dance routine, but because I was so uncool I thought they were marvelling at how very well I robot danced.[34] I danced wearing op-shop shortie pyjamas, high white heels, knee-high black lace socks and a large bow, my arms and legs perfectly coordinated in the robot school of robot dancing, step one.

Nick and his gang of bad seeds continued to throw the beer-soaked toilet paper at my head. I was going to slap one of them but stopped dead in my tracks – they were nodding off. Falling asleep. My slapping hand froze in midair. I backed away from the seedlings' table as fast as my high heels would allow, but they didn't seem to notice.

---

34 Wave your left robot arm. After you've attempted to dance in a stiff robotic fashion, repeat the same wave move on your right side. Point your arms to the right, follow them with your feet, bend, and then jerk your left arm hiiiiiiigh, up and down, up and down, three times. People should be showering you with compliments. If you're *not* receiving compliments, you're not dancing like a robot.

Uncool.

One late night in the pink fluorescent toilets at the Hellfire Club, madly reapplying lipstick in the hope it might fix my shakiness, I overheard two very beautiful arty girls talking. About me.

'Oh gawd! She's *still* at Indigo! She must be so bored. How's all that make-up she's got on? Have you seen how she bobby pins a tacky black bow on her head?'

'Did you hear she shows *her breasts* off? At nightclubs! She shows everyone her breasts, and my brothers, cousins, sisters and mother's auntie were having dinner at Spaghetti Graffiti last Friday night and apparently, *apparently*, she ripped up her top and showed everyone her breasts!'[35]

Steven's arty gang and all of Jill and John's ashram friends chanted on the same theme: 'Are you just going to be a shop girl all your life? Don't you think you should be working toward owning your own fashion shop? Vivienne Westwood and Malcolm McLaren's World's End store in London is *ab*-sarl-oooooteeeeleeeee *booming.* You should open up a store in London, you'll die on that shop floor in Chapel Street, Alannah. I cannot understand what job satisfaction you could *possibly* be having? I mean, get going! Be successful! What are you doing with your life?!'

If you were not part of the elite *Dogs in Space* film club, you simply had to die.

Anybody who was anybody *had* to be in *Dogs in Space*.

Richard Lowenstein had managed to persuade his new best friend, lead singer of INXS Michael Hutchence, to play a starring role in

35 I did show my breasts off, but not to just anybody. I had rules about my breast flashing. For one, I needed a crowd of unsuspecting, bored onlookers: I'd be guaranteed a strong reaction with a bored, straight crowd. I'd become known for my breast flashing and would often flash mid-sentence to a group I was bored with. I guess I did this for shock value. I had been told my breasts were the only good thing about me and because I thought I was ugly, I believed my breasts had to be seen!

Dogs in Space. Michael, the dazzling, hedonistic '80s rock star, a charming, complex, lionesque, rock sex god was *taking the brave leap forward*, the gamble from *rock star* to *actor*. He would be the lead role in a cast of '80s losers and complete and utter nobodies who all thought they were somebodies. Including me!

Michael Hutchence wasn't part of the smacky, punky 1979 Crystal Ballroom set, and I imagined his shame – I wasn't part of it either. Yet instead of touring America in 1986, Michael chose to disappear for eight weeks into Berry Street, a tiny one-way street in Richmond, to shine in his first-ever feature film. Instead of starting his acting career playing Blade in a Mad Max film, with a budget of $500 million, he chose to star as a drug-addled narcissist poet called Sam in a film where his pay cheque was half the budget of the movie.

Saskia Post, an actress from the long-running drama *The Sullivans*, had already won the prized female lead and I was beside myself with envy. Saskia was blonde, Polish and too straight to be anywhere near the Melbourne punk scene in the late '70s. I had black hair, was from Tasmania and hoped to become a character actress.

Richard Lowenstein was rumoured to be handpicking thousands of extras for the punk crowd scenes – *handpicking* them with Michael Hutchence. Bernadette was working in the offices of *Dogs in Space* as a part-time stenographer and a PA. She wasn't pleased with my quest to be a leading actress. I was breaking the Ten Commandment–style rules she'd set out years earlier.

The real question was, how the hell did one obtain the secret phone number, followed by *another* secret phone number that was given out only to 'special people', for the twilight castings of *Dogs in Space*?

Troy. Troy Davies held the secret phone number and he decided who would be given the secret number.

Troy was the powerbroker, the grey eminence hovering over the *Dogs in Space* shoot. He went by two names: Troy and Vanessa. Sometimes he was a gaily dressed man, sometimes a gaily dressed woman, with each of these coming in two forms – a sponge cake of intelligence or a dropped soufflé of scorn, regret and bitter irony. Troy was a troublemaker, a trickster. Troy was Richard's glittering court jester.

Troy created the illusion that he was the *only* bright star in Richard and Michael's universe. If one of his jealous eyes saw the unimaginable occurring – somebody or something with the *nerve* to hold the power of making Richard or Michael laugh or appear interested in them, Troy would begin work on a foolproof strategic plan to rid all social parasites from taking what was rightfully his.

One evening, Steven casually mentioned that he would be attending the Holy Grail, the headquarters, the nerve centre, of the *Dogs in Space* movie set, the production offices where serious people applied for serious arty work. My dreams of becoming a thespian actor were suddenly spinning toward me, ambitious devil-girl lights flickering in my eyes. The hottest ticket in town, the extra's invite for the *Dogs in Space* Ball, was right under my nose all along, in Steven's art-director back pocket.

'What do you mean, Steve? What job interview? Aren't you working on *Carson's Law*? How can you have an interview for *Dogs in Space*? *How*, Steve? Tell me how. Quick!'

Steven lived with me but also in a world of his own. He was the island with the sea all around. Impossible to reach, even with a tugboat. Steven often kept me from his thoughts and plans, withholding very important FBI information, though not deliberately. He was bored by that sort of information. Sometimes it would take seven hours to extract a paragraph from him as he wandered through his own private world, my high-pitched voice a gentle interruption that he could ignore for hours. A biscuit with a cup of tea would often perk Steve up, and so I became the quickest server of tea and a biscuit known to womankind.

'If I get the art director's job, I'll leave Crawford's and go freelance. I refuse to design another boring set for Crawford's. We could rent an apartment in Paris, Lan ... fuck ... come *on*, let's just do it. Have you got a British passport? Actually, have you got any kind of a passport?'

I had an idea what a passport was but I knew I didn't have one. I was determined to get my hands on a British one.

Richard was looking for punkettes who looked like Siouxsie Sioux, Banshees with ghostly skin, red lipstick, black hair and a fragile air of heroin addiction and vulnerability. The next day, I covered my face and most of my body in baby talcum powder. I'd read about this beauty ghoul trick from an interview with Siouxsie Sioux. I applied my smoky black eyes, I smeared cherry-bomb lipstick generously onto my uncool lips, seven ludicrous small black dots painted onto each eyelid for *more edge*, my lips outlined in black eyeliner. Long black boots, a tartan miniskirt, and a loose mohair cardigan with two small Barbie dolls pinned on the lapel – I was ready, ready for my audition as a real-life punk thespian.

I was jealous of my sister's blossoming friendship with Steven – my heart was not logical in matters of love and jealousy – and so I consigned the pair of them to blazes and made ready for my acting audition. History was in the making, and I believe Richard observed this the moment I cherry-bombed into his and Michael's casting couch office. They were wrapped in each other's arms and legs, charmingly disarming. Michael's charisma and electric enthusiasm made me feel like I was the only girl in the room. I showed myself off again and again: perky, inquisitive and brash, flicking my thin, lacquered hair across my baby-powdered white *Dogs in Space* desperate-to-be-a-somebody face.

'I think she'd be gorgeous in your film, Dick,' Michael sang.

'Nahhhhh, she wasn't even a real Ballroom girl,' the infamous Troy Davies quipped. 'Were you *really* around in the Ballroom days, Alannah? Heh? You were dancing at Inflation with all the tragic Blitz Kids, weren't you?'

'Leave her alone, Troy. Don't worry about him, Alannah, he's just a funny guy … have you ever *seriously* given any thought about acting?'

I saw the Oscar descending, it was coming straight at me … I had to remember to prepare a speech.

Richard told me I was a natural. Michael told me I was a natural. Troy, my sister and Steven told each other I was very *unnatural.* And I was!

Richard presented me with a *Dogs in Space* script for my character role as a featured extra and told me not to show that script to a single mortal soul. He asked me if I could be available and on call four days a week and four nights a week. I would be in the night shoots, the morning shoots, the afternoon shoots, the party shoots and one funeral scene.

My God, I was character actressing at full steam.

I telephoned Mum, excited to tell her all about my new starring role.

'Mum! Guess what *just* happened to me? I'm going to be a *movie* star in a film called *Dogs in Space.*'

'Oh, you are NOT, dear! You haven't even done an acting course, Lannaaah?'

'I'm apparently a natural, Mum, Michael Hutchence said so … he's a rock star.'

'A rock star, Lannah? A ROCK star? Lannah, I have TOLD you before, dear … rocks in their heads! ROCKS! Not stars! What is this Hutchence fellow anyway … is he Catholic?'

I heard Mum calling out to my father, and I froze. I wasn't a prime minister yet, I was only a character actress. This was not going to impress him.

'Jimmy! JIMEEEE! Lannah's got herself an acting job! Are you LISTENING to me, Jimmeeeee? Lannah's playing a DRUG addict in a picture movie. She's playing a dog … she's acting like A DOG … a dog in space …'

25

Torn Between Two Lovers

I was nervous about telling John and Jill that I was about to become a movie-star girl. I couldn't find the right words, the right moment, the right mood.

It all came to a shuddering, shrieking, sticky end when blue-eyed, strong-jawed John miraculously jetted in from India after spending two months on an ashram. John lived on meditation, the white light, the blue light, the red light and the after light, and after apparently not speaking a sound for two months and meditating twenty-four hours a day, John was often startled by the simplest of things. Like when I screamed with joy after my audition for a certain movie being made in Melbourne.

'John! John! *John!*' Startled! Startled! *Startled!* Solemnly, John held one finger up to his lips and pushed a homemade Indian-music cassette into my hand along with ten packets of incense, his strangely radiant eyes commanding me to place the cassette into the Indigo cassette player. Obscure bleating Indian harps and bewildering hippie sounds erupted.

I began to explain to John about the film, but his face fell and kept falling as he told me Jill's mother had had a heart attack, and Jill had flown urgently to Canberra to spend a few weeks by her mother's side. This left John and me to run the Indigo bow teek.

John didn't see the point of working, not even himself. He hadn't spent any time with customers, he hadn't worked on the shop floor and, what's more, he had no interest in working at all. His interest lay in spiritual enlightenment.[36]

For six weeks in early 1986, I ran from the film set back to the shop floor, from the shop floor to a night shoot, then, with no sleep, back to working on the shop floor, straight on to a night shoot and once again back to Indigo's small shop floor.

The Berry Street house was packed with extras and a proper film crew, who were snaking cables and red-hot lights in and around hundreds of moving bodies. The smoke machines were pumping, my heart thumping; making my way through the chaos was like walking across a minefield of unexploded Troy bombs.

Troy had the uncanny ability to quickly identify a person's deepest vulnerability, and in my case, his supernatural perception was that I felt my father's abandonment as unspeakable shame upon myself. And it was my runaway eyebrows that were the cause.

'Richard! Lynne Marie! Glenys! Michael! *Anybody!* Look at Featured Extra Number One's eyebrows again, *please*? For fuck's sake, let me *shave* them off or I'll have to call the P-O-L-EEEEEEEEE-CE!'

The on-set improvised make-up area was a whirling, seething mass of gossip and hairspray, fussed over by Troy and his minions, all of us running with scissors, terrified of his razor-sharp tongue. Troy had cleverly morphed into the Antichrist's angel child and seemed determined to shame and embarrass.

Sometimes I felt my heart was going to burst with happiness, other

36 I now understand this is actually very hard work.

times I thought my heart, at any moment, could *burst* forth with one almighty killer aneurysm or a mild, *ongoing* ten-year heart attack. To ease the boredom, often waiting up to five hours before I was called on set, I spent the time flirting. Flirting with the infamous Hugo Race, an elusive punk singer who fronted a band called Plays With Marionettes. I was like an effervescent voodoo doll with a slight ego problem – love me, adore me, look at me, *don't* look at me. I couldn't have known that decades later I would become Hugo's effervescent married voodoo doll!

My mind was working faster than a speeding bullet, my eyes constantly blinking, my mouth painted into a permanent phoney smile, and I'd wonder at times if I was real. I felt wrong and displaced, right and *replaced*. *Dogs in Space* was a new environment – a nonstop party. My Indigo world was filled with customers and buttons and Jill and John. This new film world was so different from my Indigo world, the job I was guiltily neglecting.

During breaks in shooting *Dogs in Space*, the cast and crew, along with hundreds of extras, would either be taking drugs, scoring drugs, smoking, gossiping, eating, stealing the one-of-a-kind op-shop finds from the wardrobe department or sitting on Michael's lap. Wanderlust ran through his veins. Michael's heart seemed to be always seeking, filling up for his next adventure, and when I sat on Michael's lap I tried to make my eyes flicker in time to his – the flickering of Michael's eyes told me that we cannot tether ourselves to a soul that's meant to fly. Michael had not yet become *the* Michael Hutchence, a star whose light I could never imagine burning out. I wondered if he knew he was a soul meant to fly.

Twice a day I'd wander to a phone box, dropping in my 20-cent coins to call John. I knew John would be having a hippie meltdown alone in the Indigo bow teek and this gave *me* a punk breakdown.

'Lan, we've sold out of the D600 again and I can't find any more in the stock room, why does bloody Jizz hide the D600s?'

'John, she doesn't hide them, they're under the tie-dyed velvet maxiskirts in the first change room.'

'Can you come back here, please? I need to go out.'

'Oh John, I'll be there soon as I can, five minutes? OK? I'm shooting a big scene with Michael Hutchence this afternoon, I have to pretend I'm a real live heroin addict and I don't think …'

John would hang up with a gurgle of desperation and I'd hang on to the cold telephone receiver as it beeped like a life-support system. Rushing back to the set, I'd make up an excuse that I had to leave, flinging off my Buffalo Girl costume to struggle back into my Indigo hippie clothes, torn with a desire to please everybody, torn in two, *failing* to please anyone.

Dogs in Space had a red-carpet premiere in December 1986 at Hoyts Cinemas, with anybody who was anybody invited to the after party with the promise of drugs, sex and rock and roll all mixed together in a cocktail of euphoria and chaotic good times. There was no way I was going to that after party. As soon as the credits rolled, I planned to make my escape.

Under the bright glare of the Hoyts foyer lights, Troy, with blithesome good cheer, informed twenty extras and me that my character actressing was similar to watching a car crash in slow motion. He said I'd ruined the beginning of the film by over acting and staring into the camera.

I didn't believe him, and seven extras told him to stop being such a little bitch. Richard had already told me I was exceptional and could have played the lead.

But according to Troy, I'd committed acting suicide. Only Fellini actors got away with staring into the camera.

But stare into the camera I did! Fellini style.

26

The World Tour

I knew my mother had fallen from her blissful first day of marriage into a thirty-year hole of disappointment. She had watched herself transform from a young sassy telephonist taking trunk calls on a switchboard in Hobart into a suspicious and fictitious woman, a woman she no longer recognised.

Mum had always warned me to have a nest egg in case I needed to flee my own marriage hell. 'Lan, don't get TRAPPED like I did, dear, always keep something hidden for a rainy day!'

My nest egg was growing. The pocket-sized savings booklet in my handbag of the moment (a medical doctor's leather case) noted how I'd actually saved a whopping $11,890. For five years I had consistently put a little 'extra' aside, and for five years I'd watched my nest egg grow so that one day I could own my very own flat with hundreds of crisp white doilies elegantly planted on antique tables. My nest egg was positively thriving, I thought, *positively thriving*! Steven's nest egg was also *positively thriving* with the most incredible amount of money I had ever seen written down. His nest egg had reached $25,895 with a promise from his mum to help us out if we got into any trouble on our world tour.

Yes, Steven had planned a world tour. We were packing up and leaving on a jet plane to see the world!

Our cat, Tiddles, was sent to stay with Rae, our flat rented out to strangers, all of Steven's furniture stored. I had none of my own – Steven, years earlier, had kindly let me know my Post-Nanna Op-Shop Chic style was not suited to his cooler views on decorating. I didn't own a bed, a mattress, a kettle, a pillow, a chest of drawers. Steven didn't like lacy doilies or ordiments, or distorted kitsch angels hanging from ceilings.

Steven would art direct everything on our European tour, and I gladly gave him all responsibility to organise the aeroplane tickets, my passport, accommodation, train tickets, bus tickets, the *Frommer's Guide to Europe*, a fancy Euro pass that enabled us to travel on a bus or a train, and a form that allowed Steven to drive a car on the berserk *autostradas*.

On the violet-hued and cloudless afternoon when I signed my signature more than fifty times for American Express travellers cheques, I realised after the signing I would have only one dollar to my name! I would be broke and jobless, a dollar in my handbag. Completely and *utterly* reliant on a man.

Steven was now in control of my $11,890, and I didn't care for my fraught feelings of being suspended, waiting for my own fall from nest egg heaven. Mum was right, I did feel stuck, hemmed in and panicky. My head was pounding, my hands were itching. Had I really just put my entire nest egg into a man's hands?

Holding my first passport, I braced myself into my economy World Star traveller seat. First stop, Tokyo. I watched Australia shrink into my past – the moon and stars urging me on. I stared in wonder at the TV screen in front of me and gasped loudly at the flashing horror of the flying time: Melbourne to Tokyo – twelve hours! Twelve hours?

'You have *got* to be kidding me,' I said to Steven, grabbing his arm.

'You have *got* to be kidding me,' I said to Steven, grabbing his other arm.

'You have *GOT* to be kidding me,' I said to Steven, grabbing his leg.

'Twelve hours? That's just bloody insane, Steve,' I said to Steven, grabbing his other leg.

Dressed in a 100 per cent wool-suit ensemble, I would fly into 45-degree European airports on my world ticket to Tokyo, Los Angeles, New York City, Berlin, Paris, Greece, London and Prague. Our grand world tour was about to begin.

For as long as I could remember, the Eiffel Tower in Paris, France, had been an iconic tower of hope for me – to see the Eiffel Tower in real life was something that happened only to educated people from good genes. It was a dream I had barely imagined; I mean, *really*, who the hell did this girl from an apple orchard in Geeveston, Tasmania, think she was?

And yet here I was in Paris, France, with a boyfriend who at least *pretended* to love me. And here I was again, driving through the magnificent streets of Paris at midnight in a rented Citroën. And Paris, Paris! Overwhelmingly beautiful, peaceful and exciting all at the same time.

I loved Paris and Paris loved me!

Parisian girls wore high heels while walking miniature snappy French dogs. Almost every woman I stared at was dressed in her own style. These French girls were discreetly flamboyant, and I'd overheard they never used soap on their faces or bought long-stemmed flowers.

I was awestruck. Eiffel Tower struck!

Steven told me to close my eyes and then I could open them. I closed my eyes for five minutes and didn't open them once, not even for a little stickybeak at the glorious, fantastical lights ahead. As the city came out of its Parisian darkness, we drove across the River Seine in stunned silence. I waited until I heard the car engine stop. My eyes were still shut tight.

'You can open them now, Lan.'

I knew right there and then that there must be a French God because what I saw before me was a statue of true beauty and hope. A skeleton tower reaching over 300 metres, made from steel with open lattice, a building so incredibly beautiful I thought I might levitate in the Citroën. If you're anything like me, you will understand what it means to see a vision you only dared to dream of in your lonely teen years. Upon seeing your dream as a grown-up person, *all hell* can break loose in your mind.

Suddenly I was a young French aristocrat wife with a degree in fine arts. I was an only child hosting a French cultural TV programme and I lived in a French medieval castle in the Loire Valley with servants and a 300-metre security gate to glide open whenever my new powder-blue Citroën drew near. I believed for at least a week that my name was Anaïs Valentine Paris France …

That smile lasted until the sudden shock of discovering our travellers cheques had all been lost. I still blame Steven. He still blames me. And the truth lies somewhere on a train between Florence and Paris where we misplaced all of them. The whole damn lot! I remained calm (but quietly hysterical) when it became apparent that one of us – definitely not me – had lost our joint nest egg.

Waiting for a transfer of money from Australia meant frantic reverse-charge phone calls made from a French phone box at 3 am, and twice-daily trips to the American Express Office on Rue Scribe to see if the money had come through. I called Mum to let her know I was stuck in Paris.

'All the cheques have been lost, Mum! We're stuck in Paris waiting for some money to come through from Australia.'

'Money from Australia, Lannaah? Oh, *go on* with you, dear, how can Steven's mother send money when she's not even in Paris? Where are you again, dear … Germany?'

'No, I'm Paris, France, and I've even seen the Eiffel Tower, Mum … it's *huge*!'

'I don't know why you gave away your hard-earned nest egg money, Lannaaah. Now look at the MESS you've gotten yourself into … You're stuck and I don't think THAT Steven has any idea how to be a proper man, he's a dilettante, Lan, a lazy SELFISH dilettante who's stolen your entire nest egg. I WARNED you dear, I did WARN you!'

'*Guess* what, Mum? When I get to Rome I'm going to this place called Vatican City, and I have to prove I'm an arty atheist. I don't think I'm Catholic anymore, I've learnt so much on this trip, Mum, and so … so … I'm going to go to church and then I'll renounce God at the altar. I'm not going to confession and I'm *not* going to be blessed by the Pope.'

The gasp from Mum was ironic and sudden.

'RENOUNCE God at the holy altar then, Lannaaaah. RENOUNCE your own GOD and watch yourself burn in hell for the rest of your life, DEAR! Hyphenated isn't going to save you! Hyphenated could NOT save his own soul in HELL. Are you still FAWNING all over the KIND MOTHER? Making a fool of yourself, dear?'

Steven had cleverly taken out some kind of international travel insurance. This gave us a little reprieve while we waited for almost a week – with our hotel bill covered – until the American Express Office informed us that *all* our travellers cheques had been replaced.

With a gentle push we drove toward the supernatural European light through Switzerland, Prague and other cities I'd only heard about in art movies and art books. I was slowly learning to throw away the old me and to sit impatiently with myself. Steven showed me the Berlin Wall and educated me on Marxism, Communism, World War II and an art movement called Bauhaus. As we drove toward Zurich I looked down, making sure my ten postcards of the Eiffel Tower were still tucked inside the lining of my doctor's medical bag.

After four months away, Steven and I were back from our *most* triumphant spectacular World Tour. I loved our trip but regretted it at the same time. I'd read how after a trip, emotionally intense relationships can either fall apart or flourish and grow. Detailed plans made for each other's futures, shared goals and new European career dreams are discussed at length along with joint bank accounts, wedding and baby plans. Steven's flu-like symptoms toward me turned out to *not* be a deadly and eventually fatal illness.

He was falling out of love with me.

27

Apron Strings

All of us reach breaking points in our lives, but thankfully we're provided with turning points as well. Some things are harder to let go of than others, like letting go of the past, or of sugar. For me, life-altering changes – a new home, a new job, a new boyfriend, a reinvention – were like a revolving door of spontaneous atomic sugary explosions. I was aware I was fooling myself with my reinvention of a brand-new Alannah. I could change for the world however much I liked, but deep down I feared Childhood Alannah had the power to destroy anyone in her path, anyone – *including me*!

In Steven's endeavours to educate me as part of my 'cultural renaissance', he'd tried hard to show me the world. It appeared to have worn him down. His love was slowly being replaced with impatience and a melancholic silence I couldn't understand, let alone bear to feel. I was once Steven's *glittering misfit girl*, a shiny beacon of hope he could cling to; but now I was falling short, and I watched his love retreat from my self-sabotaging, crippling insecurities. My beguiling ways were not having the same effect they had once had. Even my cups of tea with a biscuit were falling short.

One morning, the words that I'd been dying to say to Steven came tumbling from my mouth. I'd been crying and in my haste to collect the mail, I literally tripped over him lying loveless on the floor, staring at the ceiling.

'You're not in love with me anymore, are you, Steve? Please tell me, love, I can't stand the silence … You're still in love with me, aren't you, Steve? Please tell me, love, I can't stand the silence.'

I don't know if my words were a question, a statement, or some kind of announcement, but for what felt like four weeks Steven stared into my quick-blinking eyes. He didn't care for any form of confrontation. I heard him say, 'I love you *but* …

'Lan, you're like a bathtub without a plug. I'm exhausted, Lan … I love you, I don't want to let you go, *but* …'

And there it was again, the *but*.

Steven withdrew and I became clingy. He withdrew even more and I became clingier. I *tried* to withdraw but absolutely *nothing* happened. With my clinginess at *fever pitch*, I convinced myself that Steven was having, or was *about* to have, a literary affair with our literary friend, Emma. At the same time, the paradox of the so-called affair was that I *knew* I was completely wrong, I knew very well it wasn't a sexual affair, it wasn't even a love affair, it was something much worse. Intimacy.

By the time Steven merrily arrived home at dawn after a night out with friends, my imagination had run far, far, far away, to a town called *divorced*. Good Alannah and Bad Alannah were locked in mortal combat and the bad girl was winning, bringing up ghosts from my childhood to poison my mind, body and soul. Unfortunately, my true Aries colours shone through. I didn't begin my dark mood in a slow-burning build-up. Instead, I went straight to accusing Steve of all manner of untoward and unboyfriendly crimes. I also accused him of having an affair with every girl we had ever met. I couldn't stop accusing, judging and sentencing. I invented and believed around seven ludicrous crimes of which Steven surely stood guilty … My jealousy had brought up trampled-on childhood memories, and I didn't have a clue how to calm myself down.

I knew I was losing Steven and so I thought, *To hell with this, I'll quicken this whole thing up*, and I began to act and react very badly, crying my tantrum tears and pushing emotions into a place where Steven might explode. He didn't know what to do with me – I could feel his love, and at the same time I knew he couldn't close his eyes to what his heart might have been telling him: to run …

Jill and John, knowing that my World Tour had ended, invited me to meet and discuss our new futures. It was 1987 and Steven and I had been back for one month. I didn't know how to tell them that I couldn't Windex myself around the shop floor anymore, that I needed a goal to work toward.

Amazingly, Jill and John recognised Indigo needed to find a new direction. Perhaps they realised the hippie look was coming to an almighty hippie-like end and chose that very moment to give me a voice, a voice in which to speak my thoughts on styling, fashion and reinvention. I couldn't believe my ears, but Jill and John were asking for *my* advice on how to raise Indigo back up to where it belonged.

'Lan, what was the styling like in Europe? Did you and Steven notice a change in what young people are wearing in the streets, in nightclubs, in Tokyo? Paris?'

and

'Look, Lan, you're a great asset to any business, a great seller, and Jizz and I are too old to be dragging our sorry bloody arses to the other side of the world – tell us what you think we need to do …'

I was star-spangled, overawed, head spinning, and completely *beside myself*.

I covered my heart with strawberry topping, fourteen cherries atop – my silent voice was about to be heard!

'Jill! Jill! You have *no idea* how many times I've imagined this moment … I've been *dying* to tell you about this incredible scene in Tokyo in a place called Harajuku, Jill, it's the fashion capital. I was so inspired! I saw sub movements, sub sub sub movements and the new geisha fashion models. Japanese girls are so incredibly elegant. I saw a gang of girls in Shibuya and they were *all* wearing plastic clothes! Imagine that? Plastic clothing? The Indigo wedding-bell dress and caftans can *all* be replaced with plastic ones? Don't you love that idea?'

I was babbling like a newborn brook. I saw the look in Jill's and John's eyes: they could *almost* see my vision, but I worried I'd lost John with my plastic design idea. I just needed to convince them a little bit more, I had to convince them to open the design world door …

'I think we need to open another store – we need to reinvent ourselves – we need to be the first with what *everybody* wants. We need to be aware of subculture movements and art movements, collaborate with groovy people and go to *all* the important fashion events and parades. I would love to direct a fashion show – you've seen me dance, John? Do you know there are fashion movements being created right at this moment? The world can't keep up, we need Italian and Japanese fashion magazines and a real fashion shoot. If we reinvent Indigo,[37] *I don't want to be awful*, I don't want to hurt your feelings, Jill, but things will have to be shaken up … I could go to Tokyo next week, if you like?'

Thoughts and ideas that had been building up in me for years and years and bloody years came bursting into the Indigo air like champagne bubbles, and I might have even run away with myself

37 My voice may have lowered a bit here.

that afternoon, speaking wildly about secret fashion revolutions and reinvention —

I wondered if Jill and John were even listening. When I finally got the courage to look at Jill, I saw that she was taking notes on a pad. John said, 'Do what you feel's best … I'm going to read the paper …' and quickly slipped upstairs.

I had a sudden flush and was about to stop, but Jill gave me one of her incredible smiles, a smile that could light up an entire hippie commune. 'That's great, Lan … *wow*,' she said. I pulled my chair over closer to Jill and looked into her liquid brown eyes. I *had* to make her see that what I was about to propose would turn her world upside down and how that would be a good thing.

'I know you love hippies, Jill, and I love hippies too, but can I be really honest, Jill? We have to *completely* start again. We could knock out all the hippie fittings in the store – no offence to John, but the incense and elephant pictures with the guru man you love hanging in the change rooms, I think they freak people out a bit … they really have to go …'

Jill bit her lip, out of insecurity or maybe a sense of relief, I couldn't tell, but I kept going.

'We could line the change rooms with flower contact? In Tokyo, I saw one store with wallpaper covering the entire store … we could have a giant antique mirror in the middle of the shop and we could name all the outfits … like "Wall flower Girl" or, ummmmm, say … "Knock 'Em Dead" or "She's Not a Little Mongrel" … You know I saw these great new mannequins in Paris – oooh I forgot! I also know where knitwear can be made up into garments, a factory in Preston runs the entire production for you.'

'We can't get knitwear made up in a factory in Preston … John won't drive that far, and knitwear … I'm not sure if people want to wear *knitwear* in summer … do they?'

Grabbing Jill by the shoulders, I looked deeper into her flickering, velvety eyes. '*Sure*, people want to wear knitwear in summer, Jill! *Sure*, they do. The trick is … we *just* have to make the customers believe they *want* to wear it, they *have* to wear it, that's another trick, Jill. It's fashion, Jill … we design what people want to wear. We show them the way! We could even wholesale to Myer's, or David Jones? Oh my God, Jill … imagine what we could *do*!'

It took me almost a year to convince Jill and John to rebrand Indigo into a Chapel Street Destination Bow Teek – a Neo-Punk Bow Heaven. But first, I had to reveal my vision and we had to hire new staff. The Indigo Girls were my first team – I called them The Alannah-ettes. It didn't matter if the girls didn't have any experience, I'd show them what to do. I'd spend hours getting to know my new girls, learning to understand their strengths and weaknesses, teaching them how to sell clothing and approach customers in a unique sassy little manner.

I was teaching myself how to build a brand.

The day Jill showed me the first ever Alannah Hill sew-in labels and swing tags[38] was terribly strange, as I'd never seen my name used in such an exciting way before. The labels were cream silk with my name embroidered in cherry-red silk stitching! My name squealed at me and I squealed back.

Jill said I could put my Alannah Hill label on a few designs only; Indigo was still the star of the show. I could design anything I wanted, in any fabric I wanted, using any trims I wanted. I just had to run it past Jill for her approval before my designs went into production. I drew inspiration from everywhere, including the Camberwell Market, a fashion beehive that I stalked every Sunday morning, digging through car boots on the hunt for antique florals, jet buttons and original '60s Simplicity patterns.

---

38 A sew-in label is usually the name of the brand, sewn onto the back of the costume. A swing tag can be as cheap as a piece of cardboard or something fancy and ornate. It tells the customer the size of the garment, the cost, where it's made and other details, like washing instructions.

The very first outfit I designed was a fancy apron with spots and gingham all mixed together in a jigsaw puzzle of mishmash fabrics, my name embroidered onto heart-shaped pockets. Even John came running from upstairs the afternoon Kylie and Dannii Minogue bought two of my mismatched aprons for their mother and grandmother as Mother's Day gifts. I was a little disappointed but I tried not to show it. My aprons were designed to be worn as layering, to go over the top of a Harajuku-styled black frou-frou skirt, not over a mother and a grandmother on Mother's Day. But it was a start, and although I couldn't have known it at the time, it was the start of something much bigger than I ever could have imagined.

With just a few lucky rays of sunshine, Childhood Alannah was growing smaller, the doubting voices fading. I threw myself into the passion of fashion to distract myself as my heart was cracking and breaking for the very first time.

I thought I already knew about heartache, but this was different. Steven and I had turned ourselves inside out living in each other's pockets. I was part of his family and we had a group of friends, an *entire* group of friends – we were inseparable, Lan-and-Steve. He had been so many things to me, and now we were merely strangers in the night, both of us misguided love ships, lost at sea.

Steven was kind enough not to ever actually break up with me, he simply moved me from the downstairs couple's apartment to the upstairs single girl's bedsit. I arrived home from work one day to find that Steve had spent all day set-dressing my new bedsit. He'd bought me a single bed – a wrought-iron hospital bed from the op shop – a bar fridge, a couch, towels, some records and a handful of fine lace doilies. He presented my new home to me like I was being given the perfect gift of love.

He calmly told me as he arranged flowers in a floral vase that he was going to live with one of his brothers. I could stay here in the magnificent mini-Versailles singles apartment for as long as I wanted, and I shouldn't worry, for we'd be seeing each other every other day.

Steven had quietly blown out the candle of love.

I stayed in my mini Versailles for two years before I moved into a magnificent National Trust mansion in Toorak with a six-year-old girl ghost and forty-three spirits who haunted me and haunted me and haunted me. Of course, I didn't believe in ghosts; I thought people who believed in ghosts were ludicrous people: ghosts only lived in the part of our brains where fragments of madness splintered and spluttered.

Illawarra House lay at the end of a dead-end street where angels feared to tread. I was blissfully unaware of the madness within on the sun-soaked day I laid eyes on its twisted turrets and gables. I loved its antique weirdness, its majestic wraparound balcony allowing me to see far and wide and all the way to Kew.

Marching up to the door, I knocked and waited. I heard the faint shimmy of soft slippers on floorboards, then the door opened a crack, a bloodshot, piercing eye staring out at me, unblinking.

'Hello,' I said with a slight quaver in my voice. 'Hello, can I please come in, for a moment?'

The eye blinked at me and the door swung back. I stared into a magnificent lobby coated with an inch of thick dust. A tall black-haired woman was staring at me with her sharp, mad eyes. Her name was Quentin Belle, and she was wearing a neck and shoulder brace. Her face was pale and heavily rouged, her eyelids smeared with apple-green glittery eye shadow like a Mary Quant poster.

I told her I was the new tenant, that the National Trust had allowed me to rent the tower flat (the penthouse, in my eyes) for $65 a week. She glared at me and asked if I had any horrible cats.

Quentin told me just after I moved in that we needed to make a herb garden and we needed to make it now. We worked on our knees, digging delicate holes with teaspoons and filling the holes with Salada biscuits. Quentin would push one Salada biscuit into each freshly dug hole, explaining how we were making one of the most advanced herb gardens in Toorak. While we pegged autumn leaves on the clothes line, Quentin told me we both had a lot of washing and it needed to dry. She then asked me to drive her to North Melbourne where her three small children needed to speak with her. They lived in the small town's local cemetery in an underground vault; we needed to bring warm gumboots because her children were cold since they had died alongside her in the car accident.

One evening in June I heard a loud rush – a door banging – a small girl singing and Quentin. Quentin was inside my bedroom, cutting the air with scissors as she whispered that we must get dressed. She told me her scissors wanted to cut all the way to my heart! I tried to get up to run for my life but Quentin stopped me, asking why I had stolen her herb garden – why I killed her children – why I *didn't* kill myself and why hadn't I taken the autumn leaves *off the clothes line* as now they were all dead? I tried to speak but couldn't. Dried autumn leaves spilled from her white-gloved hands as she left my room in a white nightdress, snipping the air with a pair of antiquated silver scissors.

28

Romantically Incurable

It was a Friday night in 1990, 8.30 pm. I was preparing to close Indigo for the night. I could feel the eyes of a boy stranger peering in at me from outside the shop window, eyes that peered through me, around me and behind me. Perhaps he was the boyfriend of a girl I'd asked too many questions of. Perhaps he was going to hammer me to death for performing stickybeak exorcisms. He could even have been a shallow grave–digger type!

His hair was a halo of waves, black as tar. He was 6-foot, with a 2-inch stare looking into my Alannah Indigo world. I stare-beared right back at him and he disappeared from my vision almost immediately. And then he magically reappeared. Was he stalking me, I wondered?

'I've been watching you, I'm … I'm … I'm … oh God, I'm nervous, I'm so nervous just looking at you. You're beautiful, it's your eyes … I can't stop looking at you.'

My world turned into two separate time zones.

'You can't stop looking at *me*? Really? Why? I'm not *that* beautiful, you know, I'm all mirrors and strings. Tell me this, Stranger Boy. Are you a berserk murderer or are you high on the drugs? I think you're *high* on the drugs. Where are your mother and father? How old are you? Where did you *schoooooooooool*?'

He quietly interrupted me.

'I'm not on drugs. I shouldn't have come inside, I'm sorry. I've frightened you. I like sensitive girls. I hoped you'd be just like you look. I've written you a poem, so read it when you get home and ask yourself if you're prepared to take a risk: I've never fallen in love with a vision before, I didn't think it was possible but …'

Every siren in my head went off.

I was spookily intrigued but immediately on alert. I was dying to call my Indigo work friend Sarah to inform her of the crazy, beautiful stranger who appeared to have fallen in love with me on sight. Should I call the police?

The paramedics?

Lifeline?

Mum?

Behind his trickster confidence, I could see a falling-down in-love-with-a-vision boy who I didn't entirely trust with his vision-talk, poetry and stalking vibe. Despite this, I felt immediate sympathy for him; his hands shook as he offered me his handwritten love poem tied with a red ribbon and misted with Chanel.

And then I let him have the real me at full blast. I thought it best to give him fair warning.

'Mister. What's your name? Mine's Alannah and you are … ?'

I could barely hear him.

'Karl with a K.'

Pretentious, I thought. *Who says their name with the letter at the beginning*? 'Let me tell you something, Karl with a K, this is how it starts. Men see a vision, a creation of me that they've drawn inside their own mad, love-driven heads. You believe I'm a perfect vision of loveliness and glory, you'll idolise me, adore me and then you'll have to live with the crushing disappointment. I'm a bathtub without a plug. A broken window, a cracked skeleton. I fall from elegance with dull thuds onto floors. I can fly you to the moon and back in one day, and the very next I'll fly you straight to hell, where you'll stay until I feel loved again. I'm really a very plain, ordinary girl pretending to be a smashing girl. I also have a terrible affliction, Karl with a K, and it's even got a name. It's called "love cancer".' I paused to draw breath.

And then he did something that almost blew my head off.

He leant over the counter, both hands reaching for my flushed face. I was astounded. *He must be on the drugs*, I thought. *He* must *be*. With his two hands on each of my flaming-pink cheeks, he spoke.

'I can see you're hurt, Alannah. You've been crushed, bruised, battered – I understand your cracking heart. You don't feel real, your soul torn apart by what I can only guess was your childhood? Hoping nobody can see that you're not really living, that you're slowly dying a thousand deaths from a loveless world. Experiencing real love has a lot to do with ego boundaries, since it involves an extension of one's limits. To love properly we must first become committed to an object outside of ourselves, beyond the boundaries of self. It's my birthday tomorrow and I'd very much like to spend it with you, beautiful you, a paradoxical love bomb. Have you ever read Freud or Jung or Voltaire?'

Of course, I didn't believe a word of his carry on, did I?

I almost believed him.

Almost.

I knew he'd taken words from M Scott Peck's *The Road Less Travelled*, but I was kind enough and love struck enough *not* to let him know. I didn't want to know it myself.

I knew Steven would dislike this sort of carry-on – he'd tell me to be very wary of a man prancing around quoting dated philosophers. Falling in love with *me* at first sight was implausible to someone like Steven. But Karl with a K continued to speak.

'At the very least, spend some time with me on my birthday? I shall wait outside for a moment, and when you've regrouped please sign this little card with a *Yes* and hand it to me.'

I forgot to close the store. Customers couldn't believe Indigo's lights were still blazing at 10 pm on a Friday night. I believe up to five items from the bow teek *may* have been stolen. I believed I'd miraculously turned into a *Vogue* cover-girl beauty, ready to enter the Miss Universe competition.

Karl asked if he could live with me on his birthday, our very first date. He asked to *marry* me on our first date. I was surprised but pretended it was a very normal question to ask on a first date. I told him I could never marry. I told him I knew I'd be left a week after the honeymoon.[39] He held my hand over a vanilla milkshake, whispering in my ear how I'd always remain beautiful to him – even when I was fifty. He was full of love, admiration and respect for me. He knew things I'd never told a soul. He psychoanalysed me. I discovered he was a psychology student and he analysed my recurring dream. He asked me question after question. I asked him almost as many and he answered all of them.

From that day forth, my world changed from a pale powder-blue into a rainbow of colours, each colour a different version of Karl's surrendering his heart to me. I blossomed in my soul. My heart grew to a titanic size. The storm inside my head quietened.

I was happy.

But soon my wheels and heels were spinning to keep up with a boyfriend. A boyfriend who was eight years younger. A boyfriend who

---

39 The honeymoon concept is one I have never fully grasped. The honey, the moon. It doesn't make sense to me!

was trialling his psychology experiments on me. A boyfriend who told me the moment I let go of my fear would be the moment I would truly love myself.

He had me.

29

He Had Me!

Over the next few years, Karl and I fell into a social routine. Every second Sunday, there was the visit to Karl's grandparents in Burwood with the trip to Camberwell Market on alternate Sundays. We picnicked at the Melbourne Zoo 189 times, we drove to Brunswick Street for pancakes every Saturday, we took a mini break to Cairns and Brisbane, we saw arty movies, romantic dramas, romantic comedies, we watched Saturday night TV and Sunday afternoon TV. We saw his mum, we went to bed early, we fought, kissed and made up, we fought, kissed and didn't make up. I threw myself into RMIT to gain a PhD in creative writing and then I booked myself *out* of RMIT to *not* gain a PhD in creative writing.

I had also settled into a routine of long working days where I was both designing and retailing at Indigo, and I took my duties very, *very* seriously. I felt I couldn't afford to backtrack in any way, and I needed the wheels of ritual and routine. I was spinning my way through the long Indigo days, months and years, with almost no time to notice that time itself was slipping through my fingers.

The thrill I received from selling my Alannah Hill designs had validated me as a designer, but tensions at Indigo had only increased with my queries about a pay rise and business-class international travel. Jill, John and I had rarely argued, but with me requesting my own label on half the collection and no longer wanting to work on the shop floor, arguing was just around the corner.

My final day at Indigo took me by surprise, and it left me heartbroken. I saw the look in Jill's and John's eyes. After sixteen years, I had overstayed my welcome. Jill and John called their first formal meeting with me. 'It's been great working together, Lan,' said Jill. 'It might not feel like it now, but we think it's time for you – for all of us – to move on.'

'Yes,' said John. 'Look Lan, I'm nearly fifty years old and I can't be stuffed driving around stores with stock in the boot. I'm exhausted, Lan. We just want peace. If there's ever any trouble, you're in the middle of it. We're letting you go, Lan.'

I couldn't move. I was stuck to the chair. My first real family were dropping me. I told them I couldn't face the world without them. I told them I'd do anything to stay.

With the murmur of their words, the sadness hung all around us. They were setting me free.

Jill walked me to my Honda Civic in an attempt to soothe me, but at the time nothing could. I asked about my label and what would become of it. She told me it was my name and Indigo would just go back to being Indigo without my name on the designs.

I think, dear reader, I may have given Jill one last soggy, dewy look of hope but that was dashed when I heard her last words.

'Lan, you've just got bigger dreams than the rest of us. You've become impossible.'

Without my years at Indigo, I wouldn't have learnt what girls and women want or need. Jill and John gave me the chance I'd been searching for and without their care, without their love, my life might have taken a very different turn.

But the parting of the ways, the sorrow of my last day at my first real job, shook me like an evil rattle. I threw myself onto my unmade bed, turned my face to the crumbling walls and kept my eyes shut tight for eight days. Indigo had been everything to me, but I'd taken it all for granted. I couldn't see any hope – I believed I was skill-less, that I hadn't learnt a thing from my years on the shop floor. But that's how it was with me. I had trouble leaving anyone and anything. My head and my heart were at war.

After eight days, I woke up and applied for a job at the Balwyn Cinema as an usher. Five minutes into the interview a man with the smallest eyes I've ever seen informed me that I was *too* experienced for the usher job.

I applied for a job at the Astor Theatre as a candy cane girl. When I arrived for my job interview dressed in my Sunday best, I was told there wasn't any job, no jobs at all, certainly not for any candy cane girl position.

And then, Karl arrived at my Illawarra door, his pale-green car overflowing with garbage bags filled with books and clothes. I told him I couldn't possibly live with a man again. He insisted. There was simply no choice in the matter. His romantic love was forever, and living with me would prove his commitment.

30

The Girl in the Cupboard

I had never intended to be a girl in a cupboard but a girl in a cupboard I was soon to be.

A gushy hairdresser, after asking where my usual perky self had disappeared to, told me about a company called Dialogue. The main director would *love* to employ me as a production assistant, perhaps on their main label, Target.

Dear reader, I wore Target to my job interview.

I hadn't left Illawarra House in weeks, and Karl was onto me. My outbursts of emotion were becoming more regular, and the very thing he'd once found intriguing about me was now the one thing beginning to annoy him. I was bad company and, apparently, unemployable.

The interview was with two of the directors of Dialogue, Chris Rooke and Lynne Browne, veterans of the '80s-era fast fashion for Target and Big W, a world I knew nothing about. Lynne was all curly hair, smiling eyes, a hooting laugh and a big friendly face. Chris was shrewd, mysterious, witty and a smooth operator. He did his best to show me his sincerity and deep business savvy. I did my best to try to believe him.

Chris Rooke made a decision on my fashion future five minutes after our meeting. I would be installed inside a small room hidden underneath a staircase. The financial controller must never discover me in the staircase room, and it would be best if I actually didn't walk around the building. Basically, I was to stay hidden. I didn't exist. My brief was to design and produce an eighty-piece Alannah Hill fashion collection. I was to research and find my own wholesale customers throughout Australia and New Zealand, with the aim of selling my collection to David Jones or Myer.[40]

I found Chris hilarious one moment, irreverent the next. Wicked and switched on then grumpy and unapproachable. He would often pop into my cupboard office and we'd discuss fashion, Chris's desire for cashmere, his desire to be a guest in the most expensive hotel in the world and his new desire, the latest BMW. I was to be paid a consultancy fee of $2000 a week with a budget for sampling fabrics and trims. Chris said times were a bit tough so I wouldn't be able to travel overseas for inspiration. He said he'd understand if I couldn't do it; it was a big ask and hiring me was an experiment. Chris wanted to see if he could build a brand.

Thrilled, alarmed but determined, I set about designing and producing an eighty-piece Alannah Hill fashion collection.

And I did it!

I designed over 200 pieces and I loved it, dear reader. I loved everything about it, the pressure, the freedom, the Target production staff members slightly aghast at the curious busy-bee girl in the cupboard. I was shining with excellence, making my own fabric appointments, outlining the collection breakdown in my head, and busying myself with

---

40 When a designer sells their first collection to one of the giant department stores it's considered a real coup. I'd heard about the department stores' annual fashion shows and fantasised daily that the womenswear buyer would answer one of my calls. She'd tell me how desperate she was for my collection to be in the front windows of David Jones! I was fantasising. I knew it wasn't real.

how to avoid being seen by people.

I worked 100 hours a week designing my first fashion collection. I was in and out of the cupboard, occasionally dragging people in from the Target design area. I found two people to join my Alannah-ette team. Quoc, a wild and clever pattern maker, and Hanh, an intelligent, no-nonsense war refugee with a keen eye for the absurd. We were a team!

After three months, I'd filled ten suitcases with Alannah Hill sample designs. With fifty appointments in my diary, up to eight appointments a day that could last as long as four hours, I travelled all around Australia and New Zealand setting up clothing racks in humble inner-city hotel rooms. I'd carefully set the scene – the music, the lighting, the snacks, the show-and-tell, all so important for charming the new boutique customers I'd found. I was learning how to offer afternoon tea as well as share fashion gossip, personal gossip, the meaning of life and why it was so important that my client stock Alannah Hill.

The orders, handwritten on A4 pieces of paper, were dancing through the fax machine, and I danced robot style right alongside them.

The day I was released from the cupboard under the stairs, I finally met the financial controller. Chris Rooke proudly marched me into a room of men with dishwater grey eyes.

'This is her,' he said, with pride in his voice. 'This is *her*. The girl in the cupboard, the one I've been hiding from you all. She's just sold almost six hundred thousand dollars of her kooky, *spooky* Alannah collection. She designed the collection, made the samples in-house, found her own customers, travelled around Australia and, not only that, she even got David Jones to buy her collection! All on her own. Bloody hell. Scotch, anyone?'

A week later, just after lunch, twelve men descended upon Dialogue, the largest of them shouting at nobody in particular: 'This company is now in administration. Put your pens down and concentrate. Administration 98 per cent of the time leads to receivership. You will all have to be vigilant and we need you to stay here to assist us with any forward orders. Your bags will be scanned and checked upon leaving – and nobody is permitted to take a pencil, a rubber or a piece of paper from this building. It's our duty to inform you the administrators have seized all assets. There's an angry mob of unpaid manufacturers blocking all doorways. They are brandishing chains and are ready to attack. Please exit from the back only. Continue on normally until further notice. Thank you.'

Over the next few weeks, the parts of Dialogue that were seen as profitable were sold off to Myer and David Jones; other labels were passed over, looked over or left for dead.

I was the last label, the girl that nobody wanted. The administrators didn't care there were $600,000 of forward orders, they didn't care my Alannah Hill stock was already paid for and waiting to be delivered to David Jones and other fashion boutiques. If I spied a suited-up administrator-type person walking in my vicinity, I'd make sure our paths crossed. The administrators walked with their heads down, studying spreadsheets and sprinting around the hollow shell of the once thriving Dialogue. I'd do almost anything to startle them into noticing me and the $600,000 worth of blooming clobber that I had sold.

'I've worked so bloody hard, this was my *big chance* – I was about to shine like a bloody little effing star!'

On the day of Dialogue's last fashion gasp, shrewd business-savvy people hoping for a bargain were permitted to bid at the fire sale. Anything that hadn't been sold off was now at bargain basement prices. Fabrics, stock, industrial sewing machines, pattern tables, machinery, desks, chairs. It was rumoured even people were sold!

Chris, his mouth filled with a seventh dim sim, took me aside one afternoon and said, 'I'm sorry, darl, but *no one* wants you. If I had the money I'd back you. We can change all the labels from Alannah Hill to PTO – and sell it through Myer? Now there's an idea!'

That was at midday.

But come one o'clock, Chris danced into my cupboard like an excited bottle of bootleg scotch. His face was beetroot shiny. 'By fucking God, you've been saved! Some fashion cowboy wants your stock and they want you as well! Ahhh, now, can you be a love and buy ten more dim sims from over the road?'

He told me the word was the administrators were moments away from completing a deal with David Heeney from Factory X. David, the doyen of the Melbourne nightclub and fashion scene. In the fire sale held that afternoon David bought five sewing machines, my sample-machinist Hanh, my pattern-maker Quoc, my forward orders, my backward orders, my stock, and *apparently* there was a job for me as well.

'You mean David Heeney is going to *actually* give me a job? What as? What will I be doing there? I can't design for Dangerfield – he owns Dangerfield, doesn't he? Oh dear, what if he doesn't care for me? I've met him before, you know, he was never sure about me …'

Chris told me I was naive but that I was a bloody clever cookie, with a knack for knowing what the public wanted. It didn't matter that I hadn't been to design school, he told me. 'Alannah, I wish things had worked out. Go out there, and show them what you've got, you've done a great job – you know how to build a brand because you are the brand. I'm always here for you if you need me, and I mean that, Alannah.'

The driver of the Factory X truck picked up my stock, myself, Hanh and a small box of sewing possessions. We were off to greener pastures, to the land of Factory X – a land where freedom and youth had made Dangerfield one of the cutting-edge brands in the mid '90s. I couldn't know that within five years Factory X would launch ten opulent and ornamental Alannah Hill bow teeks.

I held Hanh's smooth hands, and we beamed together. With my heart bursting, we waited for the Factory X van to take us to our Factory X home, a tin shed held together by thick black tape, and with seven dogs running wildly under our feet and, sometimes, onto our laps.

31

Factory Girl

The opening of the first Alannah Hill bow teek on Chapel Street in 1997 was a moment when the stars, the moon and the sky all led to heaven.

It was the opening night party and the clothing racks rocked and swayed with beautiful and unique clothing, 150 designs I'd slaved over for six months with alabaster-skinned mannequins looking like superb versions of myself. One hundred and fifty rock-star fashionistas had been invited.

The interior design of my first Alannah Hill bow teek (and of the many more to come) was one of the most important aspects of branding Alannah Hill. I handpicked the furnishing fabrics, the wallpaper, the colour scheme, the architect, the furniture and all the fittings. I wanted customers to feel special and find a thread of solace, a rest from the world outside. I wanted every single soul who stepped inside to be completely swept away. There would be swathes of Jean-Pierre Heurteau curtains, with all the pomp and splendour, a gorgeous state-of-the-art floor and VIP service with a boudoir vibe never before seen on Chapel Street.

When we'd finished designing my Marie Antoinette–style bow teek, I hoped the store would be ready for the opening. The trouble was the architect had been replaced twice, and despite the guests arriving in ten minutes and the store opening for business on the dot of nine the next morning, the state-of-the-art floor was wet. Yes, dear reader, all the concrete floors were wet, too wet to tiptoe on, too wet to dance upon. The music system was convulsing, the beautiful bespoke curtains were late in their arrival – as in, the fabric may not have yet been ordered. Furniture designed for the store had been misplaced. David brought his own Art Deco op-shop couch and settee for the partygoers to sit on.

Everybody I knew was coming, everyone I didn't know seemed to be coming too. But the big scoop, the *huge* scoop, was that I'd convinced both Mum and Dad to make the massive international travel step across the strait to Melbourne. I don't believe my parents had any idea what they were really attending. Something about having to travel all the way to Melbourne to attend some kind of an opening with my name on a window. My mum was immediately distressed that she couldn't smoke during the party, and complained how her shoes were being ruined by the wet cement floor.

'Oh Lan, why is the floor so WET! I have never seen anything like this in my life! A wet FLOOR? What will people SAY about you, Lan? You'll be mocked and LAUGHED off the street. They'll all be laughing behind your back, Lan, laughing and talking about you behind your back … "Did you hear about Alannah Hill's floor? It was wet! Under FOOT!" I don't like these people, Lan. They're all phoneys and they're ALL USING you!'

I felt sorry for Mum. I'd seen a wealthy and elegant woman talking to her. They would have been about the same age. The well-heeled woman was twirling and inspecting Mum's pearls, her eyes zooming in for a full appraisal of their worth. In a mock Aussie accent, she asked Mum if they were Akoya pearls. Mum knew immediately what this game was. She was so sharp. I overheard her snapping that she had owned her pearls for years. She'd bought them in an op shop in Penguin. They were plastic or glass, she couldn't quite remember.

I saw Mum's social frailty and I knew she'd had enough of my bow teek opening.

'I'm tired, Lan, LOOK at your father over there carrying on with those vacuous young girls. I just overheard him tell the one with no breeding WHATSOEVER that he was a COWBOY. Oh, he makes me sick and he hasn't spoken a word to you all night, has he? He's as drunk as a lord, Lan. DRUNK as a LORD!'

One of David's deco chairs had magically made its way to the shopfront window. Mum loved to sit and smoke. A chair left anywhere was a chair for her.[41] That's where I found her, sitting uncomfortably in the front window on David's op-shop chair, with the entire shopfront area set up as a personal smoking station. She was greeting guests then immediately scorning them all behind their backs.

'Oh dear, Lan, who was HEEEE? What a crushing, drunken bore … You can't sew a thing, dear, you can't even darn a sock. Now you listen to me, Lan, you LISTEN to me. This does NOT feel RIGHT, I smell a rat and I just don't like it! Now tell me again, why IS your name on all of the clothing? WHY?'

Mum was last seen smoking and staring out onto Chapel Street, sitting alone in the shop window of my new Alannah Hill bow teek. My father was sitting on a single chair near the change room, repeating jokes to my new staff and twirling one girl's hair.

Before I knew it, my fantastical girl dream became a business machine. It had everybody talking, including me.

41 My mother didn't care for walking; in fact, I don't recall her walking anywhere. Her legs or her back were a problem with the walking situation.

32

I'll Show You

Unique, iconic, feminine and rebellious. The four golden words I hold inside my head whenever I design a new collection.

Building a successful brand is an imperfect science, with many self-appointed experts writing feverishly on how to get to the top, how to stay on top, how to design a pattern, how to minimise costs, and how to analyse your rivals' weaknesses to gain maximum market awareness. The very harsh truth is that by attempting to analyse your own success, you've unwittingly placed yourself in fashionable danger.

'How? How did you do it, Alannah? What terrific course did you attend at RMIT or Swinburne, or the Parsons School of Design in New York City? Surely you must have completed the advanced course in dressmaking at your local Sunday school or Girl Scout club?'

I suspect the truth, dear reader, lies in my favourite line from that great Australian comedy *The Castle*.

'It's just the vibe of the thing, and … no, that's it, it's the vibe.'

And perhaps this is the secret to success – there isn't one answer, there are many elusive ingredients to bake the perfect cake: self-raising flour isn't enough, you need the eggs, the chocolate powder, the chocolate chips, vanilla essence, wine, chocolate icing, cream, rainbow-coloured sprinkles. If you try too hard to define success, you may begin to fall apart with flu-like symptoms from a disease called:

PARALYSIS BY ANALYSIS.

I don't recall a moment where I congratulated myself, smiling at the berserk girl in the mirror who looked back into my own starry eyes, her smiling words falling like rose petals. 'Yep! You're a big shot now, girl, you just sit back quietly. Relax, and allow all that blooming floral success to roar through your veins like a fashion freight train.' I always felt I wasn't successful enough, that I had to try harder, *much* harder.

When I was starting out, I bought myself a daydream diary. Each night, after work at Indigo, I would skulk into KFC then sit in the park, stuffing in my chips with extra extra salt, a large bottle of Coke, mashed potatoes and six chicken nuggets.[42] My diary was full of plans, drawings, ideas, poems, inspirations on how to be the best I could possibly be. And when it happened, when the success finally arrived, it was such an enormous shock that I actually didn't see it coming, nor feel it happen. I knew that I must be doing something right, although the nagging little mongrel side of me was yelling in one ear, telling me to give up. But my *other* ear, the ear kept for the shiny Alannah in her fantastical suit of armour, refused to listen. My determination and desire to succeed were too strong. I worked up to a hundred hours a week, with weekends taken up by design ideas, parades, press – there was no time to socialise, no time for any Mickey Mouse activities, no time to remember that I'd forgotten to have a baby.

To be truly successful, your working life naturally and seamlessly falls into your hobby and into your lifestyle. You must hold the Holy Grail of instinct, drive, determination and tenacity, with a desire to never, ever,

---

42 On one fantastical stormy evening, I stole the largest chicken-salt container from KFC and poured it over every single thing I ate that week which was, in those heady fashion-girl days, fries and ice-cream.

ever give up. I honestly believe the success of Alannah Hill[43] was that I was my own best advertisement. I lived for my brand, breathed it, dreamed it, nightmared it, daydreamed it – any distraction meant I could fail. I invented the most perfect girl imaginable along with seven of her friends: they all lived happily inside my brain because my job was to design for young girls, businesswomen, working mothers, bridesmaids, starlets and unjoined fashion girls just like me. A brand needs an imaginative mind with a real person behind it. A person your customers can clearly see and believe in. I always believed my customers were my conscience, able to spot a phoney from a thousand yards away.

Alannah Hill, for me, wasn't just about clothing, it wasn't about making money, it was the fantasy world I created – *my* fantasy world. Perhaps this is why everything I attempted creatively was so over the top, dramatic, ornamental, larger than life. But within that fantasy I also relied heavily on my instincts about how to make women happy, how to make them feel special – I guess I adopted all the things that made *me* feel special. For me, marketing Alannah Hill the brand wasn't marketing at all, it was allowing people to enter a world of fantastical illusions and dreams so profound that shopping at one of my stores became an adventure, a moment in time where you could forget all the messes from your real life and step into a brand-new Alannah-in-Wonderland life.

I began working with Andrew Majzner at Paper Stone Scissors, a creative agency – Andrew became my fashion adviser and friend. We spent weeks conceiving magnificent Alannah Hill fashion campaigns together, choosing models, photographers, locations, hairstylists. I reinvented everything about myself with the arrival of a new season. Each collection had to be more spellbinding than the last. Billboards, Alannah Hill trams, campaign catalogues, Alannah Hill Christmas cards, VIP nights where I'd spend hours with my customers, asking them a million questions and giving them a million answers.

---

43 I will attend a Catholic confession after this chapter, dear reader, for I fear I could be tiptoeing on thin ice over very hot water. I could be accused of patting myself all over my crooked back, showing off, squeaking like a small bird all at the same time.

The naming of each garment for the season was a two-day process where I'd draw on memories, good or bad, with Mum. I'd call on her quirks and barbed, dark humour. Or if I felt uneasy with Karl's lack of love, he'd become the target of my design names.

The naming of a new collection went like this:

'Mum! It's me, Lan. What are you doing right at this very moment, Mum?'

'Is that YOU, Lannaaah? Are you calling me on that little silly phone you've got? That's not a phone, Lan, it's a toy. I'm just sitting here, dear, I might get my hair set, but I'm still in my dressing gown, dear. Have you been sacked yet, dear? Did you ask what I'm eating, Lan? How do you know I'm eating? I'm just eating a little SAO BISCUIT!'

And that's how it went, from Mum's mouth, straight into my collections:

– I'm just having a little Sao frock
– You can't sew, dear, frock
– He's going to jail cardigan
– Love me in the cemetery frock
– She's a little bitch coat
– Who the HELL do you think you are? frock
– Ask your father, dear, cardigan
– You'll burn in hell, Alannah, camisole
– He doesn't LOVE you, dear, skirt
– You're a disgrace frock
– Where's my pony skirt
– Read your Bible, Alannah, frock
– He's NEVER going to marry you, Lannah, cardigan

I had my fingers in every pie; I understood that to build a successful brand everything matters; one mistake could ruin your reputation within days. The Alannah Hill staff were infamous for arriving early and following a list of rules stickytaped everywhere!

No eating on the shop floor

Lipstick must be freshly applied on the hour

Nails and hands must be clean and painted

No greeting customers with 'What's the weather like out there? Cold enough for you?'

Perfume must be sprayed liberally and regularly

Do not ignore customers

Find new ways to greet customers

Do not chat idly with each other

Always look busy

I love you

I was list mad.

The girls would arrive early, spending hours primping themselves to perfection in readiness for their day on the bow teek floor. A gang of Alannah Hill girls walking toward you could knock a Tim Tam biscuit right out of your hands.

The story of my past was often the inspiration behind my catwalk extravaganzas. I didn't want to look like everybody else – I wanted everybody else to look like me! My attention was given to every detail: searching antique markets for a French trim, employing girls with a unique approach, meeting customers, working in the stores, and travelling around Australia to meet new managers and staff. I took real interest in the Alannah Hill staff's emotional lives, their breaking-up-with-boyfriends lives, their everyday lives. The area manager and I looked for staff who could embrace the belief that if you wore Alannah Hill, you could take on the world.

Alannah Hill embodied genuinely unique, ornamental, elegant, timeless designs, a visual attraction captivating the imagination. Rebellion, liberty and romance reigning supreme. My little mantra of

'I'll show you' was the perfect gift to myself, a perfect gift designed to drown out a past I had no idea was galloping ahead of me.

My success wasn't planned but, somehow, all the planets aligned, shining a beacon of hope from the Milky Way onto a milk-bar girl.

A milk-bar girl with an impossible dream.

33

Lost Years

After nine years, the cracks were beginning to show in my relationship with Karl.

He hadn't noticed I was lonely: lonely for him, lonely for love. Karl's concerns seemed immature and fey, the glamour of his smashing good looks and nightclub whirl was wearing off. I craved safety but wanted adventure, I craved adventure but needed money. He was dependent on me but wanted to lead a separate life, a life he quietly kept away from me.

I wanted to change how I was behaving but I didn't know how. I was running out of juice, the usual tricks I used to distract and give me pleasure no longer working. I wasn't necessarily sad or depressed, I just felt incomplete and alone most of the time. I disliked myself for becoming emotionally dependent on Karl, something I'd told myself I'd never do again.

Karl was edgy, tempestuous and bored. We fought, each using anything we could to topple the other into submission and guilt. The love cancer I'd self-diagnosed on the first night I met him seemed to be growing from stage four into – well, there is *no* stage five.

Evenings in my new decadent apartment in Dalgety Street, St Kilda, were part of a strange and surreal fantasy life. Karl would disappear through the 1878 faded-glory doorway dressed in his Prada, my credit card in his pocket. When I heard the large doors slam, I felt relief from the tension and self-deception.

And this is how lost moments turn into lost years filled with yearning and a fear or inability to contemplate change. There was no denying the age difference between Karl and me.

I had stopped going out.

I had stopped being fun.

I was going bonkers about his cavalier attitude, the rumours boomeranging back to me about Karl and his club affairs, and why didn't I know?

There were moments when I'd arrive home, close the door and suddenly feel like I was falling into a void. I was working my 100-hour week, arriving into work at 8 am and not leaving until 10 pm. Alannah Hill no longer seemed like work, and whatever it was it had completely taken over my life. In fact, it was my life! I was trying to feel the glory, but my insecurities about Karl were pushing us both into oblivion – aeons of time and understanding hung between us in vast cosmic rifts.

Living in a darkness such as this, you hanker for the light, and I was looking everywhere for a sunbeam, a spark, a star-speck of illumination to guide my way.

The new millennium, the brave new world of the future, was fast approaching. During the long-haul working hours at Factory X, I'd sometimes stare out the windows of my office and, instead of drawing solace from those picture-postcard scenes of summery blue skies with marshmallow-white clouds, I'd see the futility of my own life. Other people's lives taunted me with their everyday comings and goings, the simple pleasures of their friendships, birthdays, romances. Alienation had quietly slipped into my life – it grabbed me by my legs, arms, head, neck and shoulders. The Alienator had taken me hostage.

It seemed the more successful I became, the less control I had over anything that mattered to me. Frustrated and fractious, I was a nightmare dressed up like a daydream. The memories from my past were snapping at my high heels. Soon, I'd discover there was nowhere left to hide.

34

Don't Let Me Down, Lan

And then, my father died.

There is no doubt I felt unloved by my father. Unloved, and invisible. But I also understood he was one of the motivating forces behind my never-ending rattle to leave a mark in the world.

I had studied my father inch by inch, howl by howl, drink by drink, kick by kick. I had observed, along with my nan and mum, that my father only warmed to successful, vainglorious people, people who held a high-flying level of respect in society and had a trophy to prove it, or a nice car to prove it even more. For years, I'd watched my father fawning over complete strangers, strangers whose exploits had managed to secure my father's interest in them, while I'd failed to earn his love.

But after my father retired, he had rewritten his entire history. The one where he'd been a terrible father and a drinking, unloving, absent husband. He chastised men who drank and ignored their families; he grew to love a stray dog called Sam for sixteen years, never letting it out of his sight, and grieved the dog's death like a normal father; he played in golf tournaments, making three golfing friends; he wrote a letter to the editor of *The Australian* newspaper regarding Labor's scurrilous mishandling of Australia (Dad framed that letter); he started whistling ditties and said things like, 'What a beautiful day outside. You wouldn't be dead for quids, would you?' He announced over the telephone that if both Bernadette and I didn't fly over for Christmas, he'd be very disappointed in both of us.

'Now, don't let me *down*, I'll see you on Christmas Day.'

'I won't let you down, Dad, I'll see you on Christmas Day.'

He drove Mum to three garage sales and told her she could have anything she wanted. Mum bought a new fridge and grew taller. But Dad, in his retirement, paid a high price for his past with my mum. She saw his vulnerabilities and went for the jugular. My mum's fury at 'retired, reinvented dad and husband' was all-consuming. Even though he washed dishes, mowed the lawn and even attended church services in Ulverstone, Mum's fury continued to boil over. Watching my father pick us up at Devonport Airport, crying, 'Thank God you're here' into my confused hair, inspired her forgotten memories of hatred.

My father, although reinvented, still had nothing to say to me. He had stopped being angry, but his silence and my invisibility were still ghosting around us.

I'll never forget the one Christmas where he didn't ignore me. I showed Mum an article in a newspaper about me and although he didn't read it, he grabbed both my hands and stared at me. With my hands in his he said, 'You had what it took, Lanny! You cannot buy what you've got, tenacity' … and in an even gentler tone he repeated some of his words.

'You had what it took, you had what it took all along, Lanny.'

My father died exactly as Mum wanted. Unhappy, alone, cast into a lost and unused bedroom next to Mum's. He was left to die his lonely death after his one-year battle in Tumour Town – lung cancer. My brothers drove Dad to the Burnie hospital for chemo twice-weekly for a year. Mum ignored him and took no interest. She thought he was either invincible or putting it on. When Dad was at his worst, Mum had a massive heart attack, her back went again and she could walk only with a walking frame. Around the house she could walk quite normally, but if a neighbour dropped in to see how Dad was dying, Mum suddenly needed her walking frame to greet and then be rude to the 'stickybeak neighbours' with the courage to 'drop in to "see how Jim is, Aileen"'. 'The GALL of these stickybeak neighbours, Lan,' she'd tell me. 'The GALL of them!'

Mum was taking antidepressants so that 'she couldn't feel anything'. Two days before my father died, Mum told us he was his usual bad-tempered self. 'He's as lazy as a foal so STOP worrying about him! If you want to fly back, fly back, but your father is FINE! He's putting it on. Vomiting everywhere. I can't stand it, Lan! I can NOT stand it! Aren't you going away soon? Your work comes first, you know, Lan. I've ALWAYS said that, haven't I? HAVEN'T I? Anyway, your father is too tired to talk ... Jimmy? JIMMY! Lannaaaaah wants to talk to you! He's asleep, Lan, call again tomorrow, maybe?'

My oldest brother was with my father the morning he died from a burst aneurysm. That morning, my sister and I were boarding a plane from Melbourne to Devonport. Dad died before we landed.

I didn't know if I was utterly devastated, but I felt the weight of something I'd been carrying all my life. My sister and I limped to the chapel where Dad was to be cremated. The morgue day manager had said one sister at a time, and somehow I was pulled through the morgue door; someone had decided I should say goodbye first.

I stared into my father's coffin and touched his cracked skin. His eyes were half open and I wondered if he could see me. I blubbered and then stopped, I blubbered and stopped some more. I couldn't reconcile the strange dead man in a coffin with my father, the man I had feared all my life. I didn't want him to wake up. He'd wonder why I was crying over him.

I'd written him a letter that I wanted to read aloud to him. I placed my letter on his chest and bleated out, 'Dad, I forgive you. I understand you felt trapped, I'm sorr—' but just as I was about to say 'I'm sorry', the letter flew off his chest. I picked it up and placed it in his suit pocket where it couldn't fly away.

I kissed him goodbye and yet, God's honour, as I walked away, the letter fell back onto the floor. I imagined him sitting up to tell me he loved me, but all I could hear were the crackling distorted sounds of Elvis singing 'Love Me Tender' over the speakers.

After my father died, I turned on Mum. I told her how disappointing it was to watch how she had behaved in Dad's last year on earth. She said she didn't care, she didn't miss him and she was relieved. He had been a rotten father and an even worse husband and what WAS wrong with all of us crying and weeping over 'YOUR FATHER'? Didn't we remember how violent he was? How much of a lapsed Catholic he'd been?

Mum was stoic and a little sad at the chapel when Dad was cremated. I didn't understand where my father's high-flying drinking chums were; nobody had come for him except his family. Mum told me everybody had dropped him because he was a bore when he was ill. She hobbled to his coffin on her walking frame, clutching her heart and singing hymns loudly. She winked at me and put one of my hands on the walking frame with her hand. I couldn't read Mum. She seemed dead, forgotten about, even to herself.

Antidepressants were giving Mum what she needed. To feel nothing.

35

I Never Promised You a Rose Garden

Work had become my life, my separate identities all rolled in together like a spectacular Swiss roll from a Glen Iris bakery.

I stopped pretending I enjoyed being who I was. An unreal, unjoined girl. I believed a successful thirty-nine-year-old woman should be able to bury her past in a shallow grave, tying a yellow ribbon around the old oak tree to leave it all behind. And yet, it became clear to me that just when you think you're done with the past, the past isn't done with you.

I'd heard the rumours about the power of the biological clock. I'd sometimes wondered if my clock was working. Now I could hear it in the middle of the night, gilded with bright moonbeams, and I wondered to myself if this was what I was waiting for – a baby?

But who the hell did I think I was, thinking about bringing a child into the world?

But then again, why shouldn't I?

Why couldn't I?

I was thirty-nine years old. If I wanted a baby, it had to be Karl's.

My mother gave me fair yet horrifying instructions about children.

'DON'T YOU DARE get pregnant! Don't you DARE! If I had my time over again I wouldn't be bothered with men. Wouldn't have married. I wouldn't have had you lot, I wouldn't have THIS TERRIBLE LIFE, but you've got NO idea, dear! You're thirty-nine years old! It's not going to work out for you, Lan! You've left your run too late and YOU'VE CHOSEN THE WRONG MATE!'

It wasn't just my mum advising me not to do it. *Everybody* advised against it.

The odds of it all working out were looking somewhat unspectacular.

I watched Karl watching me, wondering how serious this was going to get. And so I came straight out with it. 'Karl, we can't put this off any longer. I think I really want a baby. Do you? Do I? Do you think I want a baby? Maybe I'm dreaming!'

Karl responded in a very direct manner. 'Look, Lan, I don't want a family. I know I'm your last chance and I love you enough to give you the baby you want. I can't promise you a rose garden. I don't find pregnant women attractive and I'm not interested in watching a birth.'

I believed Karl's response was completely normal. In fact, I thought Karl was being rather splendid about the whole thing. He wasn't totally against it. I repeated the conversation to Hanh at Factory X, with a huge phoney smile on my face, nodding madly while waiting for her to nod madly back to agree that it was all completely normal.

'Not normal, Lan. He no good! He not take care of you and the baby. He will leave you for sure. I feel sad for you, Lan, you spend years of your life giving him a good life and he treat you this way. It not fair, Lan, it not fair. What you going to do, you too old to have a baby with someone else. All your eggs dead anyway.'

She was right, although I had no idea. I didn't know what an ovary was. I deliberately avoided any books, TV programmes, DVDs, videos, cartoons; anything concerning the reproductive system was like holding a cross to a vampire for me. I knew nothing about eggs; I had no idea that a woman's eggs died off, possibly leaving me *barren*![44]

A girl once told me how girls who had been abused were afraid of their vaginas. They didn't want to look and had no interest in how their body worked. They often found themselves so disgusting that any reminders of being a woman were pushed aside into the darkness.

Lovely! Blooming lovely! I could hear my three little words inside my head, and they were getting louder. *I'll show you*. I wanted a family of my own. I wanted to show an innocent child a marvellous life, the opposite to my own childhood. I was going to bring a living soul into the terror and beauty of this world – and I'd somehow make the whole thing work perfectly.

And then it happened.

'Hello, Alannah, sit down. Congratulations! You're pregnant. You're in a very high-risk zone, Alannah, you're thirty-nine years old and the chances of the baby —'

I couldn't hear her words, I didn't care about the risks.

I was having a blooming little baby.

44 My mother's favourite word of all time.

METAMORPHOSIS

2001–2018

‘Why does the eye see a thing more clearly in dreams than with the imagination being awake?’

LEONARDO DA VINCI

36

Sin City International

Blondie's 'Eat to the Beat' pumped into the room of movers and shakers, bringing a little post-punk vim to the glamorous Sydney fashion set. A little ribbon-bowed bomb dallied from my fingers, a secret ready to explode. I'd chosen every upbeat pop hit and every heart-rending power ballad for my dancing girl–themed fashion show myself. My kitsch taste in music was now legendary, and audiences wouldn't have been surprised to hear a stirring rendition of an ABBA song sung by Celine Dion or a pop version of 'The Carnival Is Over' by the Seekers.

It was Mercedes-Benz Fashion Week Australia, where the femme fatales of the fashion set embraced all their weirdness and beauty, reassuring us that living in a fashion vacuum was different from living in a vacuum cleaner. Every hotel was booked out, all flights to Sydney booked out, every fashion event booked out and every sassy fashion editor's email wired to fire straight back: *I'm at Fashion Week. Do not disturb me!*

Alannah Hill the brand was in many fashion shows, but Mercedes-Benz Fashion Week Australia gave the most international exposure of them all. All the designers had to be chosen by a board of directors to take part.

And then I was chosen – it was my time to show the Alannah Hill collection to the world. I travelled from Melbourne to Sydney on my own, six suitcases full of outfits, six small heart attacks occurring every ten seconds. Upon landing, I threw my pregnant self along with my suitcases into a large taxi and headed straight to the venue. Twelve state-of-the-art Mercedes were lined up in front of giant white marquees that puffed like clouds sent from heaven. The state-of-the-art Mercedes gleamed every shade of the rainbow – they were giant matchbox toys, gleaming in Sin City's criminal sun.

I could never sleep in the weeks before a show: I was everywhere I was needed and everywhere I wasn't. I attended all fittings, performed for interviews, chose models, chased models, wrote endless lists, stayed up all night gluing sequins onto the dancers' tap shoes, all the while developing extravagant hairdos for the catwalk stampede.

The eight Alannah Hill dancers were chosen carefully with my friend, choreographer Alana Scanlan. We would allow weeks of time rehearsing the dancers and myself. (I might have been known to tap-dance down that catwalk for the finale.) A little show-off like me loved this moment. Alana and I would spend weeks perfecting the routines to sexcitable degrees of perfection. I hoped to light up Fashion Week by starting my show with the most beautiful and unique dancers. When the long-limbed, drop-dead-gorgeous girls hit the catwalk with a provocative, fully choreographed routine, you could feel the atmosphere in the room shift up several degrees.

The audience went wild. And so I went wild with them. I patted myself on the back, spoke to cameras and forgot who I was or where I was, completely overwhelmed by the five-star glamour and the international buyers interested in stocking the Alannah Hill brand in their stores.

All of the designers had been told that if we wanted international acclaim, the international buyers must come first. They were here for one week only, and so they were treated in a royal manner. They were asked to attend all the fashion shows in their gleaming Mercedes chauffeured cars. We designers were to make ourselves available to buyers for the entire week. All night long. All day long. Appointments were held at the clandestine hour of 11 pm in my hotel suite, or a bar. I loved every second of every moment of it.

And I sold my Alannah Hill collection to the world.

Browns in London, Selfridges in London, Henri Bendel in NYC, Bergdorf Goodman in NYC, and Tangs in Singapore. In the following months, I would become CK Tang's special international guest, showcasing my designs in their spring windows. I would also fly to NYC and London as a special international guest. Henri Bendel, the beautiful department store on Fifth Avenue in NYC, invited me to launch my collection in their store window. It was the most incredible moment in my fashion life, the moment where I was actually standing on the sparkling NYC pavements on Fifth Avenue, my name in flower lights. My designs in the actual window on Fifth Avenue!

But despite sending Mum aeroplane tickets, and organising car transfers and a hotel corner suite at the Sheraton on the Park, every seat I had reserved for her stayed empty. She never came. Not to anything. And on the outside I pretended I didn't care, but on the inside, my hurt grew into a saddened version of red-hot fury.

I had to tell Mum about my Fifth Avenue extravaganza.

'Mum, it's me, Lan! I'm in New York, Mum! I'm standing on Fifth Avenue right outside Henri Bendel's, you are not going to belieeeeeeeve this, Mum! My name is on the front windows!'

'Lan, is that you? What is it, dear? Who died? Who?'

'Mum, I'm standing on Fifth Avenue … New York …'

'New YORK??? Oh, you are NOT, Lannaaaah! How can you be talking to me in Ulverstone on that tiny little beeping phone of yours? From New York? WHAT clothing, dear? WHAT window? FIFTH Avenue? Didn't they want you on FIRST Avenue, Lan? You only came fifth?'

My heart sank.

And then it flew!

At that moment I decided I wouldn't read a single parenting book. I wouldn't need to because I'd be raising my child the opposite way to how I was raised. *When my child rings me from Fifth Avenue excitedly telling me their spectacular news, I'll already be there*, I thought.

In the front window!

With a sign saying, 'Mum's proud of you, darling' on top of my proud apple head!

37

What Not to Expect

The words 'mother' and 'mum' had *always* chilled my heart. Motherhood, for me, was eternal chaos, mayhem; three packets of cigarettes a day, an overcooked piece of steak thrown against a wall; scalding, heartbreaking scenes at the local RSL; grubby, lonely aprons; and unhappiness spliced with unending sacrifice, all etched against a skin-toned background of unimaginable despair. I believed the only escape from this cul-de-sac of maternal misery was through the very good fortune of having the extremely rarefied DNA of *good baby-making genes.* But when I reviewed my family history, I had *no* reason to believe I possessed any rarefied genes. None!

And yet, here I was, all dressed up in the fluorescent-lit birthing theatre of St Vincent's Hospital in Fitzroy, about to have a baby of my own. Beside me, instead of delicately folded baby clothes ready for the arrival of my cherub son, I'd chosen a perfectly laid out survival kit, a survival kit for new mothers. Christian Dior face powder, Chanel perfume, MAC Ruby Woo lipstick and lipliner, a can of Final Net hairspray, vitamins, a vintage watch for my son, an ivory vintage slip, three suitcases of costumes, a red ball gown and a hair teasing comb. I had convinced myself I was attending a Gala Baby Ball and *not* the birth of my very first child. I convinced myself even more that turning the American spelling of MOM upside down to spell WOW was a sign from the baby gods above. MOM and WOW. Wow!

Dear reader, I was totally and utterly unprepared for motherhood.

On the morning of the caesarean, wearing what can only be described as a meringue-pink ball gown with kitten heels, I applied my make-up very, *very* carefully. I wanted to show that I was a happy, shiny, excited new mum, with a Britpop boyfriend by my side and a ball gown floating across my watermelon stomach.

It was 6 am. Karl drove at what seemed to be a snail's pace along Punt Road in a squid-ink suit and tie and matching shoes, his fingers switching the dial of the radio impatiently. I wondered if whoever was in charge of this unreal baby universe would somehow see my inner chaos and, understanding the danger I posed to the baby world, mercifully kill me at birth yet spare the child; surely the baby-world universe would never have given permission for me to bring a new life into the world? Or would the baby gods be reassured by my costume that my little baby and I would become beautiful and extraordinary together, and permit me to live on into a golden, Waltonesque future, replete with christenings and birthday parties?

I had borrowed a *DO NOT DISTURB* sign from the Westin hotel in Sydney weeks earlier and, on arrival, hung it on the door of my hospital room. Supreme lengths had been gone to in preparing my St Vincent's hospital room so that my newborn angel (when his eyes finally opened) would be able to view my *glorious* interior-decorating style rather than the lacklustre, design-deprived maternity room.

Elegant French-style lampshades decorated with 166 handmade cherry-bomb pompoms were brought in from my shabby-chic home.

Marie Antoinette–style velvet cushions lay strewn across the bed along with a velvet doona cover, two vintage rose carpets, three suitcases of clothing and various ordiments on display – all to welcome my son into his new Alannah-mum world.

My anxiety at being trapped in a maternity hospital with my suit of armour torn open to prying eyes reached a paranoid intensity. The time I needed to make myself up was a very private affair, and without that time to reinvent myself into the Good Alannah, I was at risk of showing the entire hospital the little mongrel hiding underneath.

Have I mentioned, dear reader, that I was totally and utterly unprepared for motherhood?

I had been working in my design space at Alannah Hill until 11 pm the evening before the big day. Almost nine months pregnant, I was teetering on my sky-high heels and wondering what the hell tomorrow would bring. I was busily preparing work for Hanh, my guiding hand. 'Two weeks and *boom!* I'll be back,' I told everyone.

I prepared twenty patterns for grading, designed thirty-five styles for my Dancing with the Devil collection, ten bridesmaids' dresses, a camisole ensemble for a Valentine's Day special and PR samples for the David Jones Fashion Show.

I was planning on a two-week mini break after my son was born. That was all I would need, for I rarely holidayed. I felt holidays were only for overworked, disillusioned people caught up in the rat-race matrix. I'd been obsessed with my brand for so long, I didn't need a holiday, I told myself. I was managing life in other ways – I was the new immaculate conception. The deception within the immaculate conception!

Until now, I had been a whirling, spinning ball of girl-spark energy. Sourcing fabrics, art-directing and styling countless Alannah Hill fashion shows and Alannah Hill VIP events, travelling to Paris, Rome, Japan, NYC, Los Angeles and London to represent my brand in any way I could. I had no time for friends, no time to listen to music, no time to watch TV, no time to ponder, no time to eat, no time to sleep. I lived and breathed Alannah Hill until I began to feel like a Looney Tune.

I'd risen from a shop girl's merry-go-round to a designer's roller-coaster, and once this upgrade occurs in a girl's career, returning to the slow-moving merry-go-round can be catastrophic.

It would mean I had failed.

My success hadn't come from fitting in, it had come from standing out.

So I couldn't allow having a baby to slow me down. The sixty-nine stitches across my stomach would give me *absolutely* no pain and if they did, I would be on the Panadeine Forte – ten a day, and if the pain worsened, fifteen a day. I would be taking my child to work in a flower-decorated bassinet, laying him on a pink cashmere blanket underneath my desk where I could keep a close eye on my perfect, mute little angel, all the while designing next season's collection.

Did I mention I was totally and utterly unprepared for motherhood? Have I mentioned that yet, dear reader?

Guiding me through the perils of pregnancy was the meritorious Dr Judy. She was my obstetrician, my surgeon, my mothercraft consultant, my sounding board, and the only other person who heard my son's first heartbeats.

Dr Judy asked if I wanted to know the sex of the baby, and I told her it wasn't necessary, I already knew it was a girl. She told me it was a boy and I didn't believe her. I told her there must be some mistake. I wasn't good with boys. I couldn't dress a boy up and he'd grow up knowing I had love cancer, eventually shrinking away from me. A boy? She must check twice more, I said. Dr Judy checked twice more, and still I didn't believe her.

Because I was in the 'Diane Arbus' age bracket (over 35), a diagnostic test for Down syndrome would need to be performed, but it came back negative.

I told Dr Judy I didn't believe I could possibly be having a real-life baby and could she somehow please prove it to me once again? She obliged with a fetal monitor.

'Can you hear that, Alannah? Listen carefully: it's your son's heart beating, a good strong heartbeat he has, too.'

The heartbeat was loud. Astonishingly loud, and I understood the mighty heartbeat was telling me, 'Everything's going to be OK, Mum. I'll show you what to do. Just say yes to everything I ask for, and everything will work out fine.'

I honestly believe a glimmer of spiritual presence was in the room that day. I began to believe there really was a God, after all.

Dr Judy's kind hands pressed tissues into mine. She told me it was normal to weep upon hearing your child's heart. I thought I was completely abnormal. She told me it was abnormal to be wearing high heels in the last trimester, which I thought was completely normal.

'Come and sit down, Alannah, I want to talk with you seriously for a moment. No need to panic. We just have to make a few decisions. We need to get your baby's father in to have a blood test.'

'A *blood* test? Oh, no, he *won't* do that, love, Karl is very busy, Dr Judy. He hasn't got the time, Dr Judy, and to be perfectly honest, he isn't *that* interested in all of this. He's out a lot, you know, at night, he sleeps in until around two o'clock in the afternoon and then he has to go out again. He's really busy, love. Actually, I'm just going to say it, Dr Judy – he's being a real bloody arsehole, and I'm thinking of slaying him with a fire-iron. Selfish! You have *no* idea, Dr Judy.'

Dr Judy carried on in a serene, doctor-like tone. She told me I'd acquired diabetes, my little baby wasn't sitting high enough in my stomach; in fact, he was dropping and might drop right out from under me. I had malnutrition, scurvy and thalassaemia, an inherited blood disorder. If Karl had the blood disorder, our baby could be in serious danger and might not live. My baby was already threatening to reject me. Dr Judy was not only concerned about my wearing of the high heels, she also told me she was worried I didn't seem to have a friendly support group, and she told me how new mothers took great comfort and joy in having a strong, understanding support group. She asked me to start looking for one. A support group? I wouldn't be needing any kind of a support group. I'd be supporting myself.

Dr Judy produced a plastic-type situation that mirrors a girl's womb. I immediately recoiled from this plastic womb-like horror but, slowly, I became very, very interested in the inner workings of the ovaries, along with the outlandish lie that apparently after one gives birth, another birth occurs – something Dr Judy called the After Birth, which sounded like a punk band from Kreuzberg.

Dr Judy's talks about the ovaries, the placenta and my inner self's lack of lining reminded me of Mum's hysterectomy. No wonder Mum was pained and angry, working in the milk bar on her feet only four days after her 'hysteria'. I felt the ache of how I'd let Mum down in her many hours of need and wanted to thrill her with my latest pregnancy horror story.

'Mum! I've got the diabetes, the thalassaemia; the little baby inside of me is dropping, Mum! I've got the scurvy, the malnutrition, low iron readings, and the baby may leave me, Mum, at any given moment! He's dropping, Mum! I haven't got enough lining in my stomach to hold him in, Mum! He might even be a vegetable, Mum, with my blood disorder and …'

I could hear Mum's delighted squeals all the way from Ulverstone.

'Oh Lan, dear! Of course he's dropping! He's already going to drop you! He doesn't WANT you as his mother, dear, this is God's way, Lan, he's telling your body that you cannot HAVE a baby, Lannaaaah! I told you children ruin your life, Lannah! You'll probably have a *prolapse* anyway, dear, and the baby won't GROW!'

My mother didn't understand the science behind a prolapse. She thought a prolapse could occur at any time. Day or night. Pregnant or not pregnant. Dead or alive!

Dr Judy said she wanted to 'monitor' me and ordered an ultrasound every two weeks. Karl did attend a medical centre for the thalassaemia test and the results were perfect, no sign of any blood disorder, no sign of anything at all.

Perfect. It was all going *perfectly.*

I'd read that some men find pregnant women sexy and powerful, their bodies made for bearing children, but unfortunately the birth father of my child was not one of these men. Karl wasn't interested in how a woman's body changes. He liked thin women. I felt I *might* have made a colossal mistake as my girl stomach became too big to hide, so irreversible, so gigantic, that I decided I might have to disappear entirely after my little heartbeat of a baby was brought into the world.

I hadn't attended a single prenatal class, not a single pre-pre-prenatal class, not a single birthing class. I had no intention of attending any postnatal classes or post-postnatal classes. In my mind I was a rebel, a fire-starter, ready to instigate a revolution for new mothers, and rebellious, revolutionary new mothers did not attend these natal-type affairs. I wouldn't have the time to be joining any new mother's support groups. I'd be far too busy with my fashion career and my angel asleep in a corner, quiet and serene.

I'd forgotten to purchase a pram, baby clothes, a cot or bassinet. I'd kept my promise and not read a single book on motherhood, cooking or genetics. I'd heard about so-called hormones, emotional upside-down feelings, exaggerated by the pregnancy situation. Of course, I didn't believe any of these made-up stories. Hormones? Only real, *joined* girls had hormones. I had not a hormone in sight – I was hormone-less. Unable to feel a hormone, and yet there I was sobbing into my doctor's long hair in my lunch break when I heard my son's first tiny heartbeat. Maybe I did have some hormones that worked, after all?

Although Karl appeared as a well-dressed Tom Ford mirage, in reality he stood on the verge of a nervous breakdown. Studying his face in the cold blue light of the St Vincent's Hospital pharmacy, I couldn't deny his thousand-yard stare into another land, another planet, another girl. A girl he'd been seeing for months, a girl he'd met at a nightclub. He was light-years away. Light-years away from the life-changing experience of the birth of our son. I knew pregnancy had made me an outsider to him, a strange, black-haired girl with the gall to have a baby with a man who hadn't promised her a rose garden, and his only dream in life at this point was to join a band called The Morning After Girls and tour the world as far away from me as he could get.

But I still had hope. I hoped Karl's far-away look would fade and his close-up look would come back. I hoped he'd stop wanting to go out. I hoped he would start wanting to stay in. I hoped he'd be a good father. I hoped he'd be able to stay with us. I wanted to make it work.

Without hope, dear reader, I couldn't have gone on.

I bought my first supply of nappies and a disposable Kodak camera to create my own colour family snaps while Karl gazed off into the distance, cold, troubled and sad. It seemed a million years since I had been romanced by him through the gravel-coloured shop windows of the Indigo bow teek.

After eleven years, Karl and I had exhausted our firestorm of love. Worn out, defeated, exhausted by the fumes of our own self-destructive romance, what we had left were tainted scraps, the substance of our true love extinguished. We didn't know it then but we surely know it now – instead of loving each other with the nectar from a rose, we pricked each other with the thorns.

38

I'm a Mother. Forever!

The most astounding, haunting, triumphant, anxious day of my life will remain 25 October 2001. Paradoxically, just one week later I would experience the most astounding, haunting, triumphant, anxious day of another life – my brand-new life as a single, working, career-driven new mother.

Laid up on a cot bed in the birthing theatre at St Vincent's, I was numb from the waist down and yet my legs appeared to be thrashing from side to side. I had no control over them. In fact, my entire body was moving with jerky, sharp jolts, tossed from side to side. I was bouncing like a tennis ball served by the great Federer himself.

The anaesthetist bent the rules, allowing me to wear my make-up armour, my survival-kit ensemble cleverly hidden under a white sheet. Seven nurses were fussing and laughing at my cherry-red lips, pale goth foundation and powder, black kohl eyeliner and glittering showgirl lashes. My sixteen shimmering, glued-on fake eyelashes delighted the nurses even as they burned my eyes. My hope was that the glamorous disguise would convince my soon-to-be-newborn son that I was a real mother and not some dreadful imposter with no clue as to how to induct him into the World of Motherhood, according to Alannah.

To be fair, the nurses had every right to laugh uproariously. I was about to have a baby. I wasn't Ronald McDonald, and the birthing centre was not my own personal red-carpet runway.

The nurses told me in their good-morning singsong voices how motherhood changes a woman, how lucky I was to be having a baby at thirty-nine and how lucky-lucky-*lucky* I was to have such a gorgeous man by my side wearing black-fly sunglasses inside a *birthing theatre.*[45]

'You're so lucky, Alannah! You've got everything now. Who gets everything? You've got it all, haven't you? Oh, you're a lucky duck!'

I couldn't speak.

I hoped the joyful nurses in their uniforms would see through my mask, that I was in the middle of an anxiety attack engulfing my soul, and at the same time, I hoped they would break into a fully choreographed rendition of *Swan Lake* in full Black Swan costume. Or even a tap-dance routine.

Only half an hour earlier, a kindly nurse had injected my freckled white back with a spine-tingling lumbar block, promising me the bottom half of my body would be numb for years to come. Long meaningful glances and soothing, hushed words of comfort were whispered in the hope of convincing me that there *was* a real baby growing inside me.

'Now when the baby comes out, Alannah, you can hold him but he'll be very bloody. I mean, new babies are covered in blood, you know that, don't you?'

'I have heard that,' I heard my voice say. 'I don't really have time to hover around the hospital, nurse, so as soon as my baby is born I'll have to be getting straight back to work. Let's just hurry this birth along and I'll be out of your hair before you know it. Nurse, *nurse* … can you come back here a minute? I'm sure that lumbar block hasn't worked, I'm sure

45 Hiding a hangover from the night before.

I can feel the lower half of my body! Could I *please* have another lumbar puncture? Just grab that big needle, nurse. I'm not numb, you see, and I'll feel the knife slicing through me. Are you sure Dr Judy knows how to surgically remove babies growing inside women's stomachs?'

'Your baby will be crying but that's a good thing, Alannah! If the baby cries we know it's healthy, we like to make sure the baby has two arms, two legs, a heart and a good pair of lungs for all the screaming and all the crying. Now, your husband – would you like him to join us?'

Staring straight ahead, I asked for a Valium as the kindly nurse asked: 'Are you having a boy or a girl?'

'Can I have three Valium?'

'No, you'll be *fine*!'

'Maybe a Diet Coke … ?'

You're *only* having a baby. People do this all the time!'

All the time? I thought. *Really? All the blooming time? Why?*

'Did you feel that, Alannah?'

'Feel what, love? Did you stab me?'

The sound of my voice frightened me in the acoustically treated stillness of the theatre.

'See, you're numb! You won't feel a thing, Alannah. We'll just open you right up and your baby will be perfect, no pushing, no pain. It's much better for you this way, much safer. You won't be able to drive a car or lift the baby for six weeks. You will be really, really sore and uncomfortable. You won't be able to bend, sit down properly, or move. We also advise complete bed rest for ten days here at St Vincent's and another fourteen days of rest at home. You OK with that, Mum? Heh?'

No. No. That wouldn't be good for me at all, but at the very least, I was a numb soon-to-be mum.

I dared not let them know my only wish was for everyone to leave the theatre room until time started its clock again. I was numb, dumbstruck, overwhelmed and terrified. I could see no future, no past, while everyone around me was crashing into each other and laughing, nattering about their weekends and how very lucky I was.

And that is how, in the dreamlike, dramatic twilight of a birthing theatre, my little heartbeat baby arrived. There were no high-stepping *Swan Lake* chorus lines, no tap-dancing routines and —

All my fears magically vanished when Dr Judy placed E on top of my chest.

When your child is born, time changes shape, jumps the rails, moving slowly, fast, slowly, fast; you're constantly losing track of what time really is. There is never enough time, however hard we try to hold on to it. Becoming a mum doesn't change us so much as violently refurbish us, forcing naive girls to become caring, considered, well-adjusted adults. Overnight.

Karl began taking photographs with the new camera. The camera whirred and spluttered, and I think I started to cry. The team of baby experts told me that soon I would be filled with milk, and my anxieties tripled.

But I couldn't deny the part of me that left a ripple effect, a feeling that I couldn't quite place – a deep melancholic wonder at my brand-new son. From the moment E was born, I was born, and something changed in me forevermore.

I was a mother, forever.

I think both women and men have to make a conscious effort to accept being a parent. If one parent cannot accept that their life has now changed course forever, they often leave without really understanding why.

A week after E was born, Karl left.

He packed his bags and four CDs, poked his head into the bedroom where I was breastfeeding, and in a high bass-guitar voice sadly said:

'I can't do this. I'm sorry, but I just can't. I want to join the band. I've got to go, just let me go. I'm not leaving E, I want to see him. I'm leaving you, Lan. The thing is … I'm not in love with you anymore.'

I heard a thousand banshees screaming. I realised they were my own banshee screams.

'Are you *fucking* kidding me? Fucking hell, Karl, you're making a big mistake —'

and

'It's a fucking *great* time to tell me you don't love me anymore. Mum was right about you —'

and

'I'll make it work, Karl … please … I can make this work. You can't just leave … please?'

I may have kicked him, dear reader, as he slip-slip-slipped through the Victorian double doors of my apartment.[46] I held my breath and stared at the back of his head, watching him until he disappeared altogether.

'Get a nanny, Lan. I never promised you a rose garden …'

All I had left was the roaring feeling that I should have seen this coming. He'd warned me. I didn't have anyone, but I had my little baby, and so I started to care less.

Whenever I read a mother's writing about her love for her child, the juggling of her career, the what ifs, the what nots, the judgemental view we adopt if we see a mother smoking, I have to remember to stop dead in my tracks. To *stop* and make the conscious effort not to judge them, for none of us have any idea what other mothers go through; we have an inkling, a bright spark, but to walk in on another mother's life, even for a moment, doesn't give us the right to impose our thoughts on what

46 To be honest, dear reader, I *did* kick him! I wanted to kick him in the head but that was impossible with E in one arm, my sixty-nine stitches, and the worry of the door closing in on me.

a good mother is, what a bad mother is, what a great mother is, how to be a good mother, how to be an ordinary mother.

At times I wanted to tell my parents:

I'll show you, Mum and Dad, how to raise a child. I'll show you what a loving parent really does for their child, I'll show you how to become so exhausted from shrinking yourself to suit your child's every whim, every demand. I'll give him everything you didn't give me and …

And then I would stop.

I understand how hard life was for both my parents. Parents who, through poverty and bad luck, fell into a life with five children they didn't know how to really care for, five children they had no idea how to love.

I realise now the only thing that matters is love. If your child feels loved you've won half the battle. Becoming a mother didn't change me, it *made* me. I may have given E life but, in return, he gave me new life. Being a mother is filled with anguish, joy, guilt, rejection – and no matter what, your child comes first. *Am I working too much, am I staying home too much, will I be replaced at work by rushing home to feed my baby, will I hire a nanny? Will I* not *hire a nanny? What does a nanny do, anyway? And how the hell am I going to manage work, life, a newborn son?*

How? How? How?

I feel the gigantic mistakes I'm still making and I've been forced to curb my inquisitive ways. I now understand how easy it is to look the other way, because saying no to a teenager is like negotiating with a member of ISIS!

I loved staying home with E in those early weeks in our flat in St Kilda. I breastfed, soothed and fell in love. I would spend hours staring at E sleeping. I snapped a million photographs and purchased my first pair of runners. Tiddles the cat was jealous and ran for his life. I bought an obscene little breast pump that pushed Karl further away. I showed E off to everybody. I couldn't believe the hospital allowed us to actually bring him home. Didn't they know I simply had no idea?

I felt a little rejected by everyone when I had E – people didn't seem to be interested, except for Bernadette. If I was overseas or travelling for work, Bernadette would be right there for E, sometimes with the help of a nanny. I saw my sister nearly every day for the first thirteen years of E's life.

Mum didn't even want to travel to Melbourne when E was born. I had to convince her when E was six weeks old that she'd be well looked after and that everything would be paid for. 'Please just come!' I said. 'Fly over and see your new grandson and me, Mum.'

And she arrived.

Mum's views on babies, children, and how to parent had not changed since she was a young mother. Her visit was a real struggle for me. Her short temper was impossible.

After three weeks, it was decided I should go back to work. I redesigned my Alannah Hill office into a pampered nursery and installed a beeping berserk baby monitor. E slept like a perfect mute angel. Just like I'd imagined, he was beautifully quiet, gorgeous and serene.

Crying and shrieking, more like it, dear reader, crying and shrieking! Colic had set in. I struggled to stay awake and struggled to sleep. Knowing I'd be unable to perform at work at tip-top level was worrying me and keeping me awake. I wanted my career and a baby. I just had to figure out how.

39

The Giver, the Taker, the Flame-Throwing Faker

I knew the emotional torrent of my childhood would provide decades' worth of material for a psychoanalyst, psychologist, counsellor, psychiatrist type.

I knew exactly what Mum would say: 'Oh Lannaaah – you're so self-absorbed, dear. NO ONE wants to sit and listen to you wailing on about things you can't even remember, Lannaaaaah.'

I couldn't trust a stranger. I didn't know how anybody could ever fix me. I had already decided that I'd run several rings around anyone who tried to run rings around me. The only kind of fix I wanted was a quick one. I was too busy for therapy, too busy with my baby and my fashion career.

Therapy, I understood, was looking inwards, but I wanted to look outwards, into the light. I was afraid of my own bedtime, terrified of my hallways and their dark shadows. I was running away from dark thoughts and I wanted to put as much distance between myself and the dark thoughts as possible.

I knew how to pull myself up, I'd done it countless times before, but, dear reader, I had been dropped. Dropped from what I'd fooled myself into thinking was a serious relationship with a man twelve years younger than me named Moses. I'd seen the break-up coming … and yet I'd allowed the whole disaster to unfold right in front of me. I was inconsolable. I didn't seem able to look after E, I couldn't drive a car, I couldn't eat, I couldn't sleep, I forgot to feed my cat Tiddles the Third.[47] I forgot how to stand up or how to lie down. I could barely speak. I grew a foot shorter. I was crushed like a misshapen loveheart run over by a ten-tonne earthmover. I had morbid nightly thoughts of topping myself. My ungovernable subconscious ran riot and nobody knew what to do with me – even I didn't know what to do with me.

So I took myself off to a land called THERAPY.

Dressed up in my favourite polka-dot Yves Saint Laurent vintage '60s silk frock with a pair of mismatched lace socks inside my sky-high heels, I sat on a small wooden chair watching time disappear like a party princess on death row. I'd fled my crying-girl apartment in an emotional rush to make my very first psychologist's appointment on time, my hairdo styled crookedly with a black lace Dolce & Gabbana scarf that faintly suggested mourning and trailing a new fragrance – one that seemed strangely familiar: Calamity of Love.

I'd spirited all my learnt wisdom to kingdom come, but what seemed to be hurting me the most was my own unbearable truth – the truth that I should have known better, that I hadn't listened to my Oprah Winfrey inner self. I could feel Oprah looking at me, her outstretched fingers pointing at my broken heart with a rolling of her eyes, lips pursed with chronic disappointment. Dr Phil was seated beside her, both nodding at the love-struck fool who'd been warned that her fantasy of a serious relationship was just that. A fantasy!

As far back as I could remember, I'd been wary of becoming intimately entwined with any sort of man. I could flirt for hours in dimly

---

47 From the age of twenty, I'd had three different versions of Tiddles, each one identical to the other. Every time a Tiddles passed on it would be replaced by a duplicate Persian tabby. My love for Tiddles never changed, as it was always the same cat to me.

lit nightclubs and bars, but only within a group. I could flirt with cats, dogs, mice, lampshades, babies, grandmothers, paintings and girls – I was known as a mischievous little flirt but in all honesty, dear reader, I was faking it. Faking it until I felt the man I was flirting with might actually desire my Channel 9 dancing-girl body, and then I'd run at light-speed for safety, first to my spinster bedsit and now to my overstyled apartment.

I knew enough about myself to understand the power men could wield over me if they found out that my coquettish charm and beguiling nature were merely defiant camouflage to protect my own mongrel self. I'd even developed a tremor of sorts upon seeing men's clothing hanging alongside my femme fatale silks in a hidden velvet wall, my kind of wardrobe. Men's shoes reminded me of my father's so I hid my loved ones' shoes; their shaving equipment reminded me of my father's razor so I hid their shaving equipment too. I also hid any signs that I found any of this even slightly berserk!

But mostly I'd been wary of becoming dependent – because becoming dependent on a man meant diminishing myself.

And now here I was, waiting.

Waiting on a little wooden chair in a 20-watt-lit hallway, with a broken lift and a broken heart, at the top end of Collins Street. I threw my broken heart and shadowed-out-me into the small office.

'I can't eat, I can't sleep, my sister has taken my phone from me, she just took it off me! *Just* because I called him eight times yesterday. Eight times is nothing! His phone surely must be broken. He didn't pick up so I called twice more. He didn't answer any of my calls, which is so strange! Isn't that strange?'

'Alannah. I understand how you feel.' The therapist was tall, with a weathered, handsome face and piercing watery-blue eyes. 'A broken relationship is like a death, a grief that you feel will never pass. I promise you, these feelings will pass. It will take time, but they will pass.'

I stared at him hoping he could see I was in trouble.

'Alannah, do not underestimate the powerful effect your childhood has had on your life. You've suffered trauma, a trauma not many people could recover from. A catastrophic childhood that programmed you to believe you were not worthy of love.'

'But I am very lovable, I think? Are you telling me that Dad didn't love me because I'm unlovable? You *are* telling me that, aren't you?'

There was a high-pitched squeal, far off in the distance, the unmistakable sound of my mother's voice penetrating my unlovable self – she wouldn't care for this kind of psychobabble.

'Are you STILL talking to strangers about your father, Lannaaaah? And now you're seeing a SHRINK, Lannah? He's seen you coming, Lan! He's seen how you waste money on men, and new kitchens. That therapist is going to suck you dry, Lan. He'll take ALL your money and then you'll see just how GULLIBLE YOU REALLY ARE. He's laughing all the way to the bank, Lan.'

Despite this internal racket, the shrink was still trying to fix me. 'Your important emotional needs were not acknowledged or adequately responded to. You saw that your parents appeared to be overburdened in some way, unhappy and grief-struck themselves. You might have tried to become an invisible child, so as not to place any demands on them, or risk incurring painful repercussions for having any needs of your own.'

I have no idea what I looked like as a small child. As Mum enjoyed telling me whenever I asked, very few photos were taken of my parents' five children; there was no camera in our family house, no photo albums, nothing. If photographic evidence counted for anything, my childhood appeared to have never actually happened.

I tried to explain my views to the handsome therapist. 'I know all about the givers, the takers, the narcissists, the enablers, the dependent-personality disorder, the compassionates, the legacy makers. I know *all* about that vibe, but I don't quite believe in any of it because when the chips are down, we all fall into the puddle of giving up everything we've learnt, all our wisdom is lost no matter how tall our ladder of success; and there comes a time when all the movers and shakers of this world end up sitting in a psych's office off their heads with feelings of low self-esteem, regret and failure. Now I know all this, so why can't I put what I know into practice?'

'Alannah. A childhood cannot be replaced. I can't "fix" you. I wish I could. What you were deprived of is never going to come back; you can never get your childhood back.'

'You mean, do you actually, really mean that I'll never know what a loved childhood feels like?'

The room filled itself with hundreds of balloons, all ready to pop. The game was up, I had no more tricks left to play, no more cards to ace him with – I was a polaroid picture fading with time, my childhood fading right along with it.

'But Dad told me, he told me before he died that he loved me! He must have loved me a little bit? And when I do take Mum's calls, sometimes, sometimes she ends the call with "I love you, Lan" ... I'm sure I've heard her say that. I have, I *have*!'

More silence.

'I'm sorry, Alannah. That time has passed – you have to stop living in your head with your mother – it's time to let her voice go.'

And my point, dear reader, is this.

In my better moments on this earth, I understand that we are all responsible for our own lives. We can blame other people, we can lift the lid on our FBI files and expose all the people who've hurt us, but in the end the decision and the drive to forgive and evolve are ours and ours alone. I was broken over a man, a man who wasn't a bad person, a man who hadn't meant to hurt me, but hurt me he had. Broken hearts, broken promises, broken spirits – we all carry within us broken parts, feeling the same wounds afresh every day.

After I was dropped, I was celibate and single for four years. The wound was too deep. But I was happier in those four years than I'd been for a long time.

Slowly, with every ticking of the clock, every passing moment, I began to come back to life, like a patient on the ER table, ready to live, love and be hurt all over again.

Without love, without taking the risk of a new love, we allow ourselves to die a little. There is no time to sit around waiting for someone to fix us, to save us. We have to be willing to take responsibility for our mistakes and our own broken hearts. We carry the past within us wherever we go and whoever we're with – but if we're aware that through understanding and forgiveness we can forge a gentler and more serene future, the sooner life can begin again.

The two years I spent in therapy were the first time I'd ever been given the validation that my childhood had split me in two, that I was doing the very best I could with the melancholic knowledge that we can never truly start afresh.

I remember my therapist's last words as I slipped from his rooms, never to return. I believed I was finally fixed and so I was going to drop him, via text message.

'Alannah, you can't build a castle on a crumbling foundation and expect it to remain intact.'

And so I left my therapist. I broke up with him before he had a chance to break up with me. I stepped out into the clinic's dimly lit hallway, powdered my nose, glossed my red lips and, wearing my sky-high

Valentino shoes, I skipped out into the warm afternoon. My polaroid childhood memories were bleaching into a vanilla cream beneath the power of January's brightest sunbeams.

As I drove back to work, I couldn't deny what I was unable to erase from my faded childhood. I could still see the dark outline of a freckle-faced girl, who would always remain etched on my retinas.

I just had to learn to not let her haunt me.

40

Boom Boom Boom

Did I *ever* tell you about the time I bought myself a dream home in a suburb I couldn't afford? *Really?* Are you *sure* I've never mentioned the $5 million dream home I bought back in 2010, the one in South Yarra? It's gorgeous. It's huge. It's Boom style![48] Right opposite Fawkner Park. How *odd* I didn't mention it, because there was a time that I could *not* shut up about it.

Purchasing the Boom-style mansion was one of the moments in my life when I felt like a cat with cream all over me. Toorak Road West was an address I had only dared dream about. I could have *never* imagined buying a house that possessed such beauty and charm.

E and I had been living in a rooftop garden apartment in the old French Embassy on St Kilda's Fitzroy Street. E, full of boy curiosity, quickly became obsessed with the comings and goings, the stabbings and the hopeless sad scenes at the nearby Gatwick Private Hotel rooming house.

---

48 From 1875 to 1892 Victorian houses changed to reflect the prosperity of the gold rush. Boom! The style resembled traditional Victorian in form, but was grander and more ornate, incorporating part of the Italianate and filigree styles of private mansions for posh girls, like me.

One morning, on our way to school, a man barely able to walk staggered past with a knife embedded in his forehead, droplets of crimson blood falling onto the footpath. To innocent eyes, a man with a knife in his forehead dripping blood was a new kind of superhero, and E ran toward him, informing me that I'd better get cracking on 'who the hell this new superhero was'.

In the seven years we lived on Fitzroy Street we were robbed three times while we slept. On another occasion, two ice addicts broke into the garage and created a bonfire, incinerating my vintage dress collection. I didn't feel safe on Fitzroy Street anymore, weary of being burgled.

The final straw came early one Sunday morning. I woke to a man and woman screeching through walkie-talkies in the dark, in my hallway. I flew from my bed, instinctively hiding E with a blanket. I stumbled into one of the voices and realised he couldn't even see me. His mouth fell forward over his lip and what was left of his nose was a festering sore. I took a risk and pushed him toward the front door. Surprisingly, the man ran down the stairwell, shouting, 'Real bloody sorry to have scared ya, forgive me, lady. Will ya forgive me? Gotta smoke, love? Fuck you! You're a fucking bitch so FUUUUCK OOOOFFFF!'

Between fabric appointments and gossiping with Quoc and Hanh, I explained to David Heeney that living alone on Fitzroy Street with a young child was beginning to frighten me. I trusted David to help get us out of there. We both agreed it was best if I moved to a real house with a pool and a garage in South Yarra.

Business at Alannah Hill was at fever pitch; it seemed I could do no wrong no matter how hard I tried. I was kicking goals left, right and centre, and with the glittering rewards of the Spring Racing Carnival galloping toward me, the brand was at its best. I was privately triumphant that I was the It Girl of the Spring Carnival with all my hats and frocks. Cup Week trading was bigger than Christmas, and the AH fans would often have to form a queue to select their Derby Day outfit and matching ribbon-inspired hat.

David agreed on a new head office for the Alannah Hill brand right next door to Factory X. And for the love of God, why not? I had spent twenty years building the brand that bears my name, and with David's business savvy and capital, mixed with my creative vision and drive, we had ourselves a winning formula.

Boom!

The day of my Boom-style auction dawned pink; sunlit clouds drifted across the pale-blue sky – I even saw a rainbow. It was agreed I wasn't able to be trusted to bid without fanfare, so I had a devil's advocate, who bids quietly for others, showing no emotion and giving away no tricks at pricey auctions. E and I waited loudly in a cafe. An hour later the phone rang and *boom*, my devil's advocate told me I had won. I had won the blooming castle! It was mine.

What I didn't know was that my beautiful $5 million castle had seen me coming, had waited patiently for me ever since I was a slip of a Tasmanian girl.

Back then, I had been told by strangers and even 7-Eleven managers that if I lived in South Yarra or Toorak I'd be made for life. People would respect me; property lawyers would want my business, and I'd be addressed as Lady Hill Muck while I high-heeled it through the wide leafy streets wearing heart-stopping outfits. Back then, I'd stalk those wide leafy streets of Toorak with plucky courage, a pair of Kate Durham earrings and the hope that the silent eyes staring through small keyholes held some kindness toward me. If I spied a mansion that took my fancy (usually a castle with a tower and a Mercedes in the driveway), I would knock tentatively on the achingly beautiful door and – incredible and dreamlike as this may sound, dear reader – my Boom-style mini mansion was one of the private homes I'd doorknocked thirty years ago.

And now look at *meeeeeeee*!

I was Queen of the Castle.

There was only one glitch. The mortgage was a staggering $23,000 a month ($775 a day). But with assurances the colossal amount would be well and truly covered by profits from the AH brand, I was, in two words, beside myself!

I imagined draping myself in a 1940s silk kimono, half-asleep, half-awake in my elderly twilight years, reminiscing about my colourful and marvellous fashion life, how far I'd come and how *filthy* rich I was.

The very day I was given the keys to my castle in South Yarra was also the day that the first supernatural seeds of doubt were planted in my mind. I parked my black Onyx Mercedes on the kerb of Fawkner Park, the peculiarly spooky triangle of rolling green meadow studded with beautiful trees, which lay opposite my home. Autumn sun teased out the colour from the flowerbeds lining the garden path to the front door. With the tingling sensation of entering a whole new chapter in my life, I keyed open the lock and stepped inside.

The air was dusty and fell tinted into the hallway through a leadlight on the landing of the staircase. The house looked so different from when I'd seen it before the auction. Without the realtors and other prospective buyers, whose pleasantly inane chatter had lent it an air of familiarity, I no longer felt such cosy familiarity as I walked into the beautiful downstairs salon. I sat on a velvet-adorned ledge by the glamorously gloomy bay windows.

Suddenly, I felt something, a presence, an untouchable, unseeable presence shadowing my every move and suffocating all my thoughts.

I blocked it, refusing to allow anything to disturb this particular moment. I walked into the back garden to the tiny poolette sloping next to the triple garage. It was a sunny, windy afternoon and a soft light danced on the gently rippling water. I wanted to know what it felt like to lie poolside on a banana lounge in the house of my dreams in South Yarra.

At high school in Tasmania, possessing white skin with freckles was a mortal sin. Maude Brumby, the most spoilt girl in high school, was rumoured to own an Olympic-sized swimming pool with banana lounges set up alongside for all the sunbathing. I remembered my attempts to sunbake when I was a girl, hoping the results would soon see me reclining on a poolside banana lounge at the Brumby home, where Tony Howard told me once that he could smell the money as soon as he walked in the front door.

In my 'if only' girlhood world, I'd imagine my skin caramel brown. Determined to find out if all my freckles could join up to become one brown freckle like a caramel butter, I once lay down under a Hills hoist in the backyard of the milk bar and began the baking of my skin. My father, for some reason, had stored secret bottles of mutton-bird oil in a cupboard in the laundry. There were five bottles of the inky goo in total, and he poured one of the bottles of black goo all over my back while I dared to sunbake on a towel. And then he made an announcement:

'Get out of the sun! You're only going to freckle – you're as white as a ghost, Alannah, and now you're sunburnt.'

Perhaps there was part of me still wanting that rich-girl tan, but on that first day in the house of my dreams.

Boom!

I was falling and falling and fell and fell, accidentally, somehow, into the pool. I splashed to the edge and hung there, shivering, in my sopping cardigan and dress and Prada heels. I knew I'd been pushed, or rolled and thrown. I turned around and looked at the house towering above, shuddering from head to foot.

On that breezy day in 2010, I bought a $5 million haunted castle. I had never been superstitious, never even purchased a TattsLotto ticket, and I didn't buy into the phenomenon of the new-age vibe. But at some points in our lives, many of us have intuitions and visions that neither science nor the Bible can explain.

I wish I could write that I simply had *no* idea of what was to come, but somewhere inside my heart, I always knew. From the first day I stepped inside my blue-chip castle, I wasn't just paying the colossal price of a South Yarra mortgage, I was also paying the price of a colossal illusion, an illusion that would dissolve into a future where, in less than three years, I'd be forced to sell my South Yarra mansion, the one I could never stop talking about.

Boom!

Boom!

Boom!

41

Coming Apart at the Seams

I laid my battered brain on the plumped-up crisp white pillows of the Westin's hotel bed. I didn't seem able to control my pounding head. My pounding headache, along with a toothache, a stomach ache, an ear ache, a leg ache, a heart ache, a worry ache, a life ache … I was painfully aware that I'd said something irreversibly irreverent and wrong.

Through the window, the giant hands of the clock in Martin Place, Sydney, reminded me time was moving, and there was no turning back the hands of horror to restart my day. In moments of uncertainty, I resort to the one thing I know offers relief, even if only for a short time – reapplying my make-up. It quells uncomfortable feelings, almost like a cigarette for a smoker. Reapplying gives me the kind of inner strength I need to soldier on, and silences the noise in my head – if I can see myself in the mirror, I must be real. As I reapplied, I attempted to drink a Diet Coke, but I didn't seem able to swallow. There were twenty-eight messages on my phone urging me to face the music, a chorus of woe reminding me that I had wronged. But all I could do was remain still, like a mute, berserk doll.

I *thought* I knew women. I *thought* women knew me. I thought we had an understanding.

And yet the headlines were already written:

ALANNAH HILL GAFFE
HILL HORRIFIES WOMEN'S GROUPS
DESIGNER ALANNAH HILL'S BIZARRE SEX-SCANDAL OUTBURST
HILL HASN'T A CLUE

With all of my wins and the global reputation of the Alannah Hill brand, the sleepless nights and the giddy successes, I'd found myself making an ill-advised quip to a wall of fifty-plus cutthroat journalists, along with several TV crews holding giant cameras and lights, on the red carpet at a very special fashion event.

I understood I had let down an entire legion of women who looked up to me as a role model. I admired and respected my customers. I loved meeting them – the joy I received from styling customers in the Alannah Hill stores was heart-stopping. Through my tornado-black eyeliner, I would spy mothers, daughters, aunties and grandmothers tiptoeing toward me, whispering to each other. Sometimes there would be a newborn bundle of joy in a woman's arms. 'Alannah, I called my baby Alannah!'

These women would tell me their stories: stories about how a dress they'd bought from an Alannah Hill bow teek had snared a divine, loving and spectacular husband; or how one of my frocks had allowed for a spectacular entrance into a divorce court, and how empowered the woman had felt high-heeling it across Lonsdale Street wearing an ornamental Alannah Hill divorce costume, four lawyers by her side.

I believe women want to feel special, otherworldly, beautiful, magical and magnificent. I love making clothes for women and girls, the flame always flickering when I styled a customer in a pansy-print Sunday Afternoon Tea frock, with three AH cardigans to match.

I thought I knew women, but on that day in Sydney, I got it completely wrong.

It was the day of the 2010 David Jones Fashion Show, one of Australia's premier fashion events. A chilly wind whipped around my legs, as I waited outside the hotel for the David Jones driver to collect me. I loved the David Jones fashion shows.[49] Alannah Hill the brand had been sold in DJs for close to a decade, and the big fancy bosses at DJs treated their 'Australian Designer Fashion Family' with red-carpet tiptop service, including business-class tickets to fly from Melbourne to Sydney, front-row seats with your name inked in calligraphy on the back, a pick-up and delivery service with your very own chauffeur, and a special showbag holding tiny cans of hairspray, a lipstick, a David Jones fashion magazine and – if you were lucky – a small sample of Christian Dior perfume.

My driver had dropped me at the doors to the actual David Jones store where I'd been told to meet the other designers. David Bush, the head of fashion at David Jones, and Colette Garnsey, DJs' group general manager, were waiting to greet us. I liked David Bush a lot. He had taken to wearing no socks with a black Prada shoe, and we'd mull and dissect each other's state of mind on the red carpet. We used our affection for each other to fan our anxieties while overseeing everything and everyone in our field of vision, including surveillance of hemlines, who was dating who and how my collection was selling in-store.

Colette Garnsey, her make-up expertly applied, spoke to us, the David Jones Australian Designer Fashion Family. Dressed in Akira

49 To my mum's dying day she could never understand why I didn't step out to a Catholic mass with Mr David Jones or why Mr David Jones wasn't interested in marrying me! 'Oh Lan, who IS this David Jones man? Why can't you get him interested in you, Lan, dear? Flaunt yourself, Lan, you know how to flaunt yourself, dear. THROW yourself at Mr Jones until he throws you a BONE, dear? He might SPURN you, dear, but try harder, SUCK HIM DRY, Lan, take him for everything he's got!'

Isogawa, Colette was sporting a million-dollar diamond on her left finger like a miniature chandelier, her hair flawless, with threads of lilac and silver rose creating a glistening halo of queenliness. 'Don't say a word to the press. They're looking for a story today. Distract them. Do not allow yourselves to be tricked into saying anything about Mark McInnes. Of course, we're very sad about what's happened, but here at David Jones we are your family, we keep our heads up, we're proud, we're strong, we have a great team and we will get through this.'

I hadn't read the papers that day. I was far too busy preening myself in the Westin, taking twice as long as I used to to look half as good.

The designers were ushered through a white curtain to a red-carpet floor space in the shoe department of David Jones Sydney, but I couldn't find anybody to walk by my side through the white curtain, beyond which I'd spied a wall of photographers and journalists holding up the front page of a newspaper. The front cover of every major newspaper in the land showed us exactly what we were walking into, a sea of newsprint on David Jones:

DAVID JONES SUED FOR $37M OVER SEX BULLYING
THE SEX SCANDAL ROCKING DAVID JONES

I was the last doll standing outside the white curtain when the gallant Alex Perry came to my rescue. He'd arrived late but he offered me his arm and in we swanked together.

Nearby, Carla Zampatti was speaking to journalists in her marvellous accent, musing like a professor on the meaning of colour, the semiotics of a perfect black cocktail dress and the honour of being Carla. Carla's head was bowed, her tall angular body holding in everything that had ever hurt.

'Carla, you've been selling to David Jones for almost a decade. How do Kristy Fraser-Kirk's allegations affect you?'

'Black,' she replied coolly. 'You simply cannot go wrong with black. A little black dress can work from day right into the evening. A black clutch and a pair of pearl earrings are the only accessories required for a cocktail dress. Black, of course!'

Seamlessly, Carla moved to her private seat among the A-list crowd.

Suddenly, I was surrounded by the savvy society journalists, all talking at once. Usually in an interview situation, my mind would become a fizz of headaches. I'd beg the interviewer to ask me anything as long as it wasn't about fashion trends. I knew my words would hold nervous, unplanned soundbites. I tried to be funny and wicked, even irreverent. Anything to distract from the real questions about being Alannah Hill.

'Alannah! Alannah! Look, it's Alannah Hill!' excited journalists cried when they spotted me. They saw me coming; I wish I'd seen myself coming.

'What can we expect on the catwalk from you this morning? What will you be presenting? Will you have dancing girls? Where did you find the inspiration for your collection?'

Nothing. I had nothing. If I opened my mouth I didn't have a clue what might pop out.

'Alannah!' a gossip columnist snapped. 'What about the Mark McInnes case? The alleged sexual harassment?'

'C'mon, Alannah,' others were saying. 'What's your take on these thirty-seven million dollars?'

I faltered, I stuttered, I fumbled, and out came my unruly words. 'I wish he'd touched me up. I threw myself at him! He told me he didn't want to mix business with pleasure …'

And there they were. My ill-informed words.

Alex Perry elegantly tried to breeze through the conversation. Speaking of trends and colours for the following season, skirt lengths and supermodels, he was soon drowned out by the raging alarm bells in my ears. Dread was swirling all around, and just for a second I felt suspended in a black space, everything far, far away and terribly unimportant, and then I blinked, and I was back within myself, standing on the red carpet in the fallout of my very public mistake.

I spied an empty seat beside the editor of *Marie Claire*, Jackie Frank. I didn't know her very well – I didn't know many people from the Sydney fashion scene – but I needed to sit down and talk to somebody.

'Jackie, I think I may have said something a little untoward out there on the red carpet? I wasn't too bad … I hope people understand I was just trying to be funny … I was nervous with all that thirty-seven million dollar carry-on.'

All the light left Jackie's face, her eyes clouding over with several storms.

I was a little frightened of Jackie. She was a proper grown-up woman running *Marie Claire* magazine, and I was beginning to feel like a scolded schoolgirl.

'I said, I *said* … I wished he'd touched me up, that I couldn't *believe* Mark had rejected me! It was a joke, Jackie, a stupid joke! I was trying to stand up for Mark, I always liked him …'

I felt a shrinking sensation as Jackie tapped me on my red silk frock and told me to watch the show, that she'd speak to me after. I had begun to sweat, which made my hair flop, which in turn made my entire self drop. Horrified at the thought of anyone seeing my make-up panda-smudged with tears, I made my exit, hailing one of the DJs drivers waiting at the end of the red carpet. Within minutes I was back in the eerie silence of my room at the Westin.

I wished I'd had the time to explain to Jackie that I often felt imperfect and unreal. By the time I reached Sydney Airport I was on a Channel 9 loop – the ill-fated words that fell from my mouth spinning backwards, toward me and all around me.

That evening in my business-class seat back to Melbourne, I pulled all my phoney fingernails off while watching my media mishap on the cabin's TV screen. When I landed, I found the media camped outside my house. Despite being told to ignore them, E waved them in. He was delighted we finally had visitors and invited the crews from Channel 7 and Channel 9 to join us for Maggi noodles and mini Magnums. I had to shoo him away from the probing cameras and shut the curtains as calmly as I could.

The question the journalists asked the most was, 'Are you really sorry, Alannah?'

Yes, I was truly sorry.

But I couldn't say what I was really sorry about. My tongue was tied. I had been gasping it inside myself for so long I didn't know what I was sorry about. What was I sorry about?

I was sorry for all the unjoined girls who live in the darkness.

I was sorry I didn't read the mood that day.

I was sorry my flippant remark had hurt people.

I was sorry I had let *down* women and girls who looked *up* to me.

I was sorry I wasn't more grown up.

I was sorry I wasn't more normal.

I was sorry I didn't know what being myself meant.

I still didn't know how to tell anyone my dark secrets. I just knew it wasn't time. Not yet.

42

Freefalling

Dolly Parton's gigantic hit from the movie *9 to 5* had been on repeat in my car for years. It was my exhilarating theme music, my upbeat music, reminding me I was a winner, working nine-to-five. Dolly's tune always promised me hope, hope of a glittering prize or a gigantic trophy waiting for me on my desk at Factory X.

I'd been making the journey to Abbotsford along Punt Road for fifteen years, listening to Dolly in all her hopeful, sugar-coated glory. While I drove I made scrappy little notes in my diary, notes on my new collection, fabric reps I needed something from, comments regarding the online store, pattern lists for Quoc.

I'd been working nine-to-five for thirty years. Now for the first time, I suddenly wanted the car to turn itself around and transport me home to the safety of my South Yarra castle, back home to E, who was being cared for by Olivia, our multi-tasking nanny/PA/friend/housekeeper. January was E's school holidays and the guilt was stifling.

Home, Work, Child, Career: I thought of one when I was busy with the other. I was freefalling into fashion hell and all I could do was hold on for dear life.

In the six months since the David Jones incident, the workplace culture had changed and I needed to change with it. David and I were like a couple on the verge of a painful and bitter divorce, but I knew I could never leave. The personal cost and loss of my reinvention would kill me.

Karl had been working at Factory X for several years as founder/designer of Jack London, a '60s British-style mod-punk fashion label. The day David poured a glass of champagne and told me he was setting up Karl as a fashion label underneath the Factory X umbrella, I nearly passed out with indignant fury. Right next to my crown. Karl was now working in an office 5 metres away from me, and I could *not* actually believe it. At first I kept to myself and only waved to Karl when I spied him walking past, but our love for E slowly edged us toward lunch, once or twice a week. We'd natter over a sandwich, me talking wildly about how E's life was going. If we were having 'work issues', we'd gossip and swap stories. Sometimes I'd even offer advice on a Jack London design. And somehow, I made it work with Karl 5 metres from my desk.

In those days, I still had a deep connection with Karl. I don't believe that connection can ever disappear; how can it when you've created a life together? The lifeblood flowing through us connects us to our children. The hearts of small children are such delicate organs and so, for better or for worse, I pretended for a decade to be a family.

I thought we'd stay friends. But life's hurts, jealousies and mistrusts often get in the way. Karl and I had very different views on how to co-parent. We had different views on how to raise E. We had different views on always putting your child first. We stopped agreeing on things we once agreed upon. We stopped being friends because we couldn't agree on anything.

43

Confession

The day of Mum's confession was the twenty-sixth of December 2010. I was back in Ulverstone on a fleeting three-day Christmas break to see Mum. It was a frostbitten morning and Mum and I were nattering together wildly to warm ourselves up. There was a crack, a break in the glassy grey sky and feeble rays of dawn light were shining through. Our nattering began with me making Mum a cup of scalding hot tea, hoping she wouldn't ask me to rub her swollen purple feet.

I often wonder if destiny or perhaps a black angel preyed on Mum's smoke-filled train of thought that day. She stared right through me, sipping her tea, smoking, patting her head, whispering, nodding and holding her rosary beads close to her chest. Mum told me she had known all along that Joseph had molested me on that train years before. She told me she couldn't bear to admit it, even to herself – her Catholic upbringing and her belief in God would not allow it – and she sobbed like a real mother telling me how often she was paralysed with shame, fury and regret. Mum's shoulders shook with remorse, dark storms moving across her face. The moment the words were spoken, I saw Mum cry like a little girl who'd just lost a puppy or a doll.

When Joseph, who still lived at home, hovered anywhere near the lounge room, Mum screamed at him to get out and stay out, and to stop looking at me. I could do nothing more than offer Mum my pale hands, telling her it was neither her fault nor Joseph's – he was slow and he'd needed comfort. I told her I understood Dad had been a cruel, neglectful father to Joseph and that Dad's cruelty had caused Joseph to act out. I was there, I was there, sitting on that train with him. He had taken his comfort along with whatever was left of my childhood with him that day.

I consoled Mum, but very quickly she began asking questions about the exact details, what he'd done, how he had done it, what it felt like. And in a split second she plummeted further. I understood Mum's cries were for everything, everything that had ever happened to her, but also she cried for my childhood, which she said must have ruined me. I lied. I told her it wasn't so bad.

I didn't tell her that from that day on I was a sitting duck, and that when I was a girl, after the incident on the train, I didn't know if it was night or day, morning or afternoon. The old man who took me horseriding, the babysitter's uncle, a man who had taken me to the country when I was fourteen years old for modelling sessions – I had been molested by all of them. I didn't tell her that I misread men and they misread me. That I would find myself in situations with the wrong men, missing signs that I was in danger. I thought the look in my eye was a confident blaze, but I misread that, too. Some men saw it as a wayward glaze.

And how from that day on, I had no clue what was normal.

I didn't tell Mum any of that.

I told her if it was anyone's fault, it was God's doing.

She calmed down, but became emotional and excited when she remembered the tartan jacket my brother had thrown over me while he snatched my heart out of my body.

'Oh I know that JACKET, Lan. I KNOW that jacket. That was THE jacket he threw over you? It was your FATHER'S jacket, Lan. Why didn't you STOP him, Lan? I wonder why Bernadette wasn't on THAT train?'

I remember sitting in the fallout of poison smoke from her sixtieth cigarette and telling her that I didn't know the answers either.

44

Where Are You, Mum?

And then Mum died.

She died suddenly.

Alarmingly.

Unexpectedly.

A Red Cross nurse found Mum on the floor where she'd collapsed beside her bed. She had been dead for two or three days. The nurse thought Mum was taken by a heart attack, a diabetic fit perhaps, but in rural Tasmania autopsies were not performed on seventy-one-year-old diabetic women with three heart attacks behind them. Mum had willed herself into ill health. She'd had diabetes, sciatica, a nerve condition and a lifelong drilling headache.

Mum died alone in her smoke-filled bedroom. She was wearing a stained, loose cotton nightie that I'd given her years earlier, her gold-cross chain hanging limply by her side, her mother's blessed-by-the-Pope rosary beads wrapped tightly around her still and silent fingers.

When she died, I hadn't spoken to her for one month.

To telephone Mum was an act of courage, for I knew her hilariously negative comments could sweep me into oblivion. Telephoning Mum at any time was dangerous. If she sensed fear, if she glimpsed my vulnerability, any sense of hopelessness or fragment of fragility in my words, my entire day could be blown into a million little pieces. Mum would prey upon the faintest traces of raw emotion, investing them with her fierce energy until they were blown up to movie-screen size and projected onto my head for the entire world to see. After such a call I would be left exhausted, depleted, my free-floating anxiety falling heavily on my shoulders.

'Hi, Mum!'

'Oh no, Lannah, what's WRONG now? What's happened? What have you DONE now, Lannah?'

'Nothing, Mum, nothing, I was just ringing to see how you are.'

'Oh NOOOOOO! What HAVE YOU DONE NOW, dear? Have you been SACKED? How's that little shop you work in? Have you gone broke? What HAS HAPPENED? Is it E? What's WRONG with him? Why aren't you speaking to your sister? You're never in the magazines anymore, Lan, dear.'

The conversations were so wearying. I told Mum everything she wanted to hear, because the colossal energy it took to try to override her drama was never enough.

'Oh, Mum! Everything is *terrible*! My new boyfriend, Hugo, doesn't really love me. I *will definitely* go broke and lose everything and, you're right, Mum, E is *so* spoilt and he walks all over me. Just like you said he would. I can't make anything work, I haven't got a clue how to manage life, Mum! Not a bloody clue! How's your health, Mum?'

Mum was always *very* pleased with my negative tone, although in the next breath she'd tell me how I had ruined her day and how she'd have to lie back in her recliner and worry herself sick. That *all* her illnesses were signs that she would die very soon. And so I served it up to Mum like a sweet cherry pie, a packet of Peter Stuyvesants on top for good measure.

My calls to Mum were infrequent, rushed, histrionic. I knew she was lonely, haunted by her past with my father, troubled by her five children who she felt had all disappointed her. She lived with a small dog she had found on the side of the road, a hopelessly annoying dog that she didn't really care for, often kicking it out of her way and screaming at the ball of fluff to get out from underneath her feet. Her ludicrous dogette sat draped around her neck, suffocating under the haze of cigarette smoke.

I'd neglected Mum as I felt she had neglected me, but in a hairdressing salon at 2 pm on 4 March 2011, I made a very big decision. I would telephone Mum a little more often, perhaps even enquire after her health and her dogette. I vowed not to talk about myself in our future phone calls. From now on, I was going to be a good daughter with no resentments. If she told me E would end up in jail or become a famous actor, I wouldn't react. If she told me I was working too much and that I should come home, attend all the Catholic church services and work in the local newsagency, I would agree with that too. If she told me my hot rollers didn't work on my kind of apple head, I would not holler back. I wanted to see if I could make Mum happy, and it was about time I stepped up. There was only one problem – nothing seemed to make Mum happy.

I called five times that day, expecting to be assailed by outraged gasps and hysterical dramatics before I'd had the chance to say hello. But Mum didn't answer. Five times and she didn't answer? Where was she? Mum was always home. She never went anywhere.

Where are you, Mum? Why won't you answer me?

I told myself there would be an explanation, and that on some fundamental level everything would be alright. But of course I was kidding myself: nothing was alright nor would it ever be again. With the passing of my mum, a critical link to the past had been broken, along with the hope that she and I might achieve a real understanding, reconciliation or mutual redemption. Our story was frozen in time by the velocity of her death, all our words were now left unsaid, forevermore.

The nurse said Mum's hands were reaching for the Red Cross button installed above her bed, right next to her very special religious picture of the Last Supper. Knowing Mum's hands didn't reach that button, and imagining her terror as she realised she was condemned to die alone, made me want to rip my immortal soul from my body.

I know in my heart I wasn't the best daughter to my mum.

I know in my heart she wasn't the best mother to me.

But nothing prepared me for the despair and complete devastation I felt when the call came.

I was at work, choosing buttons for a velvet jacket, when my phone began ringing, beeping as if possessed. I kept ignoring it until finally I saw a text from my sister with the words: *CALL ME NOW LAN*

A distant, thundering howl galloped toward me at light-speed. Bernadette answered my call, her voice, the *sound* of her voice: it was the voice of the saddest girl in the world. I held my breath in the hope that maybe Mum's dogette had died.

My sister's words were muffled and yet brutally clear. 'Lan, Mum died! She *died*!'

And I fell and fell and *fell*. I tried to calm myself but I hollered out a scream, my voice unrecognisable to my newly motherless self. Nothing can ever prepare you for the news of your mother's death. It penetrates the heart with a burning arrow of sorrow and sometimes scorching regret. My world went black. I went black. It was the blackest day I'd lived.

I watched the crystal buttons spilling and tumbling like dice into concrete nothingness, remembering my last conversation with Mum, at Tokyo's Narita Airport.

'Mum! I *have* to go. They're paging me, Mum! They're *paging* me!'

My mum's last words to me were mocking, ironic and sad. 'Oh, GO ON then! GO ON THEN! NO ONE is paging you, dear. Who'd be paging you, DEAR? WHO? You're not a page? Why are you saying PAGING, dear? Whose PAGE are you on?'

I had called her while thumbing through insane fashion magazines. Mum, ever so funny, ever so mental and ever so alarmed that I was in Tokyo with Karl and E. We mocked Karl out of his earshot, we mocked what he was wearing, we mocked the airport, we mocked me, we mocked my brothers, we mocked ourselves stupid, we mocked and mocked and *mocked* until we both cried with laughter. I made her laugh even though she was cross with me for a hundred things, and she told me so.

I turned myself into a question mark on the floor, as my assistant grabbed tissues and I begged her to go and get help, go and get David, get someone! I sat in my office crying so hard I thought I'd never stop; I thought everything that meant anything to me was disappearing at such a fast rate that I simply wanted to lie down and never wake up.

I stared out through the gloom of my million-dollar office to the empty Abbotsford streets below; the leaves were grey, a slight rain was falling and I could see people smiling as they made their way back from lunch. Someone laughed out loud at a joke downstairs and my heart shrivelled to the size of an apricot stone.

Karl drove us both in silence back to the South Yarra haunted castle. He didn't know Mum, he'd met her only once. Karl seemed able to appear as though he was too cool to have feelings, and so he seemed like a paper bag blowing in the wind, empty and stiff and yet able to be carried along by the slightest breeze. I don't believe anybody is capable of not having feelings.

My new boyfriend, Hugo, was sitting at the pink onyx kitchen bench – I didn't want him to watch me falling apart, and so instead we hugged and I fell apart without him even knowing. I felt awkward and absurd. Bernadette and I sobbed into each other. E, Karl, David, and John Cain, a silent business partner at Factory X, were all gathered around the bench.

Cliché after cliché after cliché was thrown around that pink bench, and I couldn't seem to stand up, speak, drink, see, hear.

'Oh, she had a good life. A good innings! You didn't like her anyway. Did you?'

'Now you don't have to complain about not being loved. She's dead. Death silences everything.'

I sobbed out that I *loved* her, that I had *loved* her all along and now she was gone, and I'd be dying soon as well, I could not live without her voice. Now that Mum had gone from 'is' to 'was', all bets were off.

E stuck a handwritten Post-it note on his forehead and sat on Hugo's knee, his Post-it note staring back at me:

I am so sorry for you, Mum. You will miss your mum and she will miss you too.

45

The Funeral

My sister and I flew back to Tasmania, with our soaking tissues and morbid glances leaving us both looking slightly unhinged. I didn't think it was a good idea for E to travel to the Apple Isle. I knew I'd need him. His love. His little heart-shaped self. But he'd only met Mum a few times. He didn't know my brothers. And his mother and aunt were too grief-stricken to look after him. In times of trouble, Karl always took care of E, with me calling three times a day to hear his sleeping breath.

We had been checked into the emergency row. The air steward took one look at us and smartly moved us to seats in the middle of the plane. She knew we could barely save ourselves let alone the twenty others on board.

It hurt to smile.

It hurt to cry.

It hurt to breathe.

We'd been making this trip to the Apple Isle for almost thirty years to see Mum, and both of us knew that this would be our last trip back home. There was nothing there for us anymore – Mum's empty recliner chair, her dressing gown hanging from the doorknob, the cigarette ash piled into pyramids. Mum now existed in another dimension, her very own mother's group of despair.

I was about to face the brothers I'd barely seen for thirty years.

My three brothers presented themselves to my sister and me at the front door of Mum's house – brother against brother, sister against sister, each one suspicious of the other. Only Martin seemed quite pleased we were all together. I instructed my sister not to allow Joseph anywhere near me; if she saw him within a metre of me, she *must* insert herself between us, and if he tried to talk to me she had to stop the conversation.

Joseph had already disposed of a trailer-load full of Mum's clothing, ordiments, shoes, her worn-out op-shop handbags – they were all at the rubbish tip, he informed us.

'Bunch of bloody rubbish it was. Just a *bunch* of rubbish!'

Mum had not wanted a funeral. She'd told me this many times over. 'Just let me go when the time comes, Lan. I do NOT want a SOUL at my funeral. I DO NOT WANT a funeral, Lan, and I don't want those ghastly people stickybeaking at you, looking at you and taking you all out of twist. They'll ALL be laughing at you, Lan, LAUGHING LAUGHING LAUGHING at what you've got yourself up in. I don't want that, Lan, dear!'

My sister didn't want me to speak at Mum's funeral but someone in the family had to. Nobody else wanted to give Mum a eulogy and so I insisted. She finally agreed and told me I could speak but she was to oversee every word I wrote. My emotive words were scribbled over and crossed out, reducing my eulogy to two pages when I'd originally written six. I wasn't permitted to say this, I wasn't permitted to say that, how dare you write that, cross that out, put that in, cross that whole page out, don't fan your face like that, don't speak in that voice.

Finally, after a heartbreaking five hours, my sister had words written for me that she was happy with. I had something I was very unhappy with.

Mark, my oldest brother, sat in Mum's tattered chair, the fluorescent kitchen light falling across his face. He was angry with me for upgrading Mum's funeral. He told me I was a fucking idiot for changing the coffin to a lined coffin, a fool for ordering more food, an idiot for ordering expensive flowers. I knew to shut up. He owned a Harley-Davidson, and a pit bull terrier that rode along with him. Part of me knew that he was right. Upgrading Mum's coffin and flowers would never stamp out my sadness and guilt. Ordering more food wouldn't bring her back either.

On the morning of the funeral, I stared at my motherless face peering back at me in Mum's tiny bathroom mirror. I had slept in Mum's bed, wrapped in her dressing gown. I knew my dress was too tight, my shoes too high, my chandelier hairdo far too extravagant for a rural funeral in Tasmania.

We waited at the church for my brother Mark to arrive with his two children. He sent a text message moments before Mum's funeral started. The message said that he wouldn't be coming.

And he didn't.

I'll never understand why.

My brother said he had his reasons and I'm sure, in his heart, he did.

Mum's coffin gleamed enigmatically in the eerie modern church, raising more questions than answers.

Mum had been dead for forty-six days.

A knock at the door, a caustic email, a raised voice, movement in the park across the road from me, any interruption panicked me. Time held little or no meaning. It hung in the air like a sharp axe waiting to fall while I stood ashen and heartbroken repeating, 'Please let me die, please just let me die'.

I knew I had enough sleeping pills to kill myself. I had researched the subject thoroughly, as the shame of failing at a suicide attempt was one final blow I knew my pride could never take. In fact, I had an entire auto-euthanasia kit beside my bed and drew comfort from this late at night. I would flirt with the Xanax box, staring at the mauve tablets, forty-eight of them. They would stare back at me, friendly but neutral.

I busied myself with E, making cups of tea with four sugars, watching his Scotch Finger biscuits slowly disintegrate in the hot sugar hit while *SpongeBob SquarePants* screamed full blast from the television screen. On mornings such as these my only words were 'Can you turn it down a little bit, love? It's a bit *loud*, love! It's *very* loud, E, please *turn it down*. You know I cannot stand the sound of *SpongeBob*, E!'

It was excruciatingly painful to keep going, to place my feet one in front of the other, to see any kind of objective or goal when everything was so empty of meaning. For days I lived on the leftovers of my morning hot chocolates – cold hot chocolate, too sweet even for me.

I woke in the night looking for Mum in the sad drawer, where I keep all the saddest memories from all my saddest days, searching my two photo albums for images to keep her close. I slapped myself and took endless baths, but nothing helped. Nothing helps. Guilt mixed with remorse mixed with fear mixed with love mixed with loss ... this is the worst taste of all. The pain is sharp. It's excruciating. It's hell on earth.

The worst night came upon me like the devil. I'd felt it stalking me since morning broke. Mum had been dead for 56 days. I flopped into a 7-Eleven and bought Diet Coke and a takeaway chicken dish. The meal stuck in my throat and made me vomit. I looked at the clock – it was only 4.30 pm – and I fell, I fell onto the floor, deafened by my own deep sobs.

I gave myself two hours to stop.

In two hours, I told myself, I would stop crying.

I cried all night.

My friend Natalie came to visit one early evening. Nat had worked at Alannah Hill for years and had also been E's nanny. Nat knew me, understood me, and we sat in my overstyled lounge room, uneaten takeaway Indian food at our feet, watching three minutes of video footage of Mum. I'd wanted to film Mum and her thoughts on the world. She was eccentric, odd and irrational, animated by that soul-scorching cruel streak I never could defend myself from. Mum didn't know that a phone could film, so I'd hold the phone up and ask her questions:

'Oh look, Mum. Kerri-Anne Kennerley is on *The Today Show*. I dress her sometimes, she loves my clothes, you know, Mum, her stylist *always* rings up for clothing.'

A long, silent stare from Mum, cigarette poised, the dog snarling at me from around her neck, Mum's dressing gown pinned with safety pins as she reclined in the new reclining leatherette chair I'd just bought her.

'Oh GO ON with you, Lannah. You DON'T dress Kerri-Anne. She wouldn't wear YOUR clothes, dear. Why would she wear your clothes? WHY? You don't dress her? Where are you then, Lannah? If Kerri-ANNE is on the TV, where are you? You DIDN'T dress her today. If you'd dressed her TODAY she'd be wearing your clothes, and I NEVER see your name on the credits. EVER!'

I zoomed in a little closer, trying to capture Mum's expression, always forlorn, quizzical, distressed and highly amused at the same time. I thought she was making a joke out of me; she couldn't take me seriously. I wanted Nat to see my little video, so I let it keep rolling as I interviewed Mum, teasing out her sharp-tongued commentaries of doom.

'Poor sods, your father treated you all so badly. What a terrible life you all had. You were lucky to get out, Lan. You did the right thing by going, dear. What ARE you wearing, LAN? Show me? Go ON! Show me then?'

And I prance-asized around her, delighting her with fully choreographed circus moves and my breasts, which were still pert and sat high on my body.

Mum stared and ordered me to turn around so she could have a better look.

'Not BAD, Lan, NOT BAD! You're doing well for a forty-eight-year-old, dear. I was a size six, you know. A size six! What are you going to do today, LAN? There's NOTHING to do here, Lan! Are you going to wear that COSTUME today, LAN? You can't go down the street like that, Lan. Why don't you go down the street and see if you can get some looks? Don't go DOWN the street, Lan, there's NOTHING down there, nothing to do here, no ONE to see, but go down the street and get me some smokes, Lan. I bet the town will take a good long look at you, Lan – I'll hear ALL about it tomorrow! Everyone will tell me, Lan, that ALANNAH HILL was down the street, but don't you SAY anything to ANYONE.'

I had made such a scene out of Mum over the years – to deal with our history, I had transformed her into a tragicomic genius.

'Isn't she funny, Nat? Can you believe she doesn't believe I dress Kerri Bloody Anne?'

Nat paused and looked at me curiously.

'Look at her, Lan. Watch your mum closely, she loves you. Look at how she sparkles when she talks to you. Your mum loved you, Lan. She *loved* you! You brightened up her life.'

I looked from Nat back to the video. I could almost see what Nat had seen, I could almost see that she *did* spark up when I gave her attention, but I denied it all the same.

'No, Nat, she didn't love me. She didn't! She barely came to visit, Nat, she didn't even come and see me right after E was born.'

After Nat had gone, I seriously considered the uncomfortable thought that perhaps I'd had it all wrong. I watched the video until dawn broke. I zoomed in closer at the part where I twirled for Mum, showing off my body, watching frame by frame, trying to see what Nat had seen – the birthday-candle sparkle in her brown eyes.

My mother, for five seconds, had stopped smoking as I twirled. I could see the look of a mother's love suspended in time, I saw the longing of a mother for her daughter, a love she never dared know, the love of a mother living with intolerable sadness. The floorboards creaked; I heard the sounds of my dear E's feet coming toward me. He threw himself into my lap, his arms wrapped tightly around my neck.

The next morning, I flushed the Xanax box and its forty-eight lilac tablets down the toilet.

My mourning had only just begun.

46

Roman Candles

After my mum died, Hugo invited me to join him in Italy; he believed something true and mind-altering could halt my tears. He hoped that by intoxicating me with his parallel life in the spectacular Eternal City, where true and wild beauty lingered on every romantic and abandoned building, in every fourth-century church and every underground city, my Mum tears would stop.

And they did, for a little while.

I fell in love with the magical Italian light, the countless medieval towns in all their faded glory, the nobility of romantic Italian art, and of course the fact that *La Dolce Vita*, one of my all-time favourite films, was made in Italy. Hugo flung open thirteenth-century door after thirteenth-century door, revealing a world of museums and churches that put a spell on me. I limped in all my choked-up Mum regret through the hills of Umbria and along the Amalfi Coast, swimming with Hugo at wild beaches with black pebbles in Sardinia and where the currents meet on the island of Sicily.

Hugo convinced me to dive right under the water. I wore a dress, a slip, a bra and a pair of Spanx in the water but *still*, I went right under, head and all, something I'd never been able to do. For the first time in my entire life, I felt comfortable enough to actually dive into the terrifying sea water, head, face, body and feet ... and I didn't even mind when the last skerricks of my make-up were washed away by a giant wave at *least* two feet tall.

Hugo was on a musical tour through Europe, performing show after show after show in Italy. He had a reputation for being difficult, prickly, an Ernest Hemingway–esque romantic, dramatic musician, often on tour in Europe. Could I have found myself anybody more perfect? Mercurial, aloof, distant, moody but intoxicatingly attractive to me. Perfect!

After Karl, my romantic commandment had been to bathe in the delights of being single, and I consciously went suburbs out of my way to avoid any man associated with rock music. A man carrying a guitar is a man who can really be alone. A man who often needs to be alone.

In April 2010, I'd received a wry, shy, poetic text – it was from Hugo Race, who I'd first met on the *Dogs in Space* set and hadn't seen for twenty years. His text message was so superb that I may have forwarded it on to several people to dissect, made detailed notes on his mental state and begun a campaign of tracking him on every social-media app available. The text message did not contain one spelling mistake, he used expansive words that I had never seen written before, and it was 230 words long! And just like that, one evening Hugo was standing in my kitchen. But it wasn't the Hugo I remembered, the one who'd been in Nick Cave and the Bad Seeds, the Hugo that was in *Dogs In Space* with a speaking role: it was a battered, older, broken-hearted version.

Perfect.

I was helping him understand about loss, and that feeling helpless and angry was sometimes a good thing. Hugo had been dropped (by a much younger woman). He hadn't been dropped before, and he was forty-six years old. The feelings Hugo was experiencing often took days to torture from him. He had not changed. I fantasised that if I could make a broken-hearted guitar man love me … my God, I could rule the world! Like Oprah!

And we fell in love, over love letters.

Hugo was so blinded by love lights he failed to see the flashing amber lights beaming secret warnings into his heart. I had shown him the version of myself where I was a marvellous independent woman who could accept his career and travelling to Europe to live a parallel life for four months a year, sometimes even six. I'd even convinced him I was practical, reasonable, non-argumentative and that I drank red wine![50]

My fantastical little mirage, where I was simply perfect, was the fantastical illusion I showed Hugo. And he fell in love a little bit harder. I was the perfect girlfriend! We kissed in the canals of Venice, got lost in the deep fog of Milan and watched the sun set over the Eternal City from the balcony of the Hassler Hotel. But I limped around hotel lobbies, feeling my heart shrinking with the loss of that voice inside my head: Mum. The almighty voice that now lay silent. Grief is oceanic and subterranean. I felt raw and guilty. I wanted Mum back and I didn't know why.

And Hugo waited in churches in Rome while I lit candles for Mum, he waited in churches in Vatican City while I lit candles for Mum, he waited in churches in Umbria while I lit candles for Mum; there were so many churches, I ran out of candles.

Hugo sensed how I had unconsciously pulled the strings over his guitar eyes, and that I'm not the perfect girlfriend after all. The moment I feel humiliated, shamed, jealous or wronged, hurt, sidelined or ignored, my fury can light up all the Christmas lights in the world. But men can be

---

50 I was still drinking Diet Coke and was desperate to like red wine. Even a drop of the red wine makes my head giddy.

very sensitive, and as soon as I hear the sounds from a thousand machine guns triggering memories from my childhood, I have to remember to count backwards from ten.

I understand I bring the spirit from my past with me like a floating contagion. I know my mistakes and believe that without them, I cannot be a kinder, better version of myself. I like to believe, dear reader, that I no longer behave in such an immature and destructive manner (well, maybe once or thrice!). I have learnt over time to try my best not to overreact, to simply observe and let the feelings wash over me.

And after two weeks of candle lighting in churches it was time to come home. I was pining for E and grieving for Mum.

Hugo waited patiently for my grieving to stop.

I didn't know how to tell him grief never stops.

47

The Last Waltz

I knew something was wrong when Dolly Parton's '9 to 5' stopped working for me. Everything that had been a strength of my brand was suddenly a weakness. I was a little threadbare, frayed and tattered to be the face of the Alannah Hill brand, and I was compromising the empire by the fact that I *was* Alannah Hill. I needed a makeover. A *Woman's Day* article on Kerri-Anne Kennerley's fabulous new makeover was pushed across my desk. I needed to be cooler. I needed to be 'out there more', *out* there in all the right places, and not just staying at home. I silently agreed. Kerri-Anne looked smashing and I was a little bit jealous.

Heightened fear is a different kind of fear. It holds a great deal of power and clings to us with all its heightened glory and, just like Glad Wrap, eventually it suffocates its victim. With a red-carpet flourish and a perfectly manicured hand, I welcomed 'heightened fear' in like a long-lost baby shower.

It does not work well with feelings of zen, or spirituality. In fact, it nukes all of our more *delightful* feelings and concentrates on the negative parts of our personalities and psychodramas. I had been running away from my issues at work, E's drama classes and basketball lessons, school trips, the Alannah Hill VIP events, and attempting the impossible – attempting to be an intelligent, fun, focused and well-adjusted mother, and at the *same* time, a mysterious, unavailable, cool and 'happening' girlfriend.

I worried I was a bad mother. The small number of other mothers I came into contact with seemed to be doing a marvellous job of being a mother, making sure their children's emotional, educational, psychological *and* social needs were all being met, while I worried about whether I was too gentle or overly lenient, and that I wasn't teaching E how to be socially conscious or spiritually aware. I catastrophised over what school to send E to, I catastrophised a little bit more about whether my delivering him a Scotch Finger biscuit with a Kit Kat *on a side tray* would come back to haunt me in E's teen years. I didn't feel I was giving E the best start in life, so I made up for it by giving him everything. Easy!

But if I were to tell the *real* truth, dear reader, I felt pushed aside at work, disrespected and marginalised, with a sinking dread that I had run out of options. I was finding it harder and harder to adapt to the constant changes. Often I'd leave work early and hide in the Gold Class cinema. I tried working from home, but felt more excluded. I was planning my upcoming European Inspiration trip and working on next season's dresses, but with the constant turnover I often didn't know who the strangers were in my weekly team meetings. I was spending more and more time alone in my work space, staring into the void through falling autumn leaves and absent-mindedly searching for dress patterns.

The brand meetings were now informal cold wars. Consultants from chain stores such as Cotton On, Blue Illusion, Target, David Jones and Myer, new smiling assassins, were brought in to mull over and dissect what the problems were within the nerve centre of the Alannah Hill brand.

Everything had changed. Stores opened without my knowing, as did an online AH store, an eBay store and several factory outlets. An Alannah Hill make-up line was apparently on its way from China, a diffusion line on its way from China, swimwear on its way by boat to an Alannah Hill bow teek I wasn't aware was opening. A lawyer informed me months later that my name was in the process of being trademarked for alcoholic drinks like Alannah Teenies.

I was always angry, lately. Furious. I was blowing up at David (if I could find him), running toward his silence, demanding to know how many dresses I had to design for the Spring Carnival and why, *why*, was I suddenly taking instructions from my sample machinist?

I was dragging my friend and great supporter Andrew Majzner from Paper Stone Scissors into meetings with David. Andrew did everything he could to explain to David that I hadn't compromised the Alannah Hill brand with my David Jones remarks and lack of judgement. But David wouldn't listen. I was a blocker and he'd made up his mind that I was slipping. And blocking.

Sebastian – my assistant, good friend and E's godfather – explained on the telephone one day that I should get a doctor's certificate to prove the amount of stress I was enduring. I had never obtained a doctor's certificate, but I respected Sebastian and listened to his advice.

I sat opposite Dr Rooney in his cramped fluorescent-lit office. I wasn't listening to my GP's concerns about how stress, childhood trauma and a feeling of not having any control, can be catastrophic. I was waiting for him and his worries to finish, and to hurry up writing my certificate and a script for Valium.

Dr Rooney had seen me through my darkest and finest hours, offering medical help for stress, depression, anxiety and, once, for a broken finger. He wanted me to stop, to stop everything I was doing, but I refused. I couldn't stop. I wouldn't stop. The idea of 'stopping', the very thought of stopping, was a completely alien concept, and I was aghast with anybody who dared tell me how I should just stop.

'Yeah, yeah, yeah, give me the certificate and script, Dr Rooney, I really have to go.'

The next morning, I gave my doctor's certificate to a Factory X receptionist and, with blatant disregard for the medical news inside, I worked throughout that day. When I arrived home the same evening there was a work email in my inbox. I could go back to work, according to the email, when Dr Rooney thought I was well enough.

My doctor's certificate simply said I needed a week's rest. But I never went back to work, and I was not prepared for the ending when it finally came.

There were no goodbyes, no death-defying wails from the lipsticked pouts of the Alannah Hill girls paralysed with grief over my departure. No matter how many moments pass, no matter how many years come and go, I'm yanked back to this one event, this colossal and gigantic moment where I said goodbye without really saying goodbye.

On 15 August 2013, I became unemployed.

Factory X would continue to operate the eighteen Alannah Hill bow teeks nationwide. They would continue to operate the Alannah Hill David Jones concession stores. I would not design for, or have any further input into, the brand that bore my name.

I left Factory X without a button, a zipper, a piece of floral fabric, or a friend. Everything I had worked for belonged to Factory X. All I had left were memories, and I think we all know, dear reader, that often, memories are not enough.

48

Mortality

I fear death, dying and funerals. Priests and clergymen often say if you fear death, you fear life.

I like to imagine death is terrified of *me*. I've been known to wear death like a scowl across my face in the hope that I have the power to push it as far away as possible. I am not good with death, dear reader, and cling to the illusion that somehow, for some swivel-eyed reason, I will not be able to die: instead, I'll fall gracefully into a new category called

The Un-die-ables.

A doctor once told me that I should pinpoint the part of death I feared the most. He asked if I was afraid of death or if I was afraid I'd die a long lingering, painful, lonely, manic, feverish, berserk and *pointless* death. The doctor went on to enquire whether I was afraid of leaving my only son or, *perhaps*, I was just afraid of dying alone. Maybe I worried that I'd wake during the cremation service, burning alive with a dozen or fewer people filming it for a morbid American YouTube channel. Or, *maybe*, my death would just be swift and empty. The truth is, dear reader, I fear death and pretty much everything that goes along with it.

We live in a world of screens. Each morning insanity takes over and unthinkingly we all reach for our phones, our iPads and iPods, news bulletins and loud music darting into our minds before even a moment of acknowledgement of the shocking truth, that one day:

You and I are going to die.

My eyes looked at the bedside clock: *still* 4 am. Fuck! I swore into the clock's antique face and stuffed three more handfuls of M&M's into my wide-awake mouth. Sleep was impossible, murderously impossible. I swore again, dangling my legs half-heartedly over the cold floorboards. I wondered if staring at E while he slept would stop the agony. I hovered in his bedroom, waking up Jack the dog sleeping by his side. I stared at E for a long time but it didn't help. Nothing helped. I left a kiss on his warm cheek and hurried out before he caught me crying over him. Frozen in the silent hallway, I wondered what to do next. It seemed all I could do was stuff M&M's into my mouth and bawl my eyes out until I felt some sign of relief. Back in my sleepless room, I snuggled into Hugo's sleeping back, wet mascara tears smeared across his skin.

I catastrophised that I wouldn't be able to sleep *ever* again. Steven Jones Hyphenated Evans, the man who had influenced almost every decision I had made for the last thirty-five years, had been told he was going to die.

Bladder cancer

Incurable

The bullets ricocheted through the right side of my brain.

Bang

Bang

Bang

Steven and I cried over the telephone. He said he might be dead within six months, a year at best. He told me he was going to 'beat it', which made my heart skip a beat.

In the sad drawer, I found a black-and-white photograph of Steven when he was seven years old. I rarely open the sad drawer, especially since Mum died, but something compelled me to explore its treasure trove of shrieking horror, hoping this would somehow send me back to sleep. It didn't. Steven was smiling crookedly into the camera, his seven-year-old self already disconnected, charming and possibly already dying. A rush of memories from our decades-long friendship scattered through the thin dead air. I knew there was something wrong with me because, sifting through the sad drawer, I could only think about one person:

Me

Yes

Me.

In the mid '90s, Steven had moved to Sydney, and was now married, with three children. I missed our friendship, as he was often overseas in faraway countries designing feature films and he wasn't one for idle internet chatter. I saw Steve as family, my first real love, and although I didn't *quite* understand what family love felt like, I knew any bad news about him would impact heavily on my life. I had not expected the news about Steven to be so catastrophic. I don't think anybody did. I couldn't accept that Steven was going to die – if he could die, then I too could die just as easily. I pushed thoughts like these away with almighty force, hurling myself toward any kind of God, silently praying:

Fix this fucking nightmare, immediately!

Steven had stage-four *incurable* cancer. And here I was obsessing over how his death was going to affect *my* life. Steven couldn't just up and die. He was accustomed to irony, intelligence and distance; cancer was accustomed to mercilessly annihilating without guilt or remorse.

Something had to be done – the cancer cells were on the move, snaking their way into his bones, lymph glands and vertebrae. The surgeons had already removed one of his kidneys, but the tumours continued to perform their ghastly ritual rebirth situation, which forced cell after cell after cell into a new and very bleak town – Tumour Town.

Steven's cancer reminded me of my father. A father I knew was still impacting on my life but a father I barely thought about. My father's rewritten history when he'd retired had come as quite a shock. Who the hell had he turned into? I knew he didn't want to die. I had tried to talk to my father about his own death and whether he was frightened, but he wouldn't talk. He *couldn't* talk. He was too angry. He wanted to start his life all over again. Hearing his sorrow about his life was unbearable. His life was not the life he had intended for himself. And now he was dying. He had run out of time. Just like Steven.

Cancer and my mother had reduced my father to a shell. The brick house in Ulverstone became a cancer war zone, and the glory days of Dad conducting the '1812 Overture' a shrieking whisper from the unlovable, unlivable past. Dad lived on a liquid the colour of ink, marked *Morphine*, drinking bottle after bottle, lining the empty bottles up on the windowsill. Mum hovered in the background informing the neighbours of how my father had *not* lifted a tea towel in weeks and how he was *deliberately* making his cancer worse by smoking and sleeping and being lazy.

'Jimmy! Pick up that tea towel you just dropped on the toilet floor! How DARE you drop a tea towel on the toilet floor. How DARE you! You're as lazy as a foal, Jimmy! As LAZY as a foal!'

Mum was now 'completely in charge' for the first time in her life and she wielded her power until my father crumbled.

'Aileen, for God's sake, please STOP ... STOP, Aileen ... why are you doing this?'

Mum told me she didn't know why she couldn't feel anything but anger and resentment toward my father.

'I don't know why I CAN'T LOOK AT HIM, Lannaaaaah! God's PUNISHING him for being a rotten father and a terrible husband. I told your father YEARS ago that God would punish him! I gave your father FAIR warning! And now God IS punishing him. Not me! GOD is!'

Mum was brutal. And I looked the other way. I looked the other way and I blamed everybody else.

When we were much younger, Steven feared he would die in *agony* from an incurable arty disease, and we'd both laugh at how he wouldn't reach fifty, long dead from this 'incurable arty disease'.

And now, I started to believe I'd planted the seeds of his untimely death, a death Mum confirmed the day I introduced them on our 'Tasmanian Tour' of the North West Coast in 1983.[51] Mum, upon meeting Steven, immediately gathered a stockpile of black irony and, sitting in the fallout from her thousandth cigarette, she asked Steven questions. Questions where she turned all the answers into riddles.

'And Steven Jones Hyphenated … what do YOU do for a crust?'

'Ahhh, Aileen. I'm just a *filthy* art director.'

Mum spun herself right around to face us head on, two cigarettes blazing between her fingers.

'An art director, Steven, an ART DIIIIRECTOR! A FILTHY old art director! Well, GOOD for you, Steve, good for YOU … an art DIRECTOOOOOR … ?'

Mum's eyes darted and sparkled while she pondered Steven's job title. I wondered when she'd rise up like a histrionic phoenix, dashing all future hope for everyone. *Hurry up, Mum*, I thought, *time is slipping by*, and suddenly, there she was …

---

51 We even dropped in on my nan in Hobart. She took an immediate Catholic dislike to Steven. She blamed him for dislodging a tube of Blue Loo that became stuck in the cistern of her toilet, and she never quite forgave him!

'An art-IS-tic directooooooooor, Steve? I don't THINK that job's going to take you very far, Steve dear, you're a bit of an English Pom spending ALL THAT time at university and then WASTING all your time at UNIVERSITY … Lannah tells me you DIDN'T manage to finish your UNIVERSITY studies … WHAT A SHAME! You know you haven't got any REAL credentials, don't you, Steven … you can't even cobble together a chair. A FILTHY art director … oh DEAR!'

The rain pelted against the kitchen windowpanes. Steven was busily focusing a Super 8 camera on my younger brother, Martin, filming the back of my brother's head for an arty film he was making, *Deliverance 5*.

'Steven, you KNOW what's going to happen to you, don't you? You'll get nowhere with that stupid art job, NOWHERE … and you haven't got a DEGREE so you'll never ever ever ever EVER have a hope of making it, Steve, you'll be a forgotten old pensioner – an old CODGE! Lan, he is SMOKING! SMOKING, at YOUR age, Steven … if you keep on smoking, Steve, you mark my words, you will DIE! You're headed for an early grave, and when they slice you open, you know what they'll find? CANCER! You'll be riddled with it! RIDDLED!'

And we all laughed and laughed and laughed.

Four oncologists all said the same thing – *terminal*, incurable. Steven's left arm was held inside a green sling. If his arm wasn't held up, searing pain in his arms and shoulder sent scorching reminders, reminders that he was incurable. He couldn't sit, breathe or lie down, nor could he dress himself. His walking style had been reduced to a shuffle. Chemotherapy, they said, would extend his life by only a few months, and so Steven began experimenting with cannabis oil, hoping, hoping, *hoping*, for a miracle.

He began Skyping doctors and specialists in faraway European hospitals. The specialists often appeared in front of a bouquet of bright plastic flowers, and greeted you warmly in a hopeful over-lit video.

'Good mornink to you, my name is Dr Gerballs, velcome to you, dying person. Yes, we 'av found ze cure for cancer, make no mistake about this, we 'ave a cure, there is always a cure, do not lose ze heart … most of ze cancers are curaball.'

Nurses gathered in the background wearing 'hope' uniforms for the terminally unhopeful – crisp white medical coats, stethoscopes dangling from pockets. Germany and Israel were both offering hope through clinical trials with *immunotherapy* drugs, a brand-new army of cancer-nuking drugs, and if he could afford the $12,000 a shot, maybe, just maybe, Steven could get on a trial, but he had to get himself to Israel. And you had to be eligible for a trial.

Steven was not eligible for any trials.

None that he could find on the internet anyway.

One afternoon when I made my daily emotionally charged telephone call to Steven, he told me how a ladybird was sitting on his reading glasses.

'A ladybird just flew onto my glasses, Lan … that's a good sign, isn't it?'[52]

'A ladybird, Steve? Yep, that's a bloody good sign! Are you eating, Steve? Are you having any treatment? What can I do, Steve? What the fuck can I do? A ladybird, you said? Yep, that's a good sign.'

A ladybird! A ladybird?

For fuck's sake, Steve, I thought, *you're pinning your hopes on a bloody ladybird?*

The sad part is that he *was.* Steven was pinning his future on a *ladybird*, hoping it would bring him the miracle he so desperately needed.

And this was my darkest afternoon on the phone with Steven. He was everything you could imagine from a dying family man: angry, impatient and emotional one minute, eccentric, dark and absurdly

52 Warning: when someone you love is dying from incurable cancer, all bets are off. Navigating their hopes, dreams, fears and desires can often feel like a love-torn battlefield. Friends of the dying, cousins of the dying, distant uncles of the dying: we all often behave poorly. Our insecurities about life, death, rejection and love can bring up our deepest fears. Attempting to soothe and calm, without coming across as 'too much', 'too emotional' or 'not emotional enough', can be difficult for everyone. It's hard to remember that it's all about 'them' and not 'me'. Or 'us'.

funny the next. Steven's mum believed in miracles. Steven did too. But I didn't believe in miracles. Not anymore. Time was marching on and, in Tumour Town, cancer slows down for no one. In fact, in Tumour Town, cancer likes to speed up.

Running through my house in bare feet one morning, my foot accidentally collided with Jack the dog – he was going one way and I was going the other. I thrust my bare foot out, kicking the skirting board, smashing one of my toes. The doctor noticed a dreary old mole on my fourth toe, which I asked him to freeze off immediately. He shook his head, made some notes and an immediate biopsy appointment. It turned out my untoward freckle was only masquerading as a freckle. I had a malignant melanoma cancer.

Now, I understand how some people might have taken this news rather poorly. I apparently took my cancer news very, *very* well. I didn't for a moment believe I was in real trouble. I was invincible, my fear of death, dying and funerals giving me delusions and illusions.

There was a brief discussion about how insane it was that someone like me, someone who avoided basking in the sun or even being in the sun, and upon arrival at any beach was dressed like a spooky old beekeeper, how someone like me could possibly have the melanoma cancer.

'Just bad luck,' the doctor said. 'It must be in your genes.'

'But, Dr Forbes, how long, you know, if I hadn't had this untoward brown spotty mole on my foot checked out, would I have, I mean, could I have actually died?'

'We don't like to hand out death sentences here, Alannah. We don't like to dwell on this sort of news. I'll tell you what, let's not dwell on any terrors here today … OK?'

'But Dr Forbes, if Jack hadn't made me break my toe, well … how long before the melanoma, you know, if I'd just left it and done nothing …' My voice was distant, even to myself.

Dr Forbes told me if I had waited three months, maybe six, I could have been stage four. Incurable. Just like Steven.

Bedridden in Cabrini Hospital, a skin graft from my inner thigh forming a new ninth toe,[53] I made a secret plan to track down a cure for Steven. His family would love me forevermore, and I'd be welcomed back into the fold. I might even be honoured at a glittering awards ceremony in NYC, photographed for *Time* magazine and appear in a video like the hopeful nurses in faraway European clinics. There might even be a bloody star named after me! I was dying to call Steven to let him know he would not be dying alone, that I would be doing a little bit of dying myself, right alongside him.

If the wearer of brown brogues (an oncologist) wandered past my melanoma room, I would *pssssst*, *pssssst* at the oncologist's shadow until I had beguiled them to sit next to me on the hospital bed. The brown-brogue wearer would be forced to read and offer cures on the differences between Steve's two PET-scan[54] reports, which I'd thrust under their nose, almost like they were sniffing a homegrown pink rose.

'Oh dear, Alannah, the difference with these two PET scans is, well, his cancer is growing so damned fast, there seems to be a massive tumour on his shoulder, Jesus, it must be giving him a lot of pain. Alannah, I'm really sorry but he's just not going to make it. These two reports are only five months apart and the tumour growth is significant. None of us enjoy

---

53 One of my toes and part of my foot was cut away (to ensure the cancer had not spread). The skin graft, oddly enough, was more painful than the operation where the surgeon cut away a toe to eradicate any traces of cancer. After ten days, I was released from Cabrini on crutches. The cancer had been stopped in its tracks. The doctor insisted my entire body must be skin-checked every six months. Melanoma is fast and often goes straight to the brain. Jack the dog saved my life.

54 PET stands for positron emission tomography. It is a scan that uses a special dye with radioactive tracers to highlight the areas of cancer in your body.

telling someone they've only got a few months left. Was he a good friend of yours? Oh, by the way, did your friend smoke?'

I wanted to smack this oncologist around the head. I wanted to smack him hard for confirming that I would now be unhappy for the rest of my life. Discussing Steven in the past tense made me want to *pop* people with grief grenades. The past tense forced my head into a week-long headache.

And then it happened. A doctor emailed me the number of a bladder specialist who gave me the number of Professor Grant McArthur, the god of immunotherapy at the Peter MacCallum Cancer Centre. I pushed on, obtaining the emails of two more specialists and, after three emails and a promise to supply headscarves to Peter Mac and the Olivia Newton-John Cancer Wellness & Research Centre forevermore, Steven had his first appointment with a brilliant young oncologist, Dr Andrew Weickhardt, from the ONJ clinic in Heidelberg. I telephoned the brilliant Dr Andrew, speaking so quickly that he may not have understood a single word.

'He needs miracle news, Dr Andrew! Steven has a family. He doesn't want to die and everybody is so frightened. Four oncologists have told him he's incurable. Time is running out, love, you have to help him. When we have our meeting, can you be as ruthlessly upbeat as possible, even in defiance of reality?'

The brilliant Dr Andrew was kind, and understood he had to be as ruthlessly upbeat as possible, even in defiance of reality.

But the meeting was not as upbeat as we all had hoped.

Steven, his sister, Rae, and I sat in a grim semicircle in Dr Andrew's light-deprived office. Dr Andrew informed our worried but hopeful faces that unfortunately there wasn't a trial available anywhere in the world that Steven could participate in. He could try the chemo but … unfortunately, his cancer was incurable. I watched Steven's face hollow out, disappearing into deathly silence. Rae disappeared into deathly silence with him and, soon after, I followed. The fluorescent glow in Dr Andrew's cancer room illuminated cracks that could no longer be denied. Steven was dying faster than any of us realised. Sixty-eight kilograms of skin and bone, pale as a ghost, masking the ordeal inside. Our hopes that Dr Andrew would be filling Steven to the brim with immunotherapy drugs were not being fulfilled. The renegade, brilliant punk young doctor was not being as ruthlessly upbeat as he'd been instructed and so I started to squawk.

'He will pay for the Keytruda, Steven will *pay* … won't you, Steven? Get him filled up with that Keytruda, Dr Andrew, and let's hurry this along. The longer we wait, the deader Steven is!'

I hoped the brilliant young oncologist might see that my extroverted behaviour was masking the fallout from a lifetime of chronic insecurity. When I was nervous or afraid, my 'vivid' behaviour could be viewed by people as 'confidently showing off' or 'a little bit fucked up'.

Steven had his first immunotherapy infusion in May 2015. Dr Andrew kindly informed us it was a long shot: statistics on immunotherapy treating stage-four bladder cancer were basically nil. After the fourth infusion, Dr Andrew ordered a PET scan to monitor the cancer snaking through Steven's body, and afterwards we drove to a noisy cafe on Flinders Lane in Melbourne's CBD. I was worried sick and too shattered to eat. Attempting to be positive, I told Steven that his arm did seem slightly better, and the ladybird *had* sat on his glasses a few months earlier. We convinced ourselves that the tumours may have shrunk, just a little … and that maybe the Keytruda had done something? Maybe. I was having trouble looking at Steve. I still could not accept he was going to die, and was obsessing about my own fears. Would the light switch off when I died or glimmer on somewhere else?

Steven ordered two pastry cakes, saying his appetite was coming back. Suddenly his phone lit up. It was a call from our new hero, Dr Andrew. I braced myself for the worst. Oncologists usually only telephone the dying when the results are dire. I dragged out my hand mirror, reapplying lipstick, staring into dead space, preparing my heart to accept the awful news. Then I noticed Steven jigging and yelping into his phone. I had never seen Steven jig and he certainly didn't yelp but there he was, jigging and yelping. I heard him talking loudly and quickly into the phone; it was a voice I had not heard before.

'What ... what do you mean ... no cancer? The tumours have evaporated ... are you fucking joking me? No hot spots? The cancer's gone?'

We started to cry at exactly the same time. We stopped crying at exactly the same time. We had no words, but what occurred that day will never leave my heart. Steven is a perfect marvel in an imperfect storm. He went from the living dead to a worldwide cancer miracle. He was alive: after four infusions the cancer had disappeared, and my heart began to beat again. The bees came for honey and all the forgotten flowers laughed and laughed and laughed.

Just like Mum and Steven and I had years earlier.

The next morning, Dr Andrew's office was not a light-deprived shoebox. Instead, the light glimmered and danced around our hearts. Steven was 10 feet tall, Dr Andrew even taller. I cannot remember breathing on that morning when the miracle was shown to us on the screen. Not a single tumour. They had all dissolved. We all hugged and cried and took photographs and then, just like that, it was all over. For helping to save his life, Steven sent a bouquet of flowers so fantastical that they couldn't even fit through the front door. I cried into the smiling pink roses, and Jack the dog ran for cover.

And one by one, I snapped the flowers' heads off.

There would be no more trips to the airport to collect cancer-riddled Steve for his treatment in Melbourne, no more long talks about death and dying, no more telephone calls about immunotherapy, ladybirds and life. My Florence Nightingale experience was over and I had never felt emptier. Steven and his family went back to their busy lives in Sydney. Everything seemed to go back to normal, but I stumbled and crumbled. My purpose for more than six months had been to help find a cure for Steven. And now I felt nothing but sorrow and loss. Steven's family had revisited my life after decades apart and I realised how much I missed them.

I began to understand that if I kept staring back into the past, my future would never glimmer. Steven's cancer and my own cancer were pulling me toward the light. I wanted to stop courting my past, to look the other way, into the yet-to-become. Of course, these are just words, easier said than done, but even so I try to look toward a future, a brighter and darker, faster and slower, richer and poorer kind of future.

49

Wilt, Fall, Rise, Bloom

Skittish rain fell onto the flooded sidewalks of Flinders Lane. Black storm clouds of emotion raced helter-skelter across my pinched face, thunder *clapping* where my heart used to live. Some things in life cannot be fixed; they can only be carried.

My Boom castle in South Yarra, the one I could not shut up about once, the one with the colossal mortgage, had to be sold and my Lady Muck dreams scattered like ashes across the lush lawns of Fawkner Park. E and I were living in St Kilda bedsits, both of us waiting impatiently for my 'back to the future in St Kilda' Victorian house to be renovated. It was running six months late.

Few words, and even fewer sentences, could ever explain how I felt when my hand scribbled a signature across five A4 pieces of paper lying on a desktop in a blue-chip law office in the city. Seven months after my doctor's certificate and following 20 tonnes of legal letters with huge legal fees, and with negotiations at a standstill, I signed a document. The legal document states that I am not permitted to discuss the contents of the legal document.

But I did the right thing for E and signed it.

I felt nothing but sadness looking over at David in the lawyer's office. We hadn't seen each other for months and I missed my Factory X family. I was struck with a crushing emptiness.

Dear reader, seven months living through lawyers can send a girl into a mini delirium. I wasn't experienced with lawyers or how the legal game worked, but a team of lawyers was my only point of contact. They advised me to be strategically quiet and to lay low. I took their advice and lay still, quiet and low.

Quite suddenly, my world became dark, unlivable and very quiet.

I opened the black front door of my newly decorated St Kilda house, marched through the kitchen, stumbled up the red-carpeted stairs into the bedroom and pulled the red velvet curtains across the windows to shut out any light that dared shine in. I kicked off my black Chanel shoes and wiped my lipstick away with the back of my hand.

When I looked at my past, all I could see was heartbreak. Broken people, broken dreams, broken promises. Traumatised children, traumatised just like me. I wasn't alone anymore, but I was one of the multitude of hurt and injured people who stagger on through the hopelessness of their lives day after day, because it's the *only* thing we can do.

I lay low in my Lady Macbeth bedroom for three weeks. The suit of armour I'd carefully constructed to conceal my inner mongrel basdard had been irreparably damaged during my work battles, so I knew I was heading into heavy and one-sided negotiations with Buried-Alive Alannah.

I was astonished at how low I could go, and on really bad days I would watch myself falling into a gigantic pit of motherless, poisonous spiders.

My identity was split between a brand I no longer had anything to do with and my personal sense of self. 'Alannah Hill' had been my greatest invention, my secret weapon against the forces of the world, and so without my name, I didn't know how to go forward. I felt raw and exposed. The familiar rush I received from Alannah fans had been stilled. I was *always* trying to explain (without breaking the agreement) that I was no longer at Alannah Hill, or that I no longer was Alannah Hill. It made me terribly sad trying to explain almost two decades away.

The crunch usually came as something small, as simple as leaving the house on a trip to Bunnings to purchase a bathroom mat or a length of garden hose. I could spot an 'Alannah fan' metres away and, in my confusion at not being able to be myself, I would stammer out the fact that in reality I was no longer at the brand. Of course, my baffled fan often had little idea what to make of my attempts to explain myself.

You see, dear reader, I couldn't face the blistering truth: that I was fifty-one years old, unemployed, with an identity that no longer felt like my own. After almost thirty-eight years working within the safe parameters of an Indigo or a Factory X, where there was always a Jill, a John or a David, I found being out in the world terribly real and lonely.

I worried that I wasn't just a *little* bit fucked, I worried that I might be really, *really* fucked.

Hugo urged me to be positive, encouraging me to take it a day at a time and to embrace life beyond the brand. I had never taken anything a day at a time and I wanted to scream each time he said, 'Live beyond the brand, Lan ... you have to learn to live beyond the brand.'

Did he not know anything about me after years together? Did he not know I disliked platitudes, that they meant nothing to me? What does *live beyond the brand* even mean, I'd ask him.

Did I mention that I might have been an *emotional wreck* and really difficult to be around in these times?

Hugo had enormous faith in me and I didn't want to let him down. He told me I was a natural, a born creative, and not to mess with the process of being who I was, that new doors would open to me and I should have no fear. Of course, I didn't believe him. My confidence and vim were diminished. I felt like a rose bush on which roses could never grow. But with the elastic and elusive nature of time, little by little, a new me began to emerge.

I had begun to grow wings anew.

Because you do not just wake up a butterfly.

Online strangers who reached out to me became virtual friends with their messages of support. When a press statement was released explaining I had left my brand, social media sites tilted and crashed. I didn't have a personal internet page nor was I on any social media platform, and I wasn't able to write back to my dedicated followers. There were hundreds and hundreds of comments written on the Factory X Official Alannah Hill Facebook wall. Posts from customers, fan girls, men and women all over Australia, baffled by my sudden departure, all standing in solidarity. I was overwhelmed that my work had touched so many people, and for some rainbow reason, my character and aesthetics and sensibilities had helped girls everywhere recover from broken hearts, a mother's death, a child's illness, a ruined wedding or a funeral. The love and support that I received gave me the courage and self-belief to start all over again, to follow the path I loved and missed, the path of life, colour, design – and reinvention.

50

Reinvention

The name Louise Love came to me like a spirit one morning at dawn. It dawned on me that my second name was Louise, and with my life's work studying for a PhD in all the aspects of love, I knew it had to be Louise Love. A new reinvented Alannah was about to soar.

In December 2013, I met with some potential investors, and once upon a time I would have jumped at any lucky opportunity that came knock-knocking at my door. But I had learnt over time that what looked like luck was often a cunning wolf all gussied up in sheep's clothing. And so I decided to go it alone with Louise Love. I had already trademarked the name.

I plunged into launching my new brand, this time not as an employee but as the CEO and founder. I wanted a boutique-style brand, not mass produced. I wasn't comfortable in the chain-store model of retail, but on the other hand a stand-alone boutique in Chapel Street was too much too soon. A deluxe online website was the future of uniquely styled fashion retail.

I would hire a consultant. The very best I could find. A David, a Jill, a John. I'd hire a general manager, an assistant, a Louise Love head office. With my friend and collaborator Andrew Majzner from Paper Stone Scissors, I planned a comeback in style, a spectacular marketing campaign, a Louise Love fashion shoot with a *Vogue* photographer, *Vogue* photoshopping, *Vogue* models, *Vogue* locations and *Vogue* prices. I wrote a press release for the media in the hope my new name might catch on.

LOUISE LOVE

A new myth:

Somewhere in the fairytale forests of southern Tasmania, a girl is born.

If Alannah's childhood is a struggle to resist having her identity crushed, adolescence sees Alannah leaving home, never to return.

In Melbourne she studies the illusion of identity, gravitating to fashion as the great transformer of the self. And transform she does, projecting her image into life as an inspiration to girls everywhere, through glamour.

Glamour is magic, a weapon for a girl to wield in this world, a kabuki theatre of the high street where stakes are measured in the trajectories of people's lives. Never is Alannah seen without make-up in this dangerous scenery. It's a serious business being dressed and ready to go every day. She is what she appears to be, a dreamweaver.

And she takes up her mission, dressing the world up in her love. Beautify the sorrow, forget your despair, we're rising to an immaculate vision of the feminine mystique. It's serious business bringing joy and self-respect and humour to girls everywhere, heroines and villains in their own life dramas, cuttingly funny, bereft, blessed and bewildered. She is the director of all this.

The girls she dresses are reflections of her, yet her light is her own. A star she becomes high above the suburban yards, twinkling down on the crushed dreams of broken girls and sparking their Anti-christ with a heel, a dress to step out in, a coat for winter to keep the wolves at bay.

The girl without a name steps out into the crystalline morning to see the last star in the southern sky slowly fade. She understands the mystery of everyone's identity except her own. For a moment the bay and the beach and the tall palms are suffused with light. Always had I more than one name, she says, I was so many girls in time and yet only ever myself with so much more to give. My second name is Louise, and my gift to the world is Love.

By March 2014, I was on fire. I was more focused, more determined and more alive than I'd been for a very long time. I was lighting fires, stomping out fires, fire-starting and learning about firewalls. I didn't see myself as a fifty-one-year-old woman starting out all over again, mainly because I had fooled myself for decades about my real age. I had fibbed so often about my real age that I believed I had outsmarted the age war: in my mind, I was ageless.

My old suppliers wanted to see me succeed – I was pulling in favour after favour, sequin after sequin, vintage silk print after vintage silk print. My original idea was to design sixteen styles made locally, but my newfound freedom got the better of me and, before I knew it, I'd designed eighty styles in two months. I had a further 400 styles ready to go. I borrowed, I begged and I even borrowed against my house.

I settled on sixty-eight styles, some of which would be made offshore. I arranged with a supplier from Kolkata to fly to India and to book production for Louise Love.

One boiling afternoon in the fabric design warehouse in Kolkata, a lady named Boo offered me a dish of homemade ice-cream. *Homemade* ice-cream – vanilla! For a moment I forgot about the raging heat and humidity that had tormented me since my arrival, and I had four helpings. I love ice-cream and I thought ice-cream loved me.

Suddenly, I wilted on the streets of Kolkata. I made it back to the hotel but I knew I was seriously unwell, boiling and burning up with a 40-degree temperature. Hallucinations danced and played around the edges of my consciousness.

'I believe you have typhoid, my dear,' an ancient doctor who paid a hotel call said. 'You had shots? You have been immunised?'

I'd read the fine print but was sure it didn't apply to me.[55] In my mad rush to leave, I had forgotten to get any shots.

The watery-eyed doctor injected me with a temporary cure and I dreamt killer-girl wild nightmares, where I was either dying on the streets of Kolkata or my organs were stolen and sold on the black market. After three days I was allowed to travel home to E, who I had missed terribly. But I was burning up in a ring of typhoid fire, and for the next ten days I lived at Cabrini Hospital in the infectious diseases area. I remember the distant hum of voices while I stared into a 40-degree acid trip–like fever.

'Alannah, you have typhoid fever.'

'Really? *Is that all?* Nurse, love, is this typhoid thing serious? I have a David Jones order to supply, and I have to ship and pack that order back at the office, have I got any organs left, and who are you?'

After eleven days of fever I was released back into the world.

I was *terribly* impressed with my ability to typhoid on.

I sold the range to David Jones, and I was confident I looked the part of a high-flying businesswoman – I was even the cover girl of Melbourne's *Sunday Age*, in an article titled 'The Art of Reinvention'.

I delivered the first Louise Love order to David Jones in August that year and the clothing flew out the door. I launched a Louise Love online store, delivering all the Louise Love purchases in custom-made ivory boxes tied with a huge bright-red bow, handwritten notes hidden in the hemline of dresses as a special gift:

Because you do not just wake up a butterfly.

---

55 The fine print stated how eating homemade ice-cream, drinking water from the cool-water tap in a five-star hotel, mayonnaise, chicken, *all* meat and basically *all* food were best avoided. Immunisations were essential.

Steven's cancer miracle shook me up. My own cancer shook me up. Typhoid shook me up. The magnitude of not being part of Alannah Hill any longer shook me up.

The feeling of only half breathing, and of being stressed and not in control at Factory X had taken its toll. E was thirteen years old and needed me; he'd worked around my impossible dream for so many years. I suddenly understood what Dr Rooney had meant. To stop. To stop everything and discover where future cards may fall. I wanted to be there when E came home from school and, much to his horror, I also wanted to volunteer at the school canteen.

I had spent a year building Louise Love, often arriving home from the office well past midnight, or even at 5 am. Louise Love head office was only myself and my amazing assistant, Alicia, who stood close by to help me create the perfect new Louise Love brand. Perfection is impossible, of course, but we both took joy in pretending we were perfect, with the gentle air of butterfly wings on our lashes.

And slowly I began to develop a new appreciation for life. Alicia was having a baby and perhaps, perhaps, this forced me to rediscover the simple and rare beauty of just being alive. My cancer, the loss of my brand, typhoid and raising E as a single mother were what I needed to make me stop.

And so I decided to sell the remaining Louise Love designs and summer collection to David Jones, and temporarily close the Louise Love online store. I wanted to find out where the elusive future cards would fall.

51

Beautiful Strangers

I always held close the belief that children who had been abused or shamed wasted their lives away in a psychological deadlock of neglect, our silent screams reverberating in the ether above, below and all around us. Because of what had happened to me, I was also aware that the horror was still happening all around us – next door to you, next door to me, down the street, up the street, in the apartment downstairs, and in the alleyways of forgotten towns where forgotten people can no longer hold love in their hearts, not for anyone, or anything.

The trouble was I couldn't look away any longer. I felt the time had come to tell my story, but I didn't know how to articulate it or where to articulate it. The answer arrived, out of the blue: an invitation to freedom, to read a letter about burning bridges. Write a coming-out letter, an escape from the secret war waging within, the invitation urged. It was an email from Michaela McGuire of Women of Letters.[56]

Would I like to delve deep into my inner despair and read this very personal story of my own creation to 800 people in a ballroom, on

56 Women of Letters is a literary salon, an afternoon where 'Australia's best and brightest women come together on stage to celebrate the lost art of letter writing'. It was founded in 2010 by co-curators Marieke Hardy and Michaela McGuire.

a Sunday afternoon in September 2015? With four other high-flying women?

Irresistible

Terrifying

Rebellious

It was time to break one of my sister's Ten Commandments. They were not recorded on a piece of paper. They were not in any book. They were not saved on a computer hard drive. No, these ten golden rules were written in loud pop-art pink on a background of thin air, scored into my memory. Those rules were there to keep me safe from my dangerous self. And to stop me from *showing off*.

I knew the rules off by heart.

I had broken most of the rules, dear reader, except the one about writing and speaking in public. I would write a letter to E, to explain to him the chinks in my sequined armour, so he would understand the black gaping holes I filled with make-up, coquettish and ornamental dress-ups, and 999 cans of Final Net hairspray. I would explain why I could never *ever* allow myself to be a casual, breezy mum, a mum in a sensible car wearing sensible shoes, a mum always in a bright, sunny-mum mood with a Jamie Oliver–glazed oven-cooked chicken sitting, trophy like, on a grand dining table, hundreds of cooking utensils and a Royal Doulton tea set lined up inside a Miele dishwasher. I would explain why there wasn't a creamy-furred glorious labrador sleeping on a beige couch beside a glorious beige husband, wearing glorious beige slippers, reading the glorious despair of *The Australian* or the glorious wealth of the *Financial Review*.

I watched the words dance across the computer screen, daring me to write the truth, and I couldn't type the past out fast enough.

Hugo, his eighty-five-year-old mother and I drove across town to Northcote while I read and reread my four A4 pages, my letter to E, over and over again. I crouched in the back seat of the car, saying silent Hail Marys in case my sister discovered what I was about to do. I was hot and then cold, warm and then freezing, I wanted a drink of Diet Coke, and then a bottle of Fanta, a toilet stop-off, a hairdo tease.

I wanted to turn back. I wanted to go home. As I tumbled from the car like a frightened bird in an op-shop handbag, I felt my heart unfolding, a paper flower desperate to bloom. I was terrified, but I knew in my heart that I had a message to impart, and I knew that I couldn't hold the past back any longer. If my little letter could perhaps help somebody who was listening, maybe I wouldn't feel so sad all the time.

Perched on a little stage with high-achievers Zoë Foster Blake, Catriona Rowntree, Anni Davey and Rachel Power, I looked out over the heartwarming crowd. I drank my glass of water in one ungainly gulp. And then I stole Zoë's tumbler of water. And Catriona's. And then it was time to begin.

Each of us took our turn in reading out our letters. Tiny beads of sweat hovered on my powdered white forehead, my head ached, and I wanted it all to be over. I had made another life-changing mistake. I would be mocked and turned into a laughing-stock – I could hear my mother chastising me from the heavens above, my father groaning with boredom from an entirely different place. I was mentally planning my escape route after uttering my last word. I knew my tears would be impossible to hold back. The cracks were starting to show in my imperfectly ornamental public image.

Then something extraordinary happened.

I stood up, and I started to read. And I read and read, my rapid-exit plan vividly laid out in my mind. Suddenly, the audience rose to their feet, clapping. I could feel emotion running high, overwhelmed with gratitude that people had listened to me. The immaculate Zoë Foster Blake appeared to be crying, and in slow motion walked toward me whispering comforting words and gripping my hands. I gripped her hands back. I felt tall and then short, short and then tall.

Somehow, in some way, I had touched people's hearts. I felt embraced and understood by the warmth of people around me. My lit-up eyes sparkled with tears, but I refused to let them fall. People grabbed my wrists, notes were pressed into my hands, love notes of admiration for this little mongrel basdard. People whispered into my chandelier hairdo that my story could give a voice to other unjoined, abused girls lost in the dark shadows of life. Zoë told me how my story could give others a fighting chance, and so in the weeks after Women of Letters I sat down and began to write.

It was time, dear reader, for me to write my truth.

52

Dear Mum

Melbourne 2018

Dear Mum,

I found a photographed memory of you and Nan today, Mum. It was in the sad drawer. Look at you both. You're sitting on the swing in your bright-red pantsuit and Nan's leaning on the frame. You must have been around forty-eight years old.

I wish that I hadn't found it, because all it did was split my heart in two with a yearning I've not experienced for a long time, Mum. A yearning for my mother and my grandmother.

I miss you, Mum. And I miss Nan.

Mum, do you know that you and Nan gave me my values, my morals, my old-fashioned girly ways? You gave me more than I ever gave you credit for, and I am deeply sorry I didn't tell you that.

This story began with one of your attempted suicides, and now I'm closing with a love letter to you. On all the pages in between, my memories have shown me how our story will never end, that it cannot end, because although your heart may have stopped beating, Mum, your heartbeat is forever linked to my own.

When you died, Mum, I felt like I had been struck by lightning. Your death dislodged something inside me, memories cutting through feelings I buried a long time ago.

I have written words that are perhaps ungrateful, words that perhaps I should not have written, things I ought not to have felt. I had more love to give you, Mum, but you did the one thing I never thought possible. You died. You died the week when I'd promised myself I would try harder, and now your voice is silent, deadly silent.

But you left me with a golden key, the most spectacular gift you could leave a girl like me. You told me that you always knew what happened to me on that train, on the Tasman Limited when I was twelve years old. You allowed me to unlock the trauma of my childhood and bring it into the light to heal. You finally made it real not just for me, but for both of us.

Do you remember our last conversation in your smoke-filled lounge room, Mum? I remember every word we breathed, Mum, and I'll never let this memory go, because on that morning you gave me what I'd been searching for all my life. You gave me the truth.

You told me you'd always believed my childhood was smothered in darkness, a darkness you tried to ignore, a darkness you had to ignore because God was watching us. Did you hear both our Sacred Hearts break when you finally told me your truth? That you believed me all along? How you couldn't bear to live, knowing my childhood had been twisted and pulled out of shape?

I understand now why you let me go, Mum, why you cut me loose – it was the only way to banish your thoughts of what happened when I was twelve years old. I know you would have altered the path of my childhood if you knew how, but your broken heart could bear only so much pain. I try to remember moments when I saw you happy, or gazing into the mysteries of the universe.

I was afraid of you, Mum. Your temper and sadness and nervous breakdowns were confusing. I was angry with you too, Mum. I knew I could never tell you why. I didn't understand why you didn't stand up for me. Why you didn't believe in me. Why you didn't believe me.

I remember the fantastic love you had for your own mother, and how your father, who fought in the war, arrived home a completely changed man – a broken father and husband no longer able to smile or laugh. Your mother and father were the only two people in the universe I never heard you speak ill of, Mum. Not another living soul escaped your black wit, your wrath, your apocalyptic putdowns of everyone and everything.

I would often find you lying on your unmade bed, your head toward the wall. I knew you wanted to die, Mum. I wished I had been enough to make you happy, but nothing made you happy.

I remember you staring into space when I asked you what I was like as a little girl.

'Oh, I don't know what you were like, dear. But we did have VERY SPECIAL TIMES in Chasm Creek, Lannah.'

Were these some of the happiest days of our lives, Mum?

It was just you and me, Mum.

I loved your memories of our special times in Chasm Creek, Mum, because I have so few of my own, and they're all tinged and scorched with pain and regret. I do remember any special time together suddenly stopped when my father came home, how I'd instantly freeze if I heard Dad's car. I'd run blindly into the nothingness of Chasm Creek, hiding in my special secret spot in the mop cupboard. I do remember both of us wondering how hiding in the cupboard would make a scrap of difference – he couldn't see me in real life, so why the hell did I need to hide?

You gave me my dark, absurd, slightly berserk sense of humour,

Mum, and without it this world might have long ago killed my spirit. You and I could laugh in the face of darkness, we could laugh about the neighbours, the milk delivery boy, your three grandchildren, my four 'hopeless, supercilious, mind-numbing boyfriends'.

I ignored phone calls from you, Mum – I was afraid I wouldn't be able to make you laugh and afraid you would cry. I'd been so angry for so long I didn't know how to tell you. I couldn't understand why you didn't stand up for me. I was hurt that you didn't want to know E. Becoming a mother showed me I could love just like other mothers love.

And I do love him, Mum, E is everything to me.

We'd wonder together how you spent years leaning on the mantelpiece with your head in your hands, about your name being Aileen, and your mother's Eileen:

A lean

I lean

Both of you were leaners on that mantelpiece!

And now I lean on mantelpieces too.

I often couldn't breathe when you told me that you wanted to die, that you had nothing to live for, that you missed your mum and dad and just wanted to be with them. I knew I wasn't enough to make you want to live. Nothing made you want to live, Mum. Do you remember me crying into my Prada handbag, crying at how utterly devastated I'd be if you were the type of mother who could ever really die?

Mum, two years ago a lady grabbed my arm in Chapel Street with a knowing smile and a wink. It was Roz, your favourite hairdresser from Penguin. She knew how to tease hair professionally and she listened to you, she was the friend you needed. I greeted her with my sadness all shut up inside my heart.

'Oh Alannah, your mum just loved you, she was *so* proud of your success, it was all she talked about, she glowed when she talked about you.

Your mum would bring in all the articles you were in, she'd telephone me if you were ever on the television. Oh, don't be sad, it would only make your mum sad to see you crying like this.'

I disappeared into a side street, Mum. I tried to disappear because you never told me. You never told me you were proud of me and I couldn't tell you that I loved you.

Your death will remain the most brutal and painful lesson to me, Mum. Your passing taught me how we as humans always believe we have time to change or apologise to the people who mean the most to us. I wish I had learnt this in a different way, but sometimes, as we both know, Mum, life doesn't work out how we expect or imagine.

I cannot claim my book has been a therapeutic form of Catholic redemption, or that writing these words has healed the wounds inside my heart. I don't believe any of us can cleanse or wipe away our pasts, nor do I believe that redemption is impossible. All I can say is that in writing my story I learnt that my childhood, and all the spaces in between, have made me who I am – for what defines us isn't our childhoods, our unguarded moments, or our best-kept secrets. What defines us, Mum, is how well we rise after all our crooked falls, the odds stacked against us.

There were three little words you and I could never say, Mum, so now I will say them for the both of us:

I love you.

I cannot say goodbye, but because of you, dear Mum, I wrote a memoir in the hope that girls and mothers all over the world don't make the same mistakes that we both did.

Because
you don't just wake up a butterfly.

With love forevermore,
Lan

Thank you, dear reader, for listening.

It's 2.30 am and the light beams across the lawn from a warm October moon. E is sound asleep, Jack the dog by his side, and Hugo is on tour in Europe. I'm alone. Mum's voice has grown softer. I miss her. After writing my story, my mind still holds fear but it's a distant hum. I look out on the moonlit night and stare up into the heavens above. Perhaps in the end, we are forced to make peace with what we've lost – what we'll never get back no matter how many worlds we destroyed in our search. Pain can be borne to teach us, but loss … I think loss can be the greatest teacher of all.

Love, Alannah Hill

Acknowledgements

Firstly, I would like to acknowledge the unjoined and abused children, women and men living among us. I hope that my story gives you the courage to bring your own dark secrets into the light.

If you are suffering, please be gentle on yourself. Go quietly and gently toward someone who will listen to every single word you breathe. Shame and guilt have no place in your heart, my love. I understand that there is no greater agony than holding onto an untold secret.

To all of us parents: please listen to your child's young voice because a child rarely lies about sexual abuse.

I would like to acknowledge the giant souls who have helped me along the way. There are too many to name, but I am forever indebted and connected to you.

Thank you to Hugo Race, my man, for supporting me with the darker, more painful, memories from my past. Without your mentorship, my memoir would not contain one full stop and would be written entirely in CAPITALS.

To Edward – for your compassion, wisdom and encouraging words, 'Just keep writing, Mum, keep going! Don't give up!'

Andrea McNamara – thank you for your belief in the *Butterfly* project and in me. For your razor-sharp skills in psychoanalysis and for teaching me gentle restraint. For your editing, memoir shaping and home-made baking.

With thanks and gratitude to my literary agent, Tara Wynne at Curtis Brown. We did it!

To Arwen, Loran, Troy, Kasi, Olivia, Jessica, Evi and the team at Hardie Grant – for your faith, passion and grace, and for walking the *Butterfly* path with me.

To the Jones-Evans family – Holly, Steven, Rae, Dale, Lindsay and Ashley. Thank you for your love, acceptance and poetic licence.

To Jane Kennedy – for your wise, clever and heartwarming words. Words so powerful I cried for two hours! Superb, Jane, thank you!

Thank you to my brother Mark for the kind use of his poem.

To Zoë Foster Blake – for caring about my story so deeply, and encouraging me to write it all down that Sunday afternoon at Women of Letters. You are so damned kind, HILLarious (HILLarious!), sassy and really rather brilliant. I remain forever grateful to you, my love.

To Martin Hill – thank you for your support, Marty.

Thank you to Andrew Majzner, Georges Antoni, Jez Smith, Juli Balla, Monty Coles, Angela Ceberano, Richard Lowenstein, Janice Breen Burns, Michael Lallo, Jill Gould, John Bryan, Sebastian Hampson, Hanh, Quoc, Barbara Ward, Ame Cotton, David Bush, Alicia Gramsbergen, Lana Peden, Ayush, Steve Gration, Barbara Ward, Jean Pierre Heurteau, Julie Flemming, Paul Goldman, Tamara Bradshaw, Naree Fashions, Olivia Massimiliano Larocca, Chris Carlin,

Estelle Andrewartha, Christopher Rooke, Lynne Browne, Elaine Race, Bruce and Trevor Howard, Mark Dudek, Stephen Todd, Andrew Henderson, Stephen Angelides, Natalie Stretton, Cleo Dietrich, Tim Hobson, Sophie Jensen, Associate Professor Andrew Weickhardt and the Olivia Newton-John Cancer Wellness and Research Centre, Professor Grant McArthur, Dr Edward Upjohn, Professor Mark Frydenberg, Ron Sutton, Stephen Stern, Phillip Crutchfield, Catherine Healy, Richard Potter, Siobhan Ryan, Dr Mark Williams, Alex King, ABL, Joe, Gaston, April, our friend and nanny Liv, Vince and John.

To the Women of Letters founders, Marieke Hardy and Michaela McGuire.